Andrew Davidson is an award-winning journalist and the author of four previous non-fiction books, including *Fred's War*, an account of his grandfather's life as a doctor in the trenches. He is married to Vanessa Nicolson and lives near Sissinghurst in Kent.

'Padre McShane was told that the reason I was not given a Brigade was for being so outspoken at Loos. He said if that was so, I wear the invisible cross of military glory.'

THE INVISIBLE CROSS

Andrew Davidson

Quercus

First published in Great Britain in 2016 by Heron Books.
This paperback edition published in 2017 by

Quercus Editions Ltd
Carmelite House
50 Victoria Embankment
London EC4Y 0DZ

An Hachette UK company

A CIP catalogue record for this book is available
from the British Library

PB ISBN 978 0 85705 427 2
EBOOK ISBN 978 1 78429 218 8

CONTENTS

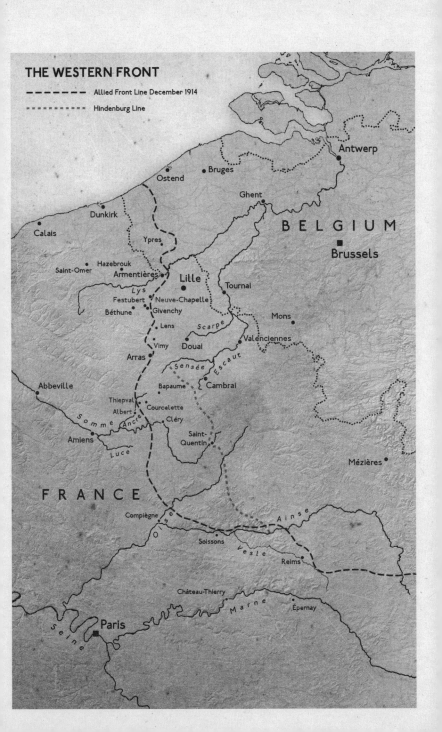

THE WESTERN FRONT

- – – – – – Allied Front Line December 1914
- ·········· Hindenburg Line

Antwerp

Ostend   Bruges

Ghent

Calais   Dunkirk   **B E L G I U M**

Saint-Omer   Hazebrouck   Ypres   **Brussels**

Armentières   Lille

Lys   Tournai

Festubert   Neuve-Chapelle

Béthune   Givenchy   Mons

Lens   *Scarpe*

Vimy   Douai   Valenciennes

Arras

Abbeville   *Sensée*   *Escaut*

Bapaume   Cambrai

Thiepval   Courcelette

Somme   Albert   *Ancre*   Cléry

Amiens   Saint-Quentin

Luce

F R A N C E   Mézières

Compiègne   *Oise*   *Aisne*

Soissons   *Vesle*

Reims

Château-Thierry   *Marne*   Épernay

Seine   **Paris**

FOREWORD

A man stares at the camera, head turned, eyes curious, his attitude un-
decided. He is weighing up the situation, unruffled enough to carry on with
the intimate task in which he is engaged, but experienced enough to assess
the risk – because every action, done by you and to you in this terrible
place, has a consequence. He is neither young nor old, his hair is thinning,
his face heavy and lugubrious, but not yet lined. At his feet stands a bucket.
His feet stand in a trench. He has washed. It is winter, and it has recently
rained, but today it is warm enough to wash outside. The thaw turns the
ground to mud, and mud already surrounds him on floor and wall. He
is buttoning up his khaki shirt against the grey cold and turning, and in
the next moment, the moment the camera cannot capture because it has
already taken its moment, he is about to ask my grandfather something . . .

This is Major Graham 'Bull' Chaplin, pictured in a muddy trench outside
Armentières, washing his face and buttoning his collar early one cold
December morning in 1914. He stands with a slight stoop, freshly shaved,
fingers on shirt, staring placidly into the lens as if he is just preparing to
go off to work on a Clapham omnibus.

He looks, as he does in many photographs from the period, simultaneously amused and unimpressed – the cameras in the battalion were wielded
by the younger men, twenty-five-year-old lieutenants like my grandfather,
who spent their teen years obsessing over cars and motorbikes and aeroplanes and the first mass-produced gadgets in the Edwardian decade
of invention. Chaplin was older, forty-one in the photograph, a veteran
of Pashtun campaigns and, by reputation, a determined, cool-headed,
no-nonsense soldier, commander of A Company, 1st Cameronians, the lead

in the Scottish battalion's five 200-strong companies of men. Chaplin was soon to become a colonel and command the Cameronians himself – part of a regiment that went on, thirty years later, to provide the British Army with more senior commanders than any other in World War Two.[1]

There has always been a slight air of mystery about Chaplin. It is clear, from memoirs and journals kept in the Cameronian archive, that he was held in the highest esteem by soldiers and fellow officers, without it being clear why. He is barely mentioned in official histories, but actually appears in two of the most famous books ever written about World War One: Robert Graves' *Goodbye to All That* and Siegfried Sassoon's *Memoirs of an Infantry Officer*. He has only a walk-on part, a Rosencrantz to two Hamlets, as commander of 1st Cameronians at a time when the battalion fought side by side with Graves' and Sassoon's 2nd Royal Welch, but he makes his mark.

Graves acknowledges Chaplin's help in dissuading their brigadier from ordering yet another pointless assault during the icy winter of 1916–17, while the Cams and Royal Welch are stationed in the frozen marshes around Cléry-sur-Somme. Sassoon, meanwhile, describes Chaplin's anguished calm during an attack on the Hindenburg Line – 'his well-disciplined face haggard with anxiety' – and depicts him as a model of restrained emotion, waiting in his command bunker for news, distracting those around him with cake, hiding his thoughts while he ponders the next move. The lack of communication, as ever, turns any decision making into guesswork.

> At the end of twenty minutes' tension the colonel exclaimed abruptly, "Good God, I wish I knew how they were doing!" . . . And then, as if regretting his manifestation of feeling, "No harm in having a bit of cake, anyhow." There was a large homemade cake on the table. I was offered a slice, which I munched with embarrassment.[2]

A colonel could not afford to show feelings. The Scottish regiments, it should be noted, were famous for their cakes.

J. C. Dunn, the medical officer who went on to write a renowned history of the 2nd Royal Welch in World War One,[3] was also a Chaplin admirer. The Cameronian colonel, he makes plain, was a man who always did the right thing – whether that be stopping the senseless murder of his men by questioning staff orders, or once, at Arras, even taking the blame for the 'failure' of an operation when some of his soldiers overran an objective and compromised a Royal Welch attack.

The memoirs and diaries written by fellow Cameronians depict a gruffer, more complex figure – a man who had fought on India's North-West Frontier and witnessed terrible things, a soldier who was deeply respected, but who never really revealed himself to others. Jacobus Hill, a trainee lawyer and Cameronian lieutenant who served under Chaplin, left this brief pen portrait in his unpublished memoir: 'The men called him The Admiral or Bull. He was clean shaven with a heavy, weather-beaten face, and was short and stocky in build. His appearance together with his stentorian voice seemed to fit him for the quarter deck.'[4]

Some of that I knew when I posted on Facebook my grandfather's photograph of Bull doing his 'morning toilet' (the photo caption in our family album) standing in that cloddy Houplines trench. But not all of it. I was pleased when the photograph got an immediate response, even more so when it turned out that the responders were assorted Chaplin grandchildren and great-grandchildren.

'Brilliant brilliant, from the great grandson!'

'This is my grandfather . . . I never met him as he married late and had just become a father for the first time, on December 13th 1914 (my dad's birthday), a few weeks before this photograph was taken. A fantastic photograph and description of him. Thank you.'

'Amazing.'

'Thank you so much!'

The Chaplin family was clearly alive and kicking. Then, days later, I received an email from Peter Roberts, another of Chaplin's grandsons, following up on the Facebook post and saying he had himself inherited Bull's album of Cameronian snapshots. 'In addition I have transcripts of (probably all) his letters to his wife for the period August 1914 to September 1917 . . . You may be interested in seeing these?'

And he sent me a scan of a batch, painstakingly typed out by his late brother, Richard. I read and read, and he kept sending. When I asked Peter how many he had, he said he had never counted. The originals were written in pencil and stacked neatly in a cardboard box, filed in date order. There were probably more than 500, making them a rare resource indeed, plus a bundle of press cuttings Chaplin's wife had kept as she followed her husband's war, and assorted papers from his army career. Few letter collections of this length exist from World War One, and none from a commanding officer who had seen front-line action for so long. They had been in the family for a century and might now, Peter thought, be of interest to others.

Why so many letters? Because Chaplin had written almost every day to his new wife, Lil, who he had only met for the first time at an army lunch in the summer of 1913. Just months later, they were dancing at the County Ball in Stirling, Scotland, by which time they had clearly fallen in love. They married in January 1914, and when parted in August, he left with a lock of her hair and promised he would write every day that he was able to. And he did. When he couldn't write a letter – when the battalion was fighting at Loos or the Somme or Arras – he would try to send one of the army's field-service postcards, circling in pencil the pre-printed, stiff-upper-lip phrase, 'I am quite well.'

The written letters are extraordinary, still in mint condition, crisp and crackly to the touch, pencilled in slanting handwriting, carefully folded into tiny envelopes stamped with censor marks and only occasionally flecked with the dirt among which they were written, deep in gloomy dugouts as senior officers waited, taking reports, planning operations. Yet the content remains so domestic in tone, as he reassures his wife with details of food, lodging, card games, horse rides, his obsession with sleep and messing (more food), plus a Mr Pooterish dissection of who he has seen, who is doing well and who isn't, with occasional bursts of description covering the fighting before more sleep and messing intervenes. The war, initially at least, could be a long way away.

At first his spirits are chipper, as if he is making every effort not to worry a wife heavily pregnant with their first child, burdened with her own worries. Whatever horrors he is witnessing, he will not discuss, because one didn't – in the same way many veterans didn't, even when the war was over (or many doctors and nurses never do, throughout their professional lives). He just puts it to one side, and carries on, craving details of his new son and then, nine months after his first trip home on leave, his new daughter. He builds another world for himself and Lil which exists only in these letters, populated by mutual friends and family, dominated by health gripes but lightened by laughs and sighs, with the war something that niggles on behind.

The letters are very different to the outpouring of grimly fatalistic memoirs that occurred a decade after the war, written with the pessimism of hindsight. What is revealed in Chaplin's letters is the authentic voice of the professional officer at the start of the war, sent over to do a job that eventually turns out to be not as advertised, and making the best of it. His British army is, by the norms of today, a brutal place, where soldiers can, in extreme cases, be shot for desertion, or chained to cart wheels for indiscipline, and an officer can feel little remorse, even for his own soldier sniped by the Germans.

> I had a man killed the day before yesterday – his own fault, contrary to orders he left the trenches in daylight. I attend the funeral at night and the parson read the service . . . It is a queer scene, a few men standing round the grave and parson saying the service in the darkness, guns and maxims firing in the distance, and the sniper firing close at hand, and wondering how soon it may be one's own turn.[5]

But it will get worse. In reality, Chaplin is entering his own Inferno, as a short war becomes a prolonged slog through the trenches, year after year, witnessing the loss of friends and the butchery inflicted on his men by guns, bombs and generals, and experiencing the exhaustion and emotional abrasion that constant exposure to war brings. No sleep, bad food, worse conditions, feeling cold and wet, night after night until his tone becomes not Pooterish but agonising.

It is hard not to be moved by the letters. For while Chaplin is always conscious of the censors seeing what he has written before Lil, so much can be read between the lines. After Chaplin takes on command of the battalion in June 1915 – and is simultaneously compiling the 1st Cameronians' daily War Diary with its clipped lists of dead and wounded, billets, battles and orders – his writing starts to darken.

In the early stages of the war it is likely that his commanding officer, Colonel Philip Robertson, took the letters on trust and signed them off, unread, as censored. Then, when the war prolongs and official systems are imposed, they will have been passed by other, nameless censors. Given the digs at other officers that appear as the fighting wears down Chaplin's resolve – his loathing of fellow Cameronian Major Vandeleur is a delicious running coda – he must have thought he could trust his censor, who would have nodded grimly at the following lines: 'I hear that Newman is now a temporary Major. It is a strange Army ours which rewards the cowards and incompetents!'[6]

Elsewhere Chaplin glosses over major incidents that must have left him shaken – not least the court martial of his friend, Captain Tom McLellan, second in command at A Company, for 'certain inactions' during a German attack in July 1915. That was just a month after Chaplin had been promoted from A Company to become colonel. What had McLellan not done? Had his nerves simply collapsed? McLellan was exonerated, eventually, but what became of their friendship? Chaplin, who finds his leave stopped until he can sort out the incident, writes only that he's angry and will tell Lil about it when he gets home: '. . . Serious trouble has occurred over an incident in the regiment – until it is settled I cannot go on leave.'[7]

Then there are the ripples created by the Cams' involvement in the Battle of Loos. Something occurs there that is to have a profound effect on his military career. Just what is not detailed initially in his letters home, but he has clearly discussed the matter with Lil on leave, and allusions to it start to pop up in later correspondence. By 1917, when he is exhausted by leadership, by abscesses and eye infections and lack of sleep, the incident has risen like a miasmic fog to infuse everything. That is why he can never leave the front line; that is why – the letters reveal – he has become, by 1917, the longest-serving front-line officer in the army. Abject and weary, he is destined to continue the cycle of trench and billet until bullet or shell removes him. Only promotion can release him, and promotion is denied him because of Loos. He is commended for it by the chaplains and padres he encounters, but he would rather be up and out.

And Lil's response? We will never know, as her letters could not return from France. Chaplin, in a Bull-like gesture, burnt every one of them in the trenches, fearing they would fall into the hands of others when – not if – he died. But with his letters, we have more than enough: a rare insight into a commanding officer's psyche, that ability to detach and focus elsewhere when the world around you has gone to hell, squaring brutality with sentimentality, glorying in the insignificant and taking succour from those you truly love. And if he clings to a single hope it is the one he expresses to Lil in his first letter – written at 5 a.m. in a railway siding at Preston as the battalion travels slowly south from Glasgow to Southampton, heading for France – and the one he reiterates in his last.

'The happiest day of my life will be when I get back to you.'[8]

Andrew Davidson

A. F. A. 2042
114/Gen. No./5248.

FIELD SERVICE POST CARD

Mrs J. G. Chaplin
ar. Brentham Park
Stirling
Scotland

Angleterre

NOTHING is to be written on this except the date and signature of the sender. Sentences not required may be erased. <u>If anything else is added the post card will be destroyed.</u>

I am quite well.

~~I have been admitted into hospital~~

~~{ sick~~ ~~and am going on well.~~
~~{ wounded~~ ~~and hope to be discharged soon.~~

~~I am being sent down to the base.~~

~~I have received your~~ { ~~letter.~~
~~telegram.~~
~~parcel.~~

Letter follows at first opportunity.

~~I have received no letter from you~~

~~{ lately.~~
~~{ for a long time.~~

Signature } Graham
only.

Date 7th Sept 1914

[Postage must be prepaid on any letter or postcard addressed to the sender of this card.]

A NOTE ON EDITING

At full length, the Chaplin letters run to over 140,000 words. The versions that follow have been edited. In deciding what to remove, I have tried to remain faithful to the tone, reducing the obvious repetitions ('My darling Lil', 'for ever your loving husband', 'no news today'), the archaic upper-casing of the first letter of general nouns, and comments of less consequence, without, I hope, losing the flavour of the conversation or the writer's mood. I have also had to remove many of the repeated thanks for foodstuffs and clothing sent, and some of the constant commentary on the movements of other officers – promotions, postings – simply because the cast of characters is too big for a reader to follow with any involvement. I have corrected misspellings of nouns and names (e.g. changing 'MacShane' to 'McShane'), inserted a limited amount of extra punctuation, and added the prefix 'PS' to additions Chaplin makes to letters after signing off. I have also corrected the spelling of certain French place names and Latin aphorisms. I have, however, left untouched his inconsistent upper-casing of the first letters of army nouns ('Brigade' and 'brigade', 'Battalion' and 'battalion').

For some periods when the battalion was at rest but the letters were still flowing, I have summarised events in the commentary and used highlights from letters which have not been included in the text, plus extracts from the battalion's War Diary, now held in the Cameronian archive at Hamilton, South Lanarkshire. I have also included and edited some letters sent to the Chaplins by other officers in the British army, which were collected by Lil and kept in the same tin box with Graham's letters. I have also quoted from original press cuttings, many clipped by Lil and kept with the letters alongside assorted photographs.

It is hoped that the Chaplin letters in full will eventually be made available online. I also hope that no relative of anyone named in these letters is offended by any of the mentions. The opinions expressed by Graham Chaplin are those of an experienced regimental officer in the British army of 1914, who had different prejudices to many of us today, but just as broad a range of likes and dislikes. Some of his views should perhaps be taken as an indicator of how much has changed.

MONS

'I sometimes think that I shall wake up and find it all a dream. I wish I could write to you every day – it would be some sort of consolation.'

Germany invades Belgium – Britain declares war on Germany – British Expeditionary Force sent to fight alongside French – BEF meets German army at Mons and begins near-fortnight-long retreat with French towards Paris – British fight rearguard action at Battle of Le Cateau – German and French forces also meet at Charleroi, Mulhouse, Lorraine and in the Ardennes

Friday, 14 August 1914 [from the train south to Southampton docks]

My darling wife,

You were very good and brave last night – it was a sad journey for me back to barracks.[1] I saw the Grahams[2] with Mrs Oakley[3] who looked appallingly ill. Mr Graham asked me to shoot with him next 12th August. I went and saw that my company was alright and then went to dinner at the Royal Field Artillery mess – it was not very cheerful. I left early and went to my room and cleared my desk. I wrote to Lindsay,[4] Col Wilson[5] and your mother. I sent you the insurance papers and the fire policy – also my card case – and Mabel[6] her bridle. We paraded at 11pm and entrained at 11.30 and left at 11.45.

The men were splendid – all sober and keen as mustard to go to the war. We marched out of the side gate – the police blocked the road – there was not a very big crowd but what there were cheered lustily. I felt leaving you much more when I got into the train and would have given all I possessed to be back with you. I only slept for an hour and have never ceased to think of you.

I started this at 5 – we have now stopped at Preston which accounts for the

---

1 Maryhill Barracks (now demolished) in Glasgow, where the 1st Cameronians are stationed.

2 Parents of 2nd Lieutenant Douglas Graham.

3 Wife of Major Richard Oakley.

4 Graham Chaplin's brother.

5 Lieutenant Colonel Alban Wilson, 8th Gurkhas, a family friend.

6 One of Lil Chaplin's four sisters: Isa, Edith, Mabel and Jessie (Baby).

improved writing – it is a beautiful day and seeing all the nice English scenery it is hard to realise that we are off to war. I sometimes think that I shall wake up and find it all a dream.

I wish I could write to you every day – it would be some sort of consolation. I am awfully glad that I have got your hair and clock. I have been wondering how you are getting on and wish that I could get a telegram.

Address letters: 1st Bn. The Cameronians (Scottish Rifles), British expeditionary force.

I have an idea that we will not be allowed to write at all.

Harriette[1] and Newman[2] are in my carriage.

The chef gave me a cold grouse as a parting gift and shook my hand warmly.

I had a very nice letter from Connie[3] in addition to her telegram to wish me luck.

I smoked one of your father's cigars, which caused a sensation.

We have lots of sandwiches and cold meat to eat. I hope that we shall be able to get tea at some station.

The block you gave me is most useful for this sort of writing.

Take very good care of yourself and rest every afternoon as you promised. By the time this reaches you we shall be in France. I wish I knew where.

I hope that your father's leg and Baby's[4] eye are better. My fondest love to you, my own darling. The happiest day of my life will be when I get back to you. Ever your loving husband, Graham

P.S. One of the transport horses strangled itself with its halter in the train.

*   *   *

So it starts. Major Graham Chaplin is forty-one years old, late to marriage, late to fatherhood, leaving his new wife, Lil, already expecting their first child when his battalion is sent south from Glasgow on that warm August

---

1 Nickname of Captain Harry Lee.
2 2nd Lieutenant E. P. Newman.
3 Graham Chaplin's sister.
4 Lil's youngest sister.

night. They have been married barely six months when they are separated, pitched into a war unlike any other.

Chaplin is a professional soldier, as are all the men sent across the English Channel in the 64,000 strong British Expeditionary Force which sails that month. He is short, stocky, stentorian, pug-faced and, to the men around him, obstinately determined – hence his army nickname: Bull. He learnt his craft fighting fierce Pashtun tribesmen in India's North-West Frontier, and seventeen years on he commands a company – 200 men – in the 1st battalion Cameronians, a regiment originally drawn from the Scottish Lowlands, but now, after many years in India, boasting soldiers recruited from every major British city. The Cams' roots stretch back to the Presbyterian Covenanters, they even issue Bibles to every recruit, but Catholics and non-believers are welcome now.

Chaplin first met Lily Dora Alexander only a year before, at a lunch given by mutual friends. It was a whirlwind romance. She is old too at twenty-seven, with four sisters and two brothers. She thought marriage had passed her by, despite being the daughter of one of Stirling's richest men, whose family is entwined in the business empire built by Sir Charles Tennant, Scotland's premier industrialist. Lily Dora is taller than Chaplin, devoted to Chaplin, as he is to her, and carrying Chaplin's child – she has overwhelmed his life only for war to capsize it again.

And change is the challenge in this era which values tradition. Graham is a London-born officer in a Lanarkshire-based infantry regiment, middle-ranking in the army's order of status, with men drawn from mines and slums, the toughest of soldiers who have served in India and South Africa and are grateful for the regular employment. All ranks believe their army is unbeatable and accept the codes within it. An officer will not speak directly to his men – only to sergeants or corporals – and a junior officer will never start a conversation with a senior. Neither will discuss army matters in the mess, in case servants overhear, and women must never be mentioned there by name, in case a row sparks a duel. Such regimental traditions are cherished. The Cameronians even post guards around their church services, a tradition from the days when they were a hunted Presbyterian sect, and they remain proud to be a Lowland, trousered regiment – not a 'kiltie' Highland group – though they have always marched to the bagpipe, and maintain a kilted pipe band, which wears the Douglas tartan. The Cams are also known by a second name, Scottish Rifles, which the 1st battalion carries only in brackets – a legacy of earlier, enforced regimental amalgamation. These are the established customs, reinforced by success in countless colonial wars won with the British army's superior discipline and technology. And for the Cameronians (Scottish Rifles), it is all about to change.

Graham Chaplin will change too. He talks as he writes, no wasted words, brief interjections, as befits his two decades in uniform. Born to an affluent family, he had once aimed to read classics at Oxford. His father, a jeweller turned Lloyd's underwriter, then lost a fortune when ships carrying horses from Argentina went down at sea. Chaplin left school at fifteen, joined the army at twenty and now holds his own counsel. Only later will he reveal himself.

Lil Alexander fills the gaps, talks about her fears and emotions – they are a rounded whole, incomplete when separate. When suddenly they are pulled apart, they have only letters to carry on a dialogue they must continue, war or no war. So he will write almost every day, and she to him, telling what each can of what is happening, allaying fears, soothing with gossip and trivialities, telling not so much the truth as a version they will live together. Before this war is over he will write over 500 letters to Lil, and she the same to him. He destroys everything from her, because the longer the war continues, the less he expects to live, and he wants no one else to read them. She keeps his every word, for us to read now.

But first, she must let him leave with his battalion, numbering over 1,000 men. They are itching to fight, worried this European war will pass too quickly for them to make their mark. They have sharpened their ceremonial swords, cleaned their Lee-Enfield rifles, drawn stores, prepared transport, packed and stacked and assembled. They are fortified by friendship. Around him, Chaplin has a group of officers and men he has served with for years, soldiers who will follow him into the toughest of situations – Captain and Adjutant 'Sam' Stormonth-Darling, best man at his wedding; Captain Harry Lee, who he teases as 'Harriette'; and Major Richard Oakley, dubbed simply 'RO'. He also has a commander, Colonel Philip Robertson, another Englishman, tall, grey and gaunt – yet only forty-eight – who relies on him. Chaplin's no-nonsense demeanour and coolness under pressure simply makes him dependable.

It is less than two months since Austria's Archduke Ferdinand and his wife were assassinated in Sarajevo on 28 June 1914. Since then the Cameronians have returned from manoeuvres at the Duke of Atholl's estate in Perthshire and readied themselves for war. Across Europe, the major powers have mobilised their armies as Austria prepares to invade Serbia. Then, to gain swift advantage, Germany strikes through Belgium at France, hoping to capture Paris, and the Cameronians' fate is sealed. Reservists are called in, old soldiers reunited; the battalion swells to full fighting strength.

And finally, with the saying of goodbyes, they begin the slow journey by rail down from Glasgow's Maryhill Barracks to Southampton's cluttered docks, one of seventy trains a day that the port is processing. A number of the dray horses used to pull the battalion's transport are simply too big for the goods wagons provided, and at least four die on the moving train, strangled by their halters: an ill omen to some. The men disembark at the port and are told they are heading for Le Havre. They wait. Chaplin has already sent his first letter. Then he sends a telegram. Then he starts to write again.

Friday, 14 August 1914 [telegram from Southampton]

Very comfortable journey. We are going to the sort of place which would please you. Writing. Graham

Fridaty, 14 August 1914 [on notepaper of Anchor Line Steamer *Caledonia*]

My darling Lil,

We had a very comfortable journey, as I wired to you. The men got hot water to make tea at Oxford and we had some breakfast there. We arrived here at the scheduled time of 3pm and had all the men aboard in no time. We are very comfortable, three in a cabin. I am with Harriette and Captain McLellan.[1] We sail or are supposed to at 6pm tonight for Le Havre where we are to guard the base, so that we shall be more safe or just as much so as in Glasgow and I expect we shall be able to write alright from there but they may stop us.

We have heard no news except that 50,000 of our men have crossed. Mrs Oakley's brother is here with the 4th Highland Light Infantry – they are guarding the docks. Everything is admirably arranged and no fuss or worry. Some of the General Staff are crossing with us but they have not arrived yet.

After I wrote this morning I slept a little more but I am short of sleep, which I hope to make up. I feel very fit however and my eyes are alright. Everyone has recovered their spirits today – all the married ones were very depressed yesterday with their sad partings.

The crossing takes 10 hours. The weather is beautiful so we ought to have a splendid passage. It is very hot here, quite a different climate. We are to be at Le Havre with the Cameron Highlanders, the 93rd[2] and 2nd Royal Welch Fusiliers. There are beside ourselves some sappers and RAMC aboard.

Boy scouts collect and post letters. I must close now to catch the post. With my fondest love, your loving husband, Graham

Thursday, 20 August [postcard]
We are all very well and comfortable, Graham

Friday, 21 August [postcard]
All very well, Graham

---

1 Captain Harry Lee and Captain Thomas McLellan.

2 2nd Argyll & Sutherland Highlanders, so called because they were created by regimental amalgamation in 1881, before which the 2nd battalion was the 93rd Sutherland Highlanders.

Extracts from the battalion War Diary,
August and September 1914,

Kept by Colonel Philip Robertson

17 August - 5.30am: entrained in one train. 7.30pm: arrived Busigny and three companies marched to Maretz and went into billets there.

18-20 August - At Maretz doing fatigues unloading trains.

21 August - A Coy[1] proceeded to Valenciennes under Major Chaplin.

22 August - B, C and D Coys with Hd Qrs also proceeded to Valenciennes.

23 August - 1pm: received orders to advance to the Condé-Mons canal and took up a position. Our right was prolonged by the Middlesex Regt. Orders received to hold position at all costs. Middlesex Regt heavily engaged.

24 August - 2am: received orders to retire at once. Very lucky to get out of this position as to do so had to march a mile and a half along enemy's front. Eventually retired to Jenlain. NCOs and men turning very foot sore and tired.

25 August - Ordered to retire. Did so at dawn and marched to Haussy. Cavalry Division engaged all round and the Battn supported them. Came under shrapnel fire for the first time. Retired to Le Cateau.

---

1 Abbreviation for Company.

26 August - Moved off. Food scarce. Shortly after leaving the
town the battle commenced. Received orders to move to the left.
Did so. Received orders to move to Montigny. Received orders
to move to Bertry. Received orders to act as rearguard towards
Maretz. No pursuit by enemy. Marched all night to St Quentin.

27 August - All ranks very exhausted. Arrived St Quentin,
many stragglers. Marched on to Ollezy, arriving about 5pm.
Discipline hard to maintain owing to exhaustion of officers
and NCOs.

28 August - 4am: received orders to relieve Royal Welch Fus.
5.30am: marched and received several contradicting orders. This
all added six miles to day's march. 11am: Started to march
to Pontoise and arrived there 11pm. Found wagons which were
supposed to have been lost.

29 August - 5.30pm: received orders to march to Carlepont at
7.30pm to go into billets.

30 August - Arrived Carlepont at 1am though only four miles.
No billets. Battn slept on the side of the road. 7am: marched
to Choisy on the River Aisne. Men v tired, had to halt every
30 minutes. Very hot. Arrived 4pm.

31 August - According to orders paraded at 5.45am. Did not
march off till 7.30am. Marched all day through Forest of
Compiègne.

1 September - Retired at 4am, as we had no maps it was v
difficult to carry out orders. Retired south and the Brigade
took up a position covering the 4th Divn. Men very tired and
horses getting very badly rubbed and thin.

```
2 September - 4am: retired as rearguard. Opened fire on
German cavalry with machine gun, which was effective. Halted
for three hours at Eve and took up a position and
entrenched. Marched on to Dammartin where we arrived
about 7pm.

3 September - 1am: paraded again and marched on to Largny
where a halt is promised. Since the 22nd the Battn has marched
every day and frequently at night, and starts have always
been very early, preventing men getting a proper meal before
starting. Rations have been scarce, especially corn for the
horses. Men are quite worn out and on the 29th 221 men were
reported missing. Today the number is reduced to 186.
```

Saturday, 29 August 1914 [letter card]

All well – very hard time – not allowed to write yet. Graham

Thursday, 3 September 1914 [letter card]

I am very well but have had a very hard time. The only letter I have received from you is that of the 20th. All well. Graham

Saturday, 5 September 1914 [FSPC (Field-Service Postcard)]

I am quite well.

Letter follows at first opportunity.

Graham

Monday, 7 September 1914 [FSPC]

I am quite well.

Letter follows at first opportunity.

Graham

Friday, 11 September 1914 [FSPC]

I am quite well.

  Letter follows at first opportunity.

  I have received no letter from you lately.

  Graham

Sunday, 13 September 1914 [from bivouac in La Carrière l'Évêque, three miles south of Soissons]

My darling,

  One of the hardest things about this campaign, and we have had a very hard time, is not being able to write to you. It is a month today since I was last able to write. However in future I shall be able to write more often as the Colonel can now censor letters. We have had two mails from home; in all I have received five letters from you – the last written were first received – the last letter was dated August 27th. They were a great comfort to me and I'm glad you are keeping so well.

  We stayed at Havre one day and then went to a place called Maretz where we stayed a few days, getting a tremendous reception and being presented with bouquets of flowers. I did two route marches[1] with my company and returned like a walking horticultural show. From Maretz we went to Valenciennes where we remained one day. We were then formed into the 19th Brigade under General Drummond[2] with Capt Johnson,[3] Rifle Brigade, as Brigade Major, and Capt Jack[4] as staff captain. We left Valenciennes on August 22nd and since then I do not suppose that the troops have ever had a harder time. We supported the Cavalry Division and took up a position along the canal[5] near Condé. My company held the lock, one of the possible crossings. A company of the Middlesex on my

---

1 Taking men on 'route marches' was the army's favourite way of keeping soldiers fit – company commanders could choose to walk or ride.

2 General Laurence Drummond, veteran of the Sudan campaign and Boer War.

3 Captain H. C. Johnson, later killed at Le Cateau.

4 Captain James Jack, 1st Cameronians, who found fame posthumously in the 1960s as author of *General Jack's Diary*.

5 Better known as the Mons-Condé Canal.

right was heavily attacked. At two in the morning we were ordered to retire and got out of a difficult situation without losing a man. A platoon of the 93rd [1] who covered our retirement were scuppered. Next day we were over the Belgium border and saw the Cavalry Division heavily engaged. We retreated to Le Cateau doing about 25 miles a day. We left Le Cateau the morning of the battle about 5.30am and were fired at by the Germans in the town as we left it. The 2nd Army and our brigade took up a position just outside Le Cateau. Our brigade was on the right with the 93rd and Middlesex in the firing line and the Welch Fusiliers and ourselves in reserve. About 11 o'clock or so we and the Welch Fusiliers were ordered to the left flank of the British position, so off we trekked about six miles and just as we were going into action we were ordered back to where we came from. We were then ordered to take up a rearguard position which we did but the Germans did not pursue, so that although we were at a big battle we never fired a shot. We remained in position till 8pm, and then marched 22 miles to St Quentin, marching all night, halting only for one hour. Next day we went on another 12 miles, covering in all 50 miles in 30 hours. We retreated until the 6th, averaging 20 miles a day and being on outposts every second or third night so that I have had little sleep. We have just our rations to live on and not always that.

We are now advancing and everything is going well.

My company had Mr Ferry[2] and 10 men wounded by shell fire. You could not recognise the regiment[3] now, ragged and dirty, but the men have marched well. We very seldom see our valises and just live in what we stand in. We usually bivouac in cornfields. The heat at first was appalling but now we are suffering from rain and have been billeted in villages the last few nights. We know little of what is going on. You probably know more about the war than I do. The things I should like you to send are cigarettes, chocolate and condensed milk and also the weekly edition of *The Times*. We never see any papers except those that come with the mail.

---

1 See footnote 2, page 8.

2 2nd Lieutenant Ernest Ferry.

3 Chaplin frequently uses the term 'regiment' to mean battalion, rather than the Scottish Rifles in their entirety.

One of my front tooth crowns has broken off and I have broken off another tooth – both by eating Army biscuits. We seldom get bread.

I was glad to hear you got your dividend. I have nearly spent the £5 I brought out. I do not know how I am going to get more. All one wants money for is for food and wine.

Mr Drew[1] has gone sick – otherwise all are well but we are all very thin.

Thursday, 17 September 1914 [postcard]

M.D.W.[2] A mail came today and there was no letter from you, which was a bitter disappointment. I hope that you're alright. I am very fit and everyone well. Graham

Friday, 18 September 1914 [FSPC]

I am quite well.

Letter follows at first opportunity.

I have received no letter from you lately.

18 September 1914 [from bivouac outside Bucy-le-Long, east of Soissons]

As I told you in my last letter it was only discovered that we could send letters censored by the Colonel the day we started to advance. Unfortunately I have no envelopes or paper. Harry gave me the means of sending the last and I have borrowed another envelope today. As a rule there is no time to write – marching all day and we generally move during the night or are on outposts and get no sleep. In the last few days we have been before a position occupied by the enemy and so have rest as far as marching goes, but I have little sleep. It has rained all the time but has cleared up today. We are in reserve but have been under shellfire the whole time. My company is along the bank of a river – pretty safe – no casualties so far. We are wet through and just sleep in the open field, sometimes we get straw and sometimes not, but everyone keeps well. We get the soldiers' ration – bully beef, biscuits

---

1 2nd Lieutenant C. F. Drew.

2 My darling wife.

or bread, tea and sugar. I have had butter once in the last month and milk in my tea twice.

It seems like years since we left home – one loses all account of time. I have not had my clothes off for a fortnight and only had my boots off twice. We occasionally get a wash and clean our teeth. My teeth give me trouble, otherwise I am very well and my eyes alright.

Hynard[1] is well but is of very little use – he is not the stuff of which warriors are made. My groom Wardrop is splendid – brave, cheery and always can produce some tea and food. The officers of A Coy would have fared badly at times but for him.

If I get back I will tell you everything about the war – at present I cannot and it would not be wise to put on paper my opinion of people. We have a good Brigadier now, Gordon[2] by name, formerly in the Gordons.

I would give anything for a hot bath and a good night's rest in a bed. We cannot buy anything, there is hardly a match in the battalion. If you can occasionally send a shirt, a vest and a pair of drawers, a pair of socks and a handkerchief or two I should like it. It is no good sending more than one of each as I cannot carry it.

Saturday, 19 September 1914 [from bivouac outside Bucy-le-Long]

Today has been a red letter day – we got our valises for the first time in a fortnight and have changed our underclothes. I have now got the waterproof sheet which I wanted badly and also envelopes and this note book so that I am in a position to write when there is a chance. It is a marked day principally because I received four letters from you – the last dated the 2nd instant.

You must not worry about me. It would be absurd to pretend there is no danger but there is no good anticipating misfortune. We have been very lucky up to date and it may continue. It would console you if you had seen me the day Mr Ferry was hit – the shells were bursting all round me and I was

---

1 Chaplin's 'servant' or batman – the soldier allocated to arrange his 'comforts'.
2 Brigadier General Hon. Frederick Gordon, of the Gordon Highlanders, replaced Lieutenant Colonel E. E. Ward of 1st Middlesex, who had temporarily replaced General Drummond, wounded at Le Cateau.

untouched. It seemed impossible that I should not be hit. One of the saddest things about this war is to see the whole countryside deserted in most places and, where the people have not left, their looks of misery.

Last night it was a foul night – it rained in torrents. A Coy captured the first prisoner the battalion has taken – an Uhlan belonging to the 10th Lancers, a nice looking man. All the prisoners I have seen so far look very decent men. I do not believe much in the stories of German brutalities – no doubt cases do occur but it is chiefly camp followers and not soldiers.

We started off messing by companies and then had a battalion mess with Vandeleur[1] as mess president. I should think we have been worse fed than any officers in the Army. I could not stand V's constant chatter and directions and have gone back to the company mess. Anything you can send in small quantities will be thankfully received, such as whisky, condensed milk, chocolate, tinned butter, cigarettes, matches, soup. We can buy nothing at present and only have our rations, bully beef, tea, sugar and biscuits, occasionally rum and tobacco.

The list of casualties in the papers received by this mail are the first we have seen. Mr Salmonson[2] arrived about a week ago with the first reinforcement. I do not think he will last long – war is not his métier. We have heard no more of Mr Drew – he may be home now.

Aeroplanes, our own and German, are constantly over us. Two German ones have been brought down by our pom-poms. You do not say where your brother[3] is going to. Are they sending Territorials to the front? Do you know anything about our 2nd battalion? We know nothing of what is going on and see no papers except the old ones. I am afraid that my hair is getting worse, but I never think of it now.

---

1 Major Crofton Vandeleur, 2nd in charge of 1st Cameronians.
2 2nd Lieutenant E. Salmonson.
3 Lil's brother, Willie Alexander, is an officer in the 6th (territorial) battalion of the Black Watch.

Wednesday, 23 September [from billets in Septmonts, south-east of Soissons]

Everything in the garden is beautiful today. The night before last we moved back from our very damp abode on the river bank six miles or so and we are now in general reserve billeted in a village. The men are packed like sardines in barns and outhouses. We (A Coy) are very lucky – we are in a 14th-century farm. We have a bedroom and the use of the kitchen to feed in and cook. I have a bed, the first I have slept in for over a month – the other fellows have mattresses on the floor. The day before yesterday we were allowed to sleep in the morning for as long as we could – the first time we have not stood to arms an hour before dawn since we left Valenciennes. With the aid of a washing tub and the tin lining of a box we have all had baths and with clean underclothes we are clean once more. It has made an awful lot of difference getting a good sleep – everyone is rejuvenated. Hynard has washed and mended all my clothes. Every one of the officers is in the best of health and spirits, and the men are very cheery. We received two drafts of 100 men from the 3rd battalion, one under Mr Hardinge who has just joined and one under Pat Hewitt[1] who I am glad to say has been posted to my company. We have been living like princes for the last two days – we have had a fowl and also a rabbit for dinner, a change from the eternal bully beef. Yesterday we were digging trenches as a precautionary measure – everything is very quiet.

I received another letter from you dated 5th September. It is a great relief to me to hear that you are so well and also Doreen.[2] I am pleased you are getting so stout – a good sign. I received your very welcome parcel with the underclothes, chocolate, cigarettes and tobacco, which were greatly appreciated. We share everything we get. Please send me some envelopes as I shall be running out of them, now that I am writing to you so often.

I have taken to walking in my sleep – I suppose the result of very little sleep. I always have the same dream that the regiment is on the march at night and

---

1 Lt James Francis Hewitt, nicknamed 'Pat', killed by a shell on 26 October 1914. See letter of 7 November 1914.
2 Chaplin's pet name for their yet-to-be-born baby.

A Coy is getting left behind. The first night here I seized all the bed clothes and walked over the end of the bed and fell on top of Capt McLellan – much to his annoyance.

You must not worry about me. So long as you get no wire you will know that I am alright. My love to all at Brentham[1] and my fondest love to yourself, darling. Ever your loving husband, Graham

---

1 Brentham Park, the Alexander family home in Stirling.

THE WANT OF SLEEP

'It is impossible with my poor pencil to convey to you any picture of what it is like – day and night rifle fire and the crashing of guns of every size and description – sometimes terrific battles going on, sometimes comparative peace. It is a life of great strain . . .'

German army halted at the Battle of the Marne — French and British attack again at first Battle of the Aisne — Germans take Antwerp and target France's Channel ports — Belgian, British and French forces fight along line from Yser in north to Arras further south — German attempts to advance around Ypres held by Allies

The Cameronians have dodged the worst. Making a ragged retreat from the Mons Canal, and watching a desperate battle at Le Cateau, they have avoided direct confrontation with the Germans. As part of an independent brigade, unassigned to an army division, the battalion is continually deployed in reserve, held back in case of enemy breakthrough. Even at the start, when Graham Chaplin predicts they will be kept at Le Havre to guard the base, their purpose is unclear. But once they reach the front, defending the Mons Canal, they find their war changes from a few hours' defending to many days of retreat. For a fortnight they footslog rapidly south as the sheer size of the German army advancing through Belgium pushes the British and French forces back to Paris.

Chaplin has witnessed a chaos unseen by many in the British army – troops flooding through streams of refugees, baggage abandoned, maps lost, rural lanes jammed, men scattered, everyone heading back in the hope of finding a line of organised defence. Across the English Channel, Lil will have seen fragmentary reports in the press, jingoistic and confused, emphasising the tactical nature of the fallback, never a flight . . . Only the death notices running front page in *The Times* indicate where this war is heading.

The British army is trained to march – young lieutenants are even taught to inspect their soldiers' feet. But the retreat from Mons, covering almost 200 miles twisting east and west to avoid the enemy, undermines the resolve of even the toughest 'old sweats'. For the first time, there is doubt in the alliance with France, doubt in the ability of the general staff plotting the campaign, doubt in the predictions of a rapid war, 'over by Christmas'. Chaplin knows the Germans have been underestimated, and, like every officer in combat, he is swiftly discovering which of his men he can trust.

And when the French and British finally turn and fight, as they do on the Marne, capitalising on German indecision, the Cameronians are again held in reserve, billeted to the idyllic village of Septmonts, a medieval hamlet nestled in a wooded valley outside the badly bombed town of Soissons, with its crumbling papal palaces and exquisite Gothic cathedral. The war is audible but away from them, as they nervously wait.

Chaplin uses the time to write more, through the early days of October, always worried about his wife's pregnancy, always anxious to reassure her with details of his 'domestic' life – food, bedding, shelter, eye infections. The war is a sideline, though he makes plain his battalion's admiration for their enemy. The Germans, he writes, are very brave soldiers.

> Their artillery is especially good – the way they conceal their guns is wonderful. The only thing is that they do not make war like gentlemen. They evidently believe that all is fair in love and war. They resort to every low trick, abuse of the Red Cross, wearing ours and French uniform, spying they have reduced to an art.[9]

Any number of spies, he adds casually, have already been shot. As to his own actions, he will only hint: 'The Colonel has sent my name for mention in despatches – do not tell anyone as it is confidential. I would not tell you but in case anything should happen to me I should like you to know that I had done my duty.'[10]

The letters to Lil are read and censored by the same colonel, Philip Robertson, commander of the battalion, son of a general, a man who has barely seen action before this war yet ascended reliably through the officers' ranks. He is also an old friend who can be trusted.

Hence Robertson – calm, aloof, happiest relaxing, cigarette in hand – shrugs off the letters' repeated digs at Crofton Vandeleur, the battalion's second in command, who Chaplin dislikes so intensely. Vandeleur, scion of an Irish military family, is later captured by the Germans, and earns fame as Britain's first prisoner of war to escape and successfully make his way home. He then attracts newspaper headlines by vociferously complaining of his treatment in enemy hands – in particular that he was made to travel with the lower ranks in a cattle truck. Yet Chaplin has long seen him as a pompous bore and garrulous pedant, whom he hopes will be promoted away. By 5 October he gets his wish: 'Major Vandeleur has gone off today to command the Cheshire regiment. We do not know if it is permanent but all sincerely hope so.'

In fact, the two will dog each other for the rest of the war.

After Mons, the Cameronians must rebuild their strength. A headcount reveals 186 men missing at the end of the retreat, lost in northern France. Fresh soldiers from the Cameronians' other battalions – they maintain two, with others formed at times of war – will be sent from Scotland. On 27 September, completing the War Diary, which every battalion commander must update daily, Robertson lists his officers by company, plus his own HQ staff:

```
Headquarters
LT COL P R ROBERTSON
MAJ C B VANDELEUR
CAPT & ADJT J C STORMONTH-DARLING
LT R C MONEY
CAPT T S RIDDELL-WEBSTER
A Coy
MAJOR J G CHAPLIN
CAPT T R McLELLAN
LT J F HEWITT
LT D G MONCRIEFF WRIGHT
LT J H C MINCHIN
B Coy
```

```
CAPT  H  H  LEE
CAPT  R  H  W  ROSE
LT  E  W  P  NEWMAN
2LT  P  R  HARDINGE
2LT  H  S  R  CRITCHLEY-SALMONSON
C Coy
MAJ  R  OAKLEY
CAPT  W  CAULFIELD-STOKER
LT  H  O  D  BECHER
2LT  C  D  ROOKE
2LT  J  D  HILL
D Coy
CAPT  F  A  C  HAMILTON
CAPT  A  R  MacALLAN
LT  E  W  J  HOBKIRK
2ND  LT  R  D  GRAHAM
QM  LT  G  WOOD
The following officers are employed or sick:
CAPT  J  L  JACK  -  Staff Capt 19th Infy Bde
appointed 23.8.14
LT  C  F  DREW  -  Sick 5.9.14
2LT  E  L  FERRY  -  Wounded 9.9.14
LT  D  C  FOSTER  -  Sick 27.9.14
```

The battalion's medical officer, Lieutenant Fred Davidson, RAMC, is left off the list – the doctor is seen as an attachment, not a regular Cameronian.

In early October 1914 the race for the sea begins. After the German army is held at the Marne, the British and French realise they can outflank their enemy by heading quickly north towards the Channel ports. From there they can strike east to cut German supply lines.

The Germans, sensing an opportunity to capture Calais and Boulogne, race north too. Finally the armies will square off around Ypres and

Armentières, straddling the Franco–Belgian border, before extending a long line of trenches from the coast to Switzerland. But before that, there is the getting there, the night-time marching to avoid spotter planes, the mile-long trains rolling slowly north at five miles per hour. Already the men are operating in a fog of whispers, never quite knowing what the strategy is, where the enemy are, who will provide the next billets, where to find the next warm food. The Cameronians rely on their jocund quartermaster, the only officer promoted from the ranks, George 'Tubby' Wood, to get things done.

As this war progresses, and soldiers die, and fresh faces are continually plucked from Britain to fill the ranks, Wood, a heavy-drinking cockney, will be a constant, an always-there, feeding and supplying and organising. Officers will leave for other regiments, promoted up to other commands, but Wood carries on, the fairy godmother who always has a tot for the men when they need it.

Chaplin too will stay, year after year, but that autumn, packing to leave Septmonts with rumours flying about where and how, misinformed by newspaper accounts of Russian victories and German defeats, he can only wonder at when the Cameronians will finally get to fight – and when he will return to his wife.

And what is Lil Chaplin thinking? Seven hundred miles away, in the seventh month of pregnancy, scouring each line of his letters for clues, she can only watch and wait. But the Alexanders are a family of doers. Her father, Thomas Alexander, has worked his way to the top of Charles Tennant & Co, one of Scotland's leading industrial groups. Her elder brother, Willie, has already started his career in business, seconded to Lever Brothers' soap works in Port Sunlight, Lancashire. The Alexanders may sit ensconced in one of Stirling's grandest mansions, Brentham Park, but they have made their own money and are the very epitome of the management elite which now pushes to break down the old upper-class mistrust of 'trade'.

So Lil is busy finding out what Graham wants, ordering supplies, wrapping and posting, as involved as an officer's wife can be, engaging daily in a dialogue over his needs – his quartermaster at home. When she married Chaplin, just eight months earlier, on a cold January Saturday in Stirling, every officer of the 1st battalion Cameronians had attended the service at Holy Trinity Church, plus the former colonel of the regiment, Major-General Lomax. Brother officers formed an archway of swords for the couple to pass under and the regimental pipers played. A silver salver inscribed with the officers' signatures was presented to the couple. All were invited back to the reception at Brentham Park.

Thus Lil marries not just the man, but his regiment too, and with that comes responsibilities that will grow with each promotion. And in a war where the officers buy their own uniform, and rely on the postal service to supply so many of their needs, an efficient spouse is a blessing indeed.

Such organising is in Lil's genes – her grandfather, William Alexander, ran the Glasgow stables for his school friend, Charles Tennant, inventor of a revolutionary 'bleaching powder' for cloth and builder of Europe's biggest chemical factory at St Rollox, Glasgow. Her own father grew up at the site and went on to run the business, starting as a salesman, rising to managing director, finally overseeing the multiple interests into which Sir Charles Tennant, the founder's grandson, rearranged the family empire – chemicals (later part of ICI), soap (later part of Lever Brothers), mining and more. As the Tennants grew increasingly distracted by wealth and power, the Alexanders happily took on day-to-day management of everything.

It means Lil Alexander is no stranger to money, and its methods. The Alexanders moved to Stirling in 1897, buying Brentham Park from tweed manufacturer Robert Smith. The house and grounds offer a more suitable base than polluted St Rollox, dwarfed by Tennant's factories. The Alexanders now hold prestige in Stirling, attend the annual County Ball each autumn, and have their guests listed in the Stirling *Observer*, as in October 1913:

This annual fashionable gathering took place in the Albert Hall, Stirling, on Tuesday evening. There was an attendance of 320 ladies and gentlemen, and the beautiful decorations of the hall, added to by the gay dresses of the ladies and the many uniforms worn, rendered the scene a very pretty one when dancing was at its height . . . Amongst those present were: – From Brentham Park, Stirling – Mr and Mrs Alexander; Miss Lily Alexander, Miss I Alexander; Captain J G Chaplin, the Cameronians, Captain Sandilands,[11] the Cameronians, and Mr J Arnott,[12] the Cameronians.

For Lily and her captain admirer it is a chance to dance the night away, just months after they first meet, introduced by mutual friends, and just months before they marry. The music that night is provided by the renowned Wilhelm Iff and his orchestra. Glasgow-based Herr Iff, a German-born, naturalised British bandmaster, is a purveyor of waltzes, polkas and ragtime, 'the most up-to-date music'. He does not have a business which will survive the war.

And by 7 October 1914, the Cameronians are on the move again, sucked back into the fighting.

Wednesday, 7 October 1914 [from billets in Béthisy-St-Pierre, twenty-six miles west of Soissons]

My darling Lil,

Do you remember this day last year and the Stirling Ball? In a way it will be like it – we shall be up all night marching.

We have made two marches since I last wrote, both by night – the first one only 12 miles. We started at 7.30pm and got to our destination[1] at 1.30am, bivouacking in the rides of an enormous wood. Last night we did 14 miles starting at 7.30 – we did not reach this place[2] till 4am – there are so many delays on a night march. It was a lovely moonlit night through beautiful country. We are better off now for bedding as the men have blankets and there are carts to carry them – all the same it is none too warm. I have found the air pillow the greatest comfort.

Toothache is my only trouble, it bothers me a good deal but I believe dentists

1 Saint-Rémy-Blanzy.
2 Béthisy-St-Pierre.

are being sent out. I never received your telegram. You see all the wires are
cut in the theatre of operations and there are only field telegraphs which do
not take private wires.

October 9th: On the 7th we again passed the night in a wood after a 14-mile
march. Yesterday we marched by day, and also today. We are now in a more
civilised country[1] and can get some provisions. Some of us had dinner last
night in a café and also dinner today. We do not know where we are off to
but you will probably get to know from the papers.

Monday, 12 October 1914 [FSPC]
I am quite well.

Thursday, 15 October 1914 [FSPC]
I am quite well.

I have received your letter dated 4th Oct.

Saturday, 17 October 1914 [from billets in Vlamertinghe, outside Ypres]
I expect that by the time this reaches you, you will know from the English
papers where we are. I think I last wrote a letter on the 9th – that night we
entrained and travelled all night not knowing where we were going to, but
having a shrewd guess as to the general direction. The men were 40 in a truck
but the officers were quite comfortable – all five A Coy officers were together.
I slept very well which is exceptional for me in a train. I woke at daybreak and
popped my head out of the window and was surprised to see that the name of
the place was where we used to go for an annual beano when I was at school.[2]
The last time I was there was 31 years ago!

We arrived at our destination[3] about midday and marched at once a few
miles where we remained till nightfall when we moved to a village[4] and were

---

1 Estrées-St-Denis.
2 Boulogne.
3 St-Omer, Pas de Calais.
4 Renescure.

billeted. My company got a nice farm and we officers lived in an old moated chateau – built in 1410 but recently restored. The country not having been passed over by troops before, we got plenty of eggs, butter, bread and milk for the first time since Condé. Next day we were moved a few miles further and camped in a wet field. We had companies on outposts but being surrounded by French troops there was not much danger. To my surprise and delight Captain Ritchie[1] arrived very fit and well and longing for battle. Next day we did a fairly long march and encamped in a field close to a village which had been severely shelled the day before. A Coy had their mess in a cottage which had had two shrapnel shells burst in it. Since that day we have been in close contact with the enemy, driving him back.

Private Blomfield, whose death you saw, belonged to my company. He was hit at the same time as Mr Ferry – poor fellow, he screamed like a wounded hare. Corporal Hester is alright – he was sick for a short time.

No, it would not do to leave Doreen's kit till too late. I shall not be happy until I hear that she has safely arrived – the time is very short now. I was glad to hear from Mabel that you are really well. I thought you might be making yourself appear well for my benefit.

Monday, 19 October 1914 [from billets in Vlamertinghe]

In my letter of the 17th I omitted a lot of things I wanted to say, owing to writing in a babel of noise. I received your letters 1–4, and have got *The Times* alright. I have got a revolver now, one which our men found – one wants a revolver at night wandering around the outposts.

Yesterday, Sunday, we thought we were going to have a late lie-in as we were to have had Church Parade at 9.30am but it was not to be. I was woken at 4am and told that breakfasts were at 6am so we had to get up. Since then we have had to be ready to move at half an hour's notice. One has some startling surprises. Church parade was cancelled and we were ordered to parade for a move at 11am in motor buses for practice. At 11.30 up rolled 50 London penny buses into which we were loaded and taken for a 12-mile run.

---

1 A Cameronian officer who had been seconded to the Indian Volunteers.

The men thoroughly enjoyed it. Our buses have all come from Antwerp and our drivers are all London busmen and gave us great accounts of the fighting there. It was a great pity Antwerp fell as that will release a number of Germans. If the war is to end soon our only hope now is a great Russian victory. I do not suppose there is much fighting in the winter owing to the difficulty of transport and you cannot bivouac in the depth of winter.

I wish I could see you and how you look. Do you wear the black teagown at night? What do you wear in the daytime? Goodbye, my darling, your loving husband, Graham

Extracts from the battalion War Diary, October 1914,

Kept by Colonel Philip Robertson

Billets, Vlamertinghe
19 October - 2.30pm: left for Laventie 22 miles. The whole
flotilla of buses did not get in till 8.45pm owing to meeting
heaving ammunition columns on road (narrow) and also being
blocked by French Cavalry baggage.

20 October - 8.30am: the Battn and RWFus sent out to entrench
a position Fleurbaix-Fauquaint. 1.30pm: received orders to
assemble Battn at Rue Du Rois. Did so and Bde marched to
Frommelles. Bivouaced in a field. V wet night.

Outside Fromelles
21 October - 5am: stood to arms. 7.05am: marched to Bas
Maisnil. Le Maisnil occupied by A&S Highrs with Middlesex R.
on left. RWFus in Fromelles and Cameronians in reserve. 4pm: B
Coy sent to support Middx. 6pm: A&S Highrs got badly shelled
and they and Middlesex had to retire. 9pm: the Bde fell back

to La Boutillerie and took up a new position there. The
Cameronians being on both flanks. Casualties were one killed.
13 wounded, one missing, all of B Coy.

Trenches, La Boutillerie

22 October - 5.50am: a position was reconnoitred by Brigadier
and Commanding Officers and the Brigade entrenched. Half C Coy
under Capt Rose and half D coy under Capt MacAllan went out as
covering party. The party became engaged at once, the Germans
allowing them to get to close range then opening fire on them
from a flank with machine guns and rifles. They fell back a
little then held on splendidly. All ranks did very well and the
trenches were dug and occupied in spite of the enemy's rifle and
shrapnel. Capt R H W Rose killed. Capt A R MacAllan missing. 2nd
Lt A H Graham wounded. 2nd Lt W D Dubin wounded. Other ranks: 14
killed, 35 wounded, 8 wounded and missing. 11 missing.

6pm: enemy attacked but easily repulsed.

23 October - Slightly shelled. 1st Coy A&S Highlanders sent up
from Bde reserve to strengthen our left.

6.30pm: enemy attacked but easily repulsed. Losses 4 wounded.

24 October - Shelled as usual. 7pm: attacked and enemy
repulsed.

25 October - 3.30am: attacked but enemy repulsed. During day
shelled as usual. 7.30pm: demonstration by enemy. Very wet
night. Casualties: 4 wounded.

26 October - Shelled heavily all day long. Lt Hewitt killed.
Night quiet. Casualties: killed 14, wounded 11.

27 October - Sent out three patrols to reconnoitre under Lt
Newman, Rooke and Hill. Hill got into enemy's trenches which
were later re-occupied. Rooke got right up to same which were
occupied. Enemy demonstrated at 10pm. No notice was taken of
him and he withdrew. Casualties: 1 killed and 4 wounded.

28 October - 2.30am: enemy attacked trenches, creeping up
ditches to close range, was easily frustrated. Each attack
lasted about 30mins. Enemy moved across our front giving good
target. Casualties: 1 killed, 11 wounded.

29 October - 2.45pm: enemy attacked and demonstrated and was
repulsed. 10pm: enemy bombarded on left.

30 October - Midnight: enemy attacked our centre which fizzled
out very soon. 12.45am: attack against C Coy began. This Coy
was holding a farm in a rather nasty part of the line, forming
a salient. Attack continued all night, enemy beaten off at
6am. Capt Ritchie was wounded and 1 man killed, 3 wounded.
The enemy got right up to the trenches and lost 30 killed and
40-60 wounded. Sir John French congratulated the Brigade on
its work. During the night, Middlesex had its line broken but
a counter attack in the morning restored line to its original
state. Lt Newman went sick.

31 October - 4am: attacked by enemy but driven off. Quiet day.
Casualties: nil.

Friday, 23 October 1914 [FSPC[
I am quite well.

Saturday, 31 October 1914 [FSPC[
I am quite well.

Monday, 2 November 1914 [FSPC]

I am quite well.

Tuesday, 3 November 1914 [FSPC]

I am quite well.

Saturday, 7 November 1914 [from trenches in La Boutillerie]

My darling Lil,

You must be wondering why I have not written. Our dreams of a peaceful time in our Belgian village were rudely shattered the day after I last wrote. I am very hazy about dates. We were given half an hour's notice to get on board our buses. We did 20 miles in them, the remainder of the Brigade marching. We started at 2pm and did not arrive till 8pm owing to breakdowns and bumping into ammunition columns and the train of a French cavalry division. We were eventually billeted in a village[1] – my company in a gendarmerie. I had a bed but did not undress. The next day we moved out as we were supposed to dig trenches for four hours and return to lunch. We then received orders for the Brigade to assemble and we marched seven miles to a village where we spent the night in a wet field. I had only my Burberry and was not too hot. Next day the Argylls and Middlesex held one village and the Welch another and we were in reserve in a central position. Towards evening Harriette was sent with his company to reinforce the line in front, but our people had already begun to retire when he arrived. He lost one killed and a good many wounded from shells. We were left in peace until nearly dark, when an aeroplane came over and gave us away and we were shelled. The shells were just lobbing over my company but not bursting and no-one was hit. We covered the retirement to this village[2] but were not pursued. We took up a position for the night. I was in charge of the right, we were not attacked, but I got only half an hour's sleep as I had to examine all the ground. Next morning I got orders to bring A and B Coys through the village and entrench. We came through the village under shell fire, drew tools and entrenched

---

1 Laventie.
2 La Boutillerie.

under fire the whole time. Half C and half D Coys under MacAllan and Rose formed a covering party about 1000 yards in front and held up the Germans to give us time to entrench. They did their job right well and had heavy casualties. Rose was killed, Dulieu (late sergeant-major) and Graham wounded. We had just got deep enough in the ground when the covering party came back. It was grand to see the way they stuck to the wounded. I said by Jove there are some brave men in the Cameronians.

No-one can hear anything of Ronnie MacAllan. He gave the order for his men to retire and went across to see Rose and was never seen again. We all hope he is a prisoner and not killed.

For the first week we got very little rest, attacked all night and shelled all day. Poor Pat Hewitt was hit by a shell. It was a great blow to me – one of the most unselfish and charming fellows I have ever met. Ritchie was severely wounded in a night attack exposing himself unnecessarily – a great pity, a splendid officer and he had done awfully well in charge of C Coy. Gordon who had only joined two days was severely wounded. We have had a lot of men hit, but fewer than you might think possible from the terrific fire which we have had poured on our devoted heads.

It is an extraordinary life we lead. Capt McLellan and myself live by the traverse of a trench, 8 feet by 4. We have it covered with a door for a roof. We have sacks stuffed with straw for a bed – we do cox and box and only require one bed. We do two-hour watches throughout the night – the men do the same, half sleep and half stand to arms. It is impossible with my poor pencil to convey to you any picture of what it is like – day and night rifle fire and the crashing of guns of every size and description – sometimes terrific battles going on, sometimes comparative peace.

It is a life of great strain which only the physically fit can stand. The want of sleep is the greatest trial. Mr Newman has gone home with a nervous breakdown, Capt Jack has also gone home sick. Capt Riddell-Webster[1] is now staff captain of the brigade. I hope to see him get on well.

---

1 Captain Thomas Riddell-Webster, later to become General Riddell-Webster in World War Two.

I am glad that Vandeleur is not killed and very glad he is not with the regiment. I was afraid that the casualty list would be a shock to you. I knew of course they had to come. I am terribly sorry for Mrs Rose and Mrs Ronnie.[1]

The German trenches are only 200 yards away so that we are very close neighbours. One night they called out "Cease Fire A Coy" as they had heard me do. My thoughts are all with you. I remember every day we have had together.

Sunday, 8 November 1914 [FSPC]
I am quite well.

11 November 1914 [from trenches in La Boutillerie]
We have been getting our letters with great regularity – they come with the rations after dark – late when there is firing – early when there is none. It does not matter, dear, if you have any news or not – your letters are the only thing I look forward to each day. I put a coat around me and read them by the electric lamp as one can show no lights with the enemy so close. Your parcel with the toilet paper was most welcome – I finished my last supply yesterday. Edith's socks for the men also arrived at a most opportune moment when they were badly needed.

Life goes on just the same – shelling all day – at night an attack somewhere. We are so well dug in now that our daily casualties are few. We have lost about 200 men here killed and wounded and have been lucky compared to some regiments.

We have had our house improved – we have made a passage behind for the men and have enlarged it – the worst is the mud. We are now sending back to a village[2] in the rear a fifth of officers and men each day to wash and have a walk. We have now been 21 days in the trenches and are all suffering from swollen feet and legs from want of exercise. Our only diversion is to go to headquarters or some other company as all the trenches are now connected up.

---

1 Wife of Captain Ronnie MacAllan – the Cameronian officer who is missing, later confirmed as a German prisoner.
2 Fleurbaix.

We know nothing about the war and get all our information from the home papers. Everyone I seem to have known has been killed or wounded. I can hardly credit Capt Fowler's report of Ronnie MacAllan[1] but hope that he is a prisoner.

It is getting very cold now. This is not a very good letter but as our guns are firing over us and the enemy are shelling it is rather hard to write. With all my fondest love and constant hope that you are well.

Friday, 13 November 1914 [FSPC]

I am quite well.

Monday, 16 November 1914 [from billets in Bac St-Maur]

The night before last, we were unexpectedly relieved out of the trenches, withdrawing in the dark with no losses. We are now in a village[2] some way in the rear of the firing line. It has been delightful being able to sleep for more than two hours at a time and not to be under fire after 25 days of it night and day, and 24 hours in the trenches. Two days before we were relieved I went back for 12 hours to a farm where we had a hot bath and good meals. I shall never forget the delight of that bath. I did not say anything about Keatings[3] as I thought it not a pleasant subject. The fact is that all of us have had unpleasant visitors for some time – it is impossible to avoid.

I hope that you were not hurt by my not writing for 10 days or so but I simply had not the heart to write in case I should be killed before you received the letter. I was in one of the trenches most exposed to the first of the heavy guns. I never cease to think of you night and day and to trust that you are well – it will be an immense relief to me when Doreen has arrived. I am afraid our rest here will not last long and we expect to go into the firing line again tomorrow. I do not know how long one can last at this game – personally I am extraordinarily well in spite of everything.

---

1 Spotted as a prisoner recovering from wounds in a Lille hospital.
2 Bac St Maur, outside Armentières.
3 A reference to fleas and lice – Thomas Keating was a nineteenth-century London chemist whose 'Persian Insect Destroying Powder' was a popular insecticide for use on animals.

We are in quite a comfortable house and have a piano. Yesterday we had a concert in the afternoon which prevented me from writing to you as I intended. Mr Hill[1] played and I had not the heart to stop them.

Tuesday, 17 November 1914 [FSPC]
I am quite well.

Thursday, 19 November 1914 [from trenches in Houplines, outside Armentières]
Our rest was not a long one. We came into these trenches the night before last, relieving the Enniskillin Fusiliers and Seaforths. The relief was carried out at night of course and we were luckily not fired on. It is rather exciting work moving in silence in the night and not knowing if there will be a blaze of fire any minute. These are not such good trenches as the ones we made at La Boutillerie. I have the best section as it lies fairly high and is therefore drier – C and D Coys are half under water. I have had a dugout built to sleep in and we are building a palatial mess but it is slow work as we have to get doors etc for the roof at night from the ruined houses behind. We have got a stove and should be comfortable.

It is snowing today pretty hard and it looks as though winter is setting in – it is awfully cold at night. Our 5th battalion has joined our Brigade – we have not seen them, they are somewhere in the rear. I shall be glad to see Billy Croft.[2]

I was sorry to hear of the death of Lord Roberts[3] but he has had a grand life and died in harness.

We have no idea how long we shall remain here. I long to see you and how you are looking.

---

1 2nd Lieutenant Jacobus (John) Hill.
2 Major William Croft, fourth son of Sir Herbert Croft, Baronet. He went on to be mentioned in despatches ten times and awarded the DSO four times in World War One. In 1919 he wrote a book of his experiences, *Three Years With The 9th (Scottish) Division*, published by John Murray.
3 Former commander-in-chief of British forces and hero of the Boer War.

Saturday, 21 November 1914 [FSPC]

I am quite well.

Monday, 23 November 1914 [FSPC]

I am quite well.

Monday, 23 November 1914 [from trenches in Houplines]

Three mails have come in with no letter from you – I hope that it does not mean that you are ill. The last two days we have spent in getting our house[1] ready. First we built quite a decent house in the trench for the servants and Hynard built me a hole in the trench to sleep in – just a six-foot hole, about three wide and three deep. It is fairly comfortable but not warm enough.

We have not been shelled since we have been here or attacked but their snipers fire all day and we have had a few casualties. I had a man killed the day before yesterday – his own fault, contrary to orders he left the trenches in daylight. I attended the funeral at night and the parson read the service. It was very simple, the soldier was buried just as he was. It was a queer scene, a few men standing round the grave and the parson saying the service in the darkness, guns and maxims firing in the distance, and the sniper firing close at hand, and wondering how soon it may be one's own turn.

With all my love – my darling, ever your loving husband, Graham.

---

1 He uses the term 'house' ironically to mean dugout.

ARMENTIÈRES

'I have felt very depressed since I came back . . . The change from Stirling is so violent. All the others have gone to bed. It is 9 o'clock, a late hour for us. You have all my thoughts.'

Trench line established from French coast to Swiss border — British forces suffer from lack of manpower, equipment and shells — first German airship seen off east coast of England — Hartlepool and Scarborough bombarded by German cruisers — bitter fighting at Ypres ends in stalemate — Franco—British forces fail in attempt to advance on German-held Lille

Armentières, twelve miles south of Ypres, one mile south of the Franco-Belgian border, has survived unscathed – so far. Sprawling and prosperous, studded with linen works drawing on the River Lys that winds around the town, it goes about its business untroubled by the violence unleashed by war. Beyond Houplines, its red-brick, eastern suburb, where rows of cobbled streets house the town's factory workers, the German army has retreated to higher ground and left the boggy fields to the British. The trench line that will hold for most of the war is already established. The Germans are determined to hold Lille, just ten miles to the south-east, but they leave Armentières be. In time it becomes known as 'the nursery front', where new battalions learn the art of trench warfare away from the threat of sudden offensives. But for now, on its outskirts, it is lethal, as the Cameronians, exhausted from the battering they took at La Boutillerie, dig in for prolonged trench defence – vulnerable to snipers, to exhaustion, to lice and trench foot, to cold and filthy conditions.

Yet in Armentières life goes on, beer flows, the brothels multiply, the shops are full of pastries, the estaminets sell omelettes and chips. For Graham Chaplin and his battalion, it will be a strange on–off existence, five days misery, five days relief, as they alternate with other units in the 19th brigade, now part of the 6th division, in and out of trenches. A routine is established, experience is gleaned, and the realisation creeps in of just how pitifully ill-prepared they are for this type of warfare. Down in the hastily dug trenches, they have no hand grenades, no rifle grenades, no periscopes, no mortars, too few machine guns, inadequate digging tools, no waterproof clothing or footwear. The Cameronians struggle in an army that is used to fighting ill-armed natives in colonial territories and winning. Now their opponents are better prepared, with better weapons and better discipline. They have met an immovable force, and do not have a strategy to overcome it.

As commander of A Company, strung out in the waterlogged line, Chaplin faces extreme peril. Robertson has no choice but to stretch all four of his companies across the front, with little in reserve. The enemy is only eighty yards away in places, clearly audible at night. Their snipers take aim from ruined houses across churned fields. Yet the trenches are often poorly linked, forcing officers like Chaplin to scramble up and over to visit different platoons. For a company commander must check his positions, reassuring his men, always vulnerable to snipers, exposed to shelling, fearful of raiding, living a shanty town existence in gimcrack shelters built from doors pulled out of badly bombed houses, using buckets for toilets and braziers for cooking, piling up vast parapet walls where the ground is too wet to dig. Every night drinking water must be carried in under cover of darkness from the town behind. And every dawn each man must stand to arms, peering to the east to check no attack is imminent. Sleep is hopelessly broken. Trenches must be repaired. Supplies dragged in. Reports written. Soon everyone is exhausted.

Then on 19 November the first snow arrives, and as temperatures tumble, frost becomes the new enemy, freezing fingers, numbing toes, eventually maiming and debilitating. Five days later, a thaw, and the trenches fill with more water, more misery. By 25 November Robertson is writing in the battalion's War Diary: 'Very wet – trenches in an awful state. Parapets and traverses begin to give way.' Then the frost and snow return.

Houplines in winter is a long way from the Indian sub-continent which Chaplin loves. He spent his formative army years there, escaping London in the 1890s, and a family that had hit hard times. His father, James Hopper (Jimmy) Chaplin, at one time a member of the Honourable Artillery

Company, had amassed his wealth sourcing gems abroad for the family jewellery business, and spent the 1880s as a wealthy underwriter at Lloyd's of London, insuring the vessels that carried Britain's overseas trade. Then the loss of one shipment changed everything.[13] Years later, the family would tell of a ship carrying Argentinian polo ponies lost at sea, which cost Jimmy Chaplin his fortune. The worst thing, Graham would add, telling the story, was the thought of those poor ponies drowning. Polo was one of the many things he loved about army life in India.

Before the loss, his parents ran a household that buzzed with the gossip of London's artists, craftsmen and businessmen – his mother, Alice Landells, was the daughter of illustrator Ebeneezer Landells, founder of *Punch* magazine. His uncle, Robert Landells, was a renowned war correspondent and photographer. His elder brother, Robert Chaplin, went on to become an evangelical Christian and photographer, his younger brother, Lindsay, a vicar, and his sister, Florence, an accomplished painter. Florence would later marry Ernest Shepard, the artist who made his name illustrating *Winnie The Pooh*.

So Chaplin's is not the usual army home, such as that experienced by most officers in British regiments, with long traditions of service. Quite the reverse; it is liberal, artistic, devout in parts and rooted in the wealth created by generations of London's jewellery craftsmen, drawn from Huguenot stock. In the 1880s and 1890s the Chaplin family lives with four servants in a fine six-storey house at 28 Penywern Road, Earl's Court. It is an area popular with artists and actors – Ellen Terry, London's most famous actress, lives just around the corner.[14] The Earl's Court showground by the railway station hosts exhibitions which draw vast crowds. Buffolo Bill Cody rides the arena in 1887, when Graham Chaplin is just fourteen.

And here Jimmy and Alice bring up eight children in all – but when the ship sinks, the money goes and the household shrinks. By 1897, when Jimmy Chaplin dies, the household includes paying lodgers. Before then, Graham has left, joining the army and serving in India. His education at St Paul's, the day school of choice for the newly affluent business classes, has been brief. He leaves in 1888, at barely sixteen, later telling his children that he had argued with his Classics teacher and refused to attend his lessons, and of necessity switched to 'Army classes', for those targeting a service career. He later joins the 4th Militia battalion of the Royal Fusiliers, a City of London reserve unit, training young men for an army commission. He has made his own rebellion from a family that cherishes art and craft. He is not nicknamed 'Bull' for nothing.

By the end of 1894 he is commissioned as a 2nd lieutenant in the Cameronians, a regiment with which he has no direct connection, as its base is in Lanarkshire, but which he likely chooses simply because it has a vacancy and is less expensive in terms of uniforms and mess bills than some of the more glamorous names closer to London (Guards, Cavalry).

And so, on 10 January 1895, while he is at home in Earl's Court, a letter arrives from the War Office telling him to report to the transport ship *Dilwara* in Southampton docks for passage to Bombay and join the battalion at its Indian posting. A fortnight later, he has gone.

By the time he is dragged back to Scotland in 1909, serving as adjutant in the Scottish Rifles' 3rd battalion, overseeing a unit of Special Reserve – the part-time force that replaces the Militia – he can speak Hindustani and is addicted to India's habitual warmth. But he has money problems. The Cameronians may be cheaper than the Guards, but they still make requirements on an officer's purse, and a private income of at least £150 a year is needed to supplement salary – mess bills must be paid (every officer chips in for a good chef and proper drinks), polo ponies must be stabled, tailors must be sought for multiple uniforms. Rare is the officer without a private income, and indeed, without a major boarding school to his name. But Chaplin is a signifier of how the army is already changing, even before 1914. After experiencing 1897's fierce fighting on the Afghan frontier, seconded to the 2nd battalion Yorkshire regiment for the campaign, he determines a simple credo: live well while you can, for you never know what tomorrow will bring. So, for much of his early army life, he operates in debt.

He also remains unmarried, as traditionally wives are not encouraged in the army until an officer attains senior rank. Then there is no shortage of eligible daughters looking for a major, which Graham Chaplin becomes in 1913. And one hot day that summer, Harry Lee's wife invites her friend Lil Alexander to accompany her to a lunch at Stobs military camp, near Hawick, where the Cameronians are briefly stationed. Herr Iff's polkas, two months later, do the rest.

Lil will have no qualms at Graham's impoverished circumstances, as the Alexanders have money enough. What Chaplin offers is a life outside factories and chemical works. He is droll, determined and pugnacious. He is also immediately smitten by the tall, anxious woman with the languorous eyes and pilaster-like Alexander nose.

With Lil comes love and the prospect of financial security – Graham owes money to his sister, Connie, younger brother, Lindsay, and friends in India. Engagement to Lil before Christmas 1913 is followed by marriage in January 1914, pregnancy in April, then, unexpectedly, just when he hoped for some stability, war. Just when he hoped to be by Lil's side.

All of which he carries to Houplines through months of fighting in that wet, cold winter of 1914. So when the British Expeditionary Force realises, in late November, that deadlock has been reached, that its brigades must be restocked and its serving men revived, and it allows officers ten days' home leave[15] – three at a time from each battalion – Chaplin pleads to go so he can see Lil again. Robertson accedes, choosing himself and Lieutenant Hobkirk for leave too. Chaplin travels in the hope of attending the birth of his first child, yet he is now anxious about his dreams of being left behind on the march, and his recurring bouts of sleepwalking. They are the first clear symptoms of war neurosis.

Thursday, 26 November 1914 [telegram from Folkestone]
Just arrived on ten days leave. Will arrive Stirling tomorrow morning. I will try telephone tonight. Graham

Saturday, 5 December 1914 [telegram from Folkestone]
Good journey, Graham

Sunday, 6 December 1914 [from billets in Houplines, outside Armentières]

My darling Lil,

I did not have any difficulty catching my train at Glasgow. I went into the Central and had a whisky and soda. I did not see anyone I knew as I thought I might. I warned the guard I might walk in my sleep as I had promised you that I would. I did not sleep much. I felt so miserable at leaving you again especially at such a time. In the morning I found that Stevenson of the HLI[1] – known as the Red Mullet – was in the next sleeper to me, also returning off leave, so we taxi'd together to Victoria. We put our things into the train and I walked about the platform until Mrs McLellan turned up with Hope Urquhart. The Colonel and Mrs Robertson then arrived and we all talked until the departure of the train. Mr Hobkirk only caught the train by two minutes, the Scotch train having been late. We had a rough passage. We got to Boulogne at 12.30 and had lunch and left at 1.45 in our buses. It was amusing to see the change in people from the homeward journey, everyone looking smart and clean. We were very late reaching the end of the bus journey and had to wait for some other officers before proceeding in the ration lorries.

I finally got to my billet at 2am. I was delighted to find that I had a bedroom to myself and quite a good bed. In the only other bedroom Capt McLellan has a bed and Mr Wright[2] and Mr Minchin[3] share a bed. I turned in pretty quickly and was woken by Harriette at 8am looking very well and very anxious to hear all the news. Nothing has happened whilst we were away and the trenches were relieved without a shot being fired.

I got all your letters and read them – they were a comfort though old news. It is horrid to think I shall get none from you for a week. I received all the parcels – your watch which I will return, the waterproof which is a topper and the very thing I want, the glasses which are splendid ones, the haversack and water bottle, underclothes, pipe and cigarettes, shirts and collars. Altogether,

---

1 Highland Light Infantry.
2 2nd Lt Douglas Moncrieff Wright.
3 2nd Lt James Cotton Minchin.

darling, there is absolutely nothing that I require now, thanks to you. I cannot thank you sufficiently for all your care for me.

The men are in mills and pretty comfortable and have got clothes, any amount of waffles, milk etc and have all had hot baths in a laundry. I walked into the large town with Harriette this afternoon to see Billy Croft and the 5th Bn – the King inspected them when he was here.

With all my love – all my thoughts are with you, dearest.

Monday, 7 December 1914 [from billets in Houplines]

Everything is very quiet but it was unpleasant after being at home to hear the old guns again and the occasional rifle fire. After lunch I went for a walk with Capt McLellan into the big town – there are lots of people about and it was hard to realise that it was war, so different from anything we have known before. It has been raining all day and the mackintosh proved a great boon, it is not too long.

It is very hard to settle down to this life after being at home. I think of you all day and wonder how you are – what the home life is like and if you are very dull and whether you have lots of people to see you. I shall not be happy till I hear of Doreen's safe arrival.

Tuesday, 8 December 1914 [from billets in Houplines]

I slept very badly last night – I wondered if it was anything to do with you and if your bad time had started. We were the company on inlying piquet so we could not go far away. Capt Stirling[1] who used to be in the regiment and is now in the 3rd Bn arrived last night with a draft of 130 men so we are nearly up to strength. He is in charge of C Coy – I hope he will have more luck than his predecessors.[2]

It amuses us to see some optimistic inhabitants repairing their houses and hope that they will not be disappointed. It is extraordinarily mild weather now and fine today – it is just as well as we have not got our fur-lined coats yet.

---

1 Jock Stirling, killed a month later by a sniper.
2 Capt Ritchie, wounded at La Boutillerie, later died of his wounds in hospital.

I wonder if you have got the photos[1] from Ballantyne's? St Vincent's Square is his address.

The Colonel heard from Major Vandeleur's mother today. He is – as we guessed he would be – running the messing of the officers who are prisoners.[2] We hope that they are more pleased than we were!

All the others have gone to bed. It is 9 o'clock, a late hour for us. You have all my thoughts.

Thursday, 10 December 1914 [from billets in Houplines]
All leave has been suspended, which shows how wise I was to take my leave whilst I could get it. I am very sorry for those disappointed.

This morning instead of going for a walk I remained in to give evidence as to a man's character who was being tried by CM.[3]

We go into trenches tomorrow, earlier than we expected but one company will remain here – I do not know yet whether it will be mine. I am sitting up late tonight as half my company are digging in the trenches and I feel like an anxious mother. I am never quite happy until I see them all safely back.

Of course I cannot think of anything but you and how you are getting on and how soon Doreen is to arrive. With all my love, ever your loving husband, Graham

---

1 A number of officers in the battalion are now taking photographs of the campaign, using small 'vest pocket' cameras.
2 Vandaleur had been promoted out of the Cameronians to command 1st Cheshire, and been wounded and taken prisoner.
3 Court martial.

Extracts from the battalion War Diary,
December 1914,

Kept by Colonel Philip Robertson

Trenches, Pont Ballot, outside Armentières

11 December - relieved A&S Highlanders in trenches near Pont
Ballot.

12 December - trenches very wet especially those on our left
where there were quite 18 inches of water for 30 yards.

13 December - Captain Jack rejoined.

14 December - GOC 19th Infantry Bde went round trenches in the
evening.

15 December - improving trenches - enemy sniping but doing
nothing else. Two men wounded.

16 December - Royal Field Artillery shelled farms on our front
and enemy's trenches.

17 December - one man killed.

18 December - kept up heavy sniping in enemy's trenches.

19 December - trenches very much improved, especially in the
centre by A Company (commander Major J G Chaplin).

20 December - nothing to send.

21 December - received confidential orders of an attack to be

carried out by the Battalion against a portion of the enemy's
trenches. Kept up heavy sniping of enemy's trenches.

22 December - orders received cancelling the orders to attack.
One man killed.

23 December - draft of one officer (2Lt Bannerman) and 36
other ranks joined. One man wounded. Lt PR Harding wounded.

24 December - GOC 18th Infantry Bde went round trenches.
Sniping as usual.

25 December - enemy very noisy during night. One man wounded.

26 December - 4.45pm: the battalion was relieved by the East
Yorkshire regiment. The whole relief was finished by 7.45pm.
The Battn was out of the trenches before any of the other
Battns of the Brigade. The Battn went into billets in the west
end of Armentières.

Tuesday, 15 December 1914 [from trenches at Pont Ballot, outside Armentières]

My darling Lil,

I am sorry that I have not been able to write since the 10th. On the night of the 11th we went into trenches – it was raining hard and has rained ever since. The trenches were chaos, all falling in from the rain and in some places up to our knees in water. Our dugout was a pond and the roof a sieve. We were wet up to our middles the whole time and got very little sleep. We had nowhere to lie and slept in chairs. We came out to billets last night for three days. The trenches we go into are much drier.

Capt Jack[1] arrived last night – I have not seen him yet – so that he was not kept long at Nigg.[2]

We are in quite a nice house and I have a very nice bedroom and beautiful bed – a startling change from the trenches. I had a hot bath too and I feel more like a Christian. The 12th was my regimental birthday – 20 years of soldiering. I hope the next will be spent at home.

Wednesday, 16 December 1914 [from trenches at Pont Ballot, outside Armentières]

When I descended from my really luxurious bedroom to find Hynard to bring me some tea this morning and entered the room where all the others slept I was greeted by Capt Hamilton with the words "I congratulate you." I replied "What on – having a bed to sleep in?" and he said "No, on having a son."

He then told me that Mrs H had a wire and a letter – I suppose from Mabel – and that you were both well. You can imagine how pleased and surprised I was and what a relief it was to know that you are well and that it is all over. I hope that you did not have a bad time. I am awfully pleased that Doreen was a boy after all and I know that you will be.

I did not get the telegram until this afternoon. It was rather funny as it was worded "son arrived PAISLEY. Both well." I slept splendidly last night and all this afternoon and have nearly made up for lost time.

There is so much that I want to know – if you had a bad time, what weight the infant is and if up to standard, how you feel, if you are nursing it. It is very hard to write as the room is full of people talking. I cannot express how thankful I am that you are well and that we have now a son.

Thursday, 17 December 1914 [FSPC]

I am quite well.

A Happy New year.

---

1 Sent home with pneumonia.

2 Army training camp on the Cromarty Firth, north of Inverness, where the 3rd battalion Scottish Rifles were temporarily based.

17 December 1914 [from trenches at Pont Ballot, outside Armentières]

I am wondering how you are and how you are getting on with the infant and if he cries much. I could not get to sleep last night for a long time thinking all about it. The Colonel came in this morning for the day – he and everyone have been congratulating me. Get the finest perambulator you can for the boy and pay for it out of my account as a present from his father. I cannot think of anything else which would be useful at his early age. You will be pleased that he was born on the 13th as a lucky day.

There is a lot of wit being expended on what the boy should be called but I would be pleased with James Alexander as anything, unless you have other ideas.

There has been a lot of activity the last few days on our part but I do not know what it all means. We go back to the trenches tonight for nine days and then have another three days out. I should think that at some time in the New Year, the Brigade should be sent back for a rest. There is a general impression that leave will be re-opened again soon.

Sunday, 20 December 1914 [from trenches at Pont Ballot, outside Armentières]

It has been impossible to write for the last three days owing to being in the trenches and it raining hard. We are covered in mud. I had your letter dated the 12th – it was jolly good and plucky of you to write at such a time. I wish I could see you both.

Things are a bit more lively – we seem to be making a push in some quarters. Our General is going home on leave so I presume we are not moving at present.

Yesterday I was out of the trenches being President of a court martial in the big town.[1] Harriette is in billets at present. I meant to write to you but went to sleep in Harriette's bed and when I woke it was time to return to the trenches. I was very tired as we are at present up half the night on watch – also we have a very bad place to sleep in and I cannot sleep very well.

---

1 Armentières.

Monday, 21 December 1914 [from trenches at Pont Ballot, outside Armentières]

I wrote to you yesterday and gave the letter to Capt Darling who was going home on leave but he was stopped at the last moment and so I had to post. Harriette is now going instead so I am giving this to him to post – he is in a state of unbounded excitement so I hope that he will not forget.

I have received both of nurse's letters and am greatly relieved to hear that both of you are going on well. I gather from nurse's letter that you are nursing him yourself so I suppose that you were wrong when you anticipated that the dairy department would be no use. I think of you both all day and all through the long watches of the night.

The General's leave has been stopped so there is evidently something up, we do not know what it is. There is a great deal of activity all round us. We have had an easy time as regards fire and only had a few casualties.

How do you like being a mother? Of course it is very difficult for me to realise – I hope that the boy's eyes remain blue but they often change don't they?

Wednesday, 23 December 1914 [from trenches at Pont Ballot, outside Armentières]

I received your letters of the 16th, 17th, 18th and 19th – they were of enormous interest to me. I am sure you had a jolly bad time. I cannot tell you how glad I am that it is all over.

We have got our house[1] finished today and are now more or less in comfort with a table and chairs and I have a nice bed of straw. It is dry, so with my nice blankets, waterproof sheet and air pillow I sleep warm and in comfort except that one's feet are always wet and I have to wrap them in a waterproof sheet. You will be glad to hear that the Brigade goes back into reserve on the 26th, so we shall have some rest which I think we deserve.

Harriette goes on leave tonight. He has been almost off his head with excitement – poor little chap. When I said goodbye I never expected to see him again as I knew that the regiment was under orders to make a raid on

---

1 Chaplin's ironic term for a dugout.

the enemy's trenches at 3pm today. Fortunately the order was cancelled last night. It would have been a most foolish and futile enterprise and we should have probably lost most of the officers and hundreds of men. There has been pretty desperate fighting along the line. I am afraid the 2nd Bn will have caught it but we have heard nothing.

Mr Hardinge[1] has been slightly wounded and we have lost a few men by snipers. I have been very busy trying to get the trenches into good order and safe – today has been the first day I have been able to sit down.

I had a lot of letters of congratulation including one from Sandy.[2] I received the cake from Skinners – it was a beauty.

Friday, Christmas Day 1914 [from trenches at Pont Ballot, outside Armentières]

I am delighted to hear that you still both continue to do well. I am sending you the King and Queen's Christmas Card – which will be of value some day I suppose. Mrs MacAllan has heard from Ronnie, I am thankful to say – he is wounded in the left thigh and is at Weimar. We are having regular Christmas weather, a hard frost, much better than the wet. With our new house we are in comparative comfort.

It is a queer thing, war. Last night our men and the Germans were chaffing at each other, shouting across to each other's trenches and both sides singing songs. I must say that most of the shouted messages were not complimentary, such as "Go back to the Fatherland!", "Where is the ------- Kaiser?", "Waiter! Hurry up with my beer!" Capt McLellan shouted out for them to give a song and they sang very nicely in chorus. During the whole time both sides kept up a constant fire. One of my sergeants amused me by coming up to me last night and saying "Can I have a day's sniping tomorrow?" There is a ruined house in front of our line to which they crawl. One man killed three Germans from it in a day.

---

1 2nd Lt P. R. Hardinge.

2 Major Vincent Sandilands, engaged to Lil's sister, Bee, later becomes commanding officer of 2nd battalion, Cameronians.

What ages seem to have passed since last Christmas when I was at Bath and you at Turnberry. Talk about "one crowded hour" – we are having it with a vengeance. With all my love to you both. Ever your loving husband, Graham

*   *   *

Christmas in the trenches. It brings singing, and some abuse, as the Cameronians refuse to fraternise with the Germans, unlike others in the British front line. Many are curmudgeonly, disinclined to drink with anyone who regularly takes potshots at them. Few expected to be here; none believed the war would last this long.

For Chaplin, missing the birth of his son by just a few days while home on leave, it is particularly poignant. The army's postal service is extraordinarily efficient, showing a control of logistics well-honed by a century of empire, but even it cannot give him the information he wants – a child is born, but he is 700 miles away.

When he finally gets the news that his first child, born on 13 December, is a boy, fellow officers joke that he must name it after their theatre of war – John Houplines, or Jim Armentières – and carry their exploits with him for the rest of his life. Chaplin laughs them off, proud but anxious, ever conscious that he is simply a sniper's shot away from never seeing his son at all.

For the Cameronians it is an uneasy time, facing death yet guarding a quiet front where the Germans are content simply to hold and shoot. Out of trenches, the town of Armentières still maintains its attractions, 20,000 inhabitants still bustle to work, many growing rich living beside a front line with so many soldiers to entertain.

The 19th brigade at least has a stable command structure now, headed by Brigadier Frederic Gordon, former 2nd division staff officer and a fifty-three-year-old Scot who takes pride in all matters Scottish. He tells Robertson that it's a shame so many of the Cams' ranks are drawn from south of the Tweed, a result of the Cameronians spending so long in India, and he launches a recruitment drive for the regiment with a letter to the Scottish press in late December, acclaiming the battalion's feats:

Now is the time to seek the co-operation of all who are or should be interested in getting Scottish recruits for the Cameronians. I can assure any young man who contemplates adopting a military career that he cannot do better than to apply for the Cameronians – Believe me. Signed Frederic Gordon, Brigadier General, Comdg -[th] Infantry Brigade.

The open letter concludes with a eulogy to the Cameronians' feats so far – 'WHAT THE BATTALION HAS DONE' – extolling their role in the Battles of Mons and Le Cateau, and holding firm at La Boutillerie. Back home in Stirling, Lil dutifully clips the article. Quite what Robertson (English) and officers like Chaplin (English) think of it is not recorded.

Chaplin is fully occupied anyway. His routine as company commander is now established, overseeing disciplinary cases each morning at 'orderly room', scuttling around exposed trenches by day, standing to at dusk and dawn, inspecting positions, detailing work, writing up reports, then moving back into billets. Excitements are rare but the threat of change is constant. Orders from divisional HQ to carry out a large-scale raid on 23 December are issued then cancelled, to relief from all, as the German position opposite is so well defended that many officers privately believed it would have been a massacre. It is symptomatic of the distance now developing between those at the front and those behind who control their destinies and often have unrealistic expectations of what can be achieved. Chaplin simply takes pride in constantly improving his section of trench, as if grasping what control he can in a war where the participants frequently feel disempowered, ignorant of what is really taking place.

Gradually the number of court martials – usually for offences such as drunkenness, insubordination and petty thieving – will increase, then fall. The soldiers will slowly get accustomed to this war, and their officers will adapt too. The old British army, stretched across Flanders, holding the northernmost parts of a trench line that zigzags south then east to Switzerland, has fought itself to a stalemate and now has time before the weather improves to consider its options. Weak points must be strengthened, quirks in the line straightened out, the ground prepared for bigger battles ahead. To the men in the trenches, the consequent decisions from on high to remove 'salients' – protrusions in the line – will seem arbitrary at best, nonsensical at worst, and usually lethal.

Sunday, 27 December 1914 [from billets in Armentières]

My darling Lil,

I got your letter today dated the 22nd. I am sorry that you are not able to go on feeding the youth but it does not matter so long as he thrives. I am very glad that you have passed the time for any anxiety and the wound has healed so famously. We got out of the trenches last night without any trouble. I was glad to get into billets – the dirt and mud and filth generally were very unpleasant. We were not given a very good billet but we have taken the house next door to live in by day. There is a very comfortable dining room and good kitchen but the top of the house has been destroyed by a shell so we cannot use the bedrooms. We all had a rare good sleep last night and this morning I had a hot bath and complete change of clothes.

Have you heard that Major Vandeleur has escaped and is at home? We all hope that he will not come back to us.

Monday, 28 December 1914 [from billets in Armentières]

I have received your letter of the 24th today. I am glad indeed that you are both making such good progress. I cannot write much of a letter today. I have so many to write thanking people for things for the men besides heaps of un-answered private letters. I am longing to see a photograph of you and the boy.

Tuesday, 29 December 1914 [from billets in Armentières]

Last night I sat up quite late answering letters referring to the company and thanking people for presents . . . Today has been fine for a change. This morning I was on a court martial and this afternoon I went for a route march with my company and afterwards went shopping with RO and Sam Darling. The latter goes on leave tomorrow and RO probably on the 2nd. Could you send me a pair of mackintosh overalls to pull over my legs when in the trenches? Mr Hill has started to play the piano!

Wednesday, 30 December 1914 [from billets in Armentières]
I got your letter of the 26th today – enclosing picture of the pram. No, Mrs Oakley has not written to me – I imagine that she has only just heard of the boy and has probably now written to you as she said in her letter to Richard today "how pleased and excited Major Chaplin must be – please give him my congratulations etc".

The Colonel is trying to arrange for a trip to see the 2nd Bn tomorrow – I hope it comes off.

Thursday, 31 December 1914 [from billets in Armentières]
Our trip to the 2nd Bn came off alright. The Colonel called for us in his car – it took us about a three-quarter-hour run to reach them. They were out of the trenches. We saw Col Bliss, Major Carter-Campbell, Majors Lloyd, Ellis, Hayes, Capts Maunsell and Clarke.[1] They were all very fit except Majors Carter-Campbell and Ellis, both of whom we thought looked very seedy. Major Hayes had had a lucky escape – his dugout fell in on him. He was got out with great difficulty and did not recover consciousness until two hours afterwards. We stayed to lunch and had a great talk. Major Lloyd was very rude when we came away. He said "Give my love to your wife. I have never met her but she must be a very brave woman."

Col Bliss had heard from Mrs Vandeleur that Van escaped by visiting a dentist, slipping away from there, appropriated a bicycle, rode 35 miles into Holland where he was arrested as a German spy and after various adventures was handed over to the British Consul.

I dined with RO tonight and found on my return a large party here and Mr Hill playing the piano. It makes me feel terribly old when I come in and everyone shuts up and one feels that one has reached the wet blanket stage.

---

1 Bliss, Lloyd, Ellis and Hayes are killed three months later at the Battle of Neuve Chapelle.

Friday, 1 January 1915 [from billets in Armentières]

I am sorry to say this is our last night here. We go into trenches tomorrow, at least the regiment does but my company will be in a farmhouse for three days in reserve. They have now reduced the leave to eight days which just hits RO. I am sorry for those whose leave is yet to come.

Saturday, 2 January 1915 [from billets in Armentières]

We are all in the chaos of moving – everything being packed. As we shall not have time to write tonight I am writing in the middle of the day. The weather is now poisonous – wet and cold. I am afraid that we shall have a poor time in the trenches.

We are going to wear the men's equipment in future – we are wearing it for the first time today. It was absurd that we did not do so from the first, as we know that the Germans tell their best shots to shoot down officers.

Sunday, 3 January 1915 [from trenches near Bois-Grenier, outside Armentières]

Harriette turned up last night about midnight in the ruined farm which is our home and gave me your letter of the 31st – doubly welcome as we had had no mail owning to the move into the trenches. I was much relieved to hear that you were so well and had been up all day and also to hear that the boy had taken a trip abroad.

Poor Stirling was killed last night – shot dead through the heart – such a nice fellow, the best go first. It is an extraordinary coincidence that every fellow who has come from the 3rd Bn at Nigg has been killed or wounded.

We have just one room here for everything and sleep on mattresses on the floor – luxury of course compared to a wet trench.

Sunday, 10 January 1915 [from billets near Bois-Grenier]

We had a bad time in the trenches – wet up to the middle, no sleep and perished with cold. We came out the night before last and this farmhouse seemed a perfect paradise. Mr Salmonson has been sent home – he is very bad – they feared rheumatic fever. Capt Jack fainted coming out of the trenches – I do not think he will last long.

Monday, 11 January 1915 [from billets near Bois-Grenier]

I received your letter of the 7th today and also the overalls (or waders really). I think that they will do splendidly but have not tried them on yet. Yesterday I simply could not write a letter and that was why it is particularly dull. I suppose the cold in the trenches freezes one's brain.

I also saw two proofs of snapshots of myself performing my toilet in the last trenches which Capt Davidson[1] took. They are very good. He has told Ballantyne to send you two of each. One of which is for Mrs Lee as Harry was there and asked for one for her.

As to war news I know no more than you or perhaps not so much – things are comparatively quiet here.

With all my fondest love to you both, ever your loving husband, Graham

---

1 The Cameronians' medical officer until March 1915, when he was wounded and sent home.

HERE WE ARE,
HERE WE ARE,
HERE WE ARE
AGAIN

'At present the Germans are a good deal too bobbish. As I write we can hear them cheering in their trenches . . .'

French continue offensives in Artois and Champagne — Zeppelins raid Britain while U-boats attack shipping — Britain retaliates by blockading German ports — Allied attempt to break German line at Neuve Chapelle, south of Armentières, ends in costly failure — German forces use poison gas for first time at Ypres — first New Army divisions of Kitchener recruits arrive to swell British numbers

A man can dream. For Graham Chaplin, these dank days around Armentières, marshalling exhausted troops in deep trenches overlooking flat fields, are a time of gnawing worry. He has a sick colonel to support – he can see Robertson shrinking in his skin from cold, worn down by stress and the sudden increase in paperwork that floods the army as it tries to adapt and control the situation. But Chaplin also has friends to whom he can cleave: Sam Darling, Harry Lee, RO, RW, Hammy. They already have a sense that the real war now rumbles on elsewhere, up at Ypres, down below at Neuve Chapelle. Yet around Armentières, the town famed for its breweries and brothels, they must hold the line and wait, their losses sporadic but not wholesale, their anxiety palpable as they watch to see what unfolds, when it will be their turn.

This is unlike any war Chaplin has known. He learnt his army trade on India's North-West Frontier, where the Yorkshires fought in the 2nd brigade, 1st division, part of three divisions sent under Sir William Lockhart to suppress Afridi tribesmen in 1897. The Yorks led a head-on attack on the Sampaga pass and later climbed ravines to gain the heights at Ashaga, driving back a tenacious enemy who fought and fled and sniped with uncanny accuracy, capable of hitting a man at 1,000 yards. Camps at night on the Tirah Campaign were especially dangerous places, always overlooked, always subjected to rifle fire from lone tribesmen who preferred to fight at night – a tactic noted by the wily Lockhart who briefed his commanders to attack at dawn, when many Afridi preferred to sleep.[16] And the British forces there always pushed on, inspired by glorious charges over dry terrain against an enemy who preferred to shoot then dash, hoping to fight again another day, and who lacked any artillery or any degree of organisation. Sitting in cold, muddy trenches dug into long, flat plains facing the industrialised might of another European nation is a very different kind of fighting. The lack of movement saps an old soldier's soul.

So Chaplin continues to write daily, February, March and April, as the Cams take their turn in the line. At times like these his letters become those of a prisoner, serving a sentence of unknown length, with unforeseeable consequences. He counts the days – five months since we left Glasgow, six months since we left Glasgow. The same letters are also spiked with gossip and grumbles: losing a crown in his teeth, building a new iron-roofed trench shelter, coping with the cold, training the incoming Canadians, burning one of his own letters thinking it was hers, not getting mentioned in despatches, logging all known sightings of Vandeleur. Will the dreaded officer return to the front? Or has he been given a new role 'ameliorating the lot' of prisoners of war? 'For which the Gods be thanked.'[17]

Then there are the antics of his junior officers – those he likes, Cotton Minchin and Wright, both twenty-one, who he nicknames 'the children', and those that simply perplex him. 'I have a youth named Wedderburn from the 3rd Bn attached to my company, wears spectacles and I should think is quite useless. We have several of these youths attached to the regiment.'[18]

Then there is handsome Lt Becher's engagement, and poor Lt Wedderburn's death, sniped – all this is related in a matter-of-fact way, as a continual narrative of battalion front-line life. What rouses him is life elsewhere. He reads the same war news as Lil, scours the same papers, shipped out to the brigade HQs. When the Germans send a Zeppelin to drop bombs on Norfolk, his fury is palpable that this war should spread closer to home: 'I think the bomb-dropping is a low down game – the Germans ought to be wiped out as a nation.'[19]

And when factory workers on the Clyde, provoked by rent rises, go on strike, his response is immediate: 'I hope that the organisers of the strike will be shot and the men too if they do not return to work. I do not believe that the people at home realise what this war is.'[20]

In every letter he asks for news of Jim, absorbing her anxiety that the baby will not feed or grow. Each of her letters carries Jim's latest weight, up or down, then the details of doctor visits, of new recommendations. He worries in return. Why won't he feed? When will he put on weight? The letters are a dialogue that keeps him sane as he searches for what he can share, leaving out the daily horror of wounding and illness. She sends snapshots of the baby. In return, he sends pictures of his men – photographs taken initially without permission by young officers in the Cameronians, later (briefly) with official sanction. Occasionally he includes a picture of himself, posing on his own in his floppy hat, or with McLellan and others of A Company. In each, he looks rumpled and sardonic, only his exhausted eyes showing the toll he is taking.

Then he tickles her with news of concert parties and follies that spring up in Armentières, or allusions to the all-too-brief shared memories they have banked: 'I was amused to see a notice of a concert to be held in the town and giving the list of performers. The first name was "Lieut. The Maclaine of Lochbonie". I wondered if he would bore the audience as much as he did me at the Stirling Bazaar.'[21]

Back in Stirling, Lil reads these with an ailing baby to nurse, army wives to see, food, fruit, cakes and confectionary to send, clothes to order and, always, the worry that every letter she receives from Graham will be his last. She also frets that he is losing his love for her – she reads too much into each line, delighting when he is more affectionate, worrying when he is clipped, her own emotions frayed by childbirth, war and worry, with only jingoistic newspaper reporting giving her a picture of conditions at the front. Graham explains how hard he finds it writing at all: 'You said in your last that one of my letters was much more affectionate. You must remember, darling, that one cannot very well express one's feelings in a letter which one knows is liable to be opened and read by some censor.'[22]

Other fears assail her. Her father, Thomas Alexander, is now seventy-eight and in slow decline, with his own worries as to the war's effect on his business. Her elder brother, Willie, is now destined for France, called up by the 6th battalion Black Watch (a rather grander and more expensive Scottish regiment than the Cameronians). A younger brother, Tom, is with the army in Africa. Who will oversee the family's interests?

And Lil, despite living in her parents' home, now has her own notional household to run, her family allowance of £200 per annum cut off on marriage. She tries to get a grip on Graham's erratic finances, hoping to start a home for the three of them but struggling to understand the Chaplin debts, the army allowances, the £35 per month he says he is banking as an infantry major. He attempts to explain where they stand:

I am sorry for your sake that your father has taken away the £200 but I am not surprised as he must be hard hit. We are to get lodging and light allowance whilst the war lasts – about £5 a month extra, so if you want to you can always draw up to £25 a month on my account, which will leave me £5 for my own expenses and £5 for Lindsay.[1] You will remember that when I borrowed the £700 from Lindsay I had to pay £60 for depreciation of his capital and also the law expenses, so that I was nearly £100 short and could not pay off the Wilsons.[2] As I have saved £100 now I am going to pay them as soon as I can find out the address of their bank. I was going to start paying my bills which amount to about £100 but as you will now want money I will not do so but will send you the bills and you can pay them gradually out of my account. I think that I should pay for the nurse and all the baby's expenses.[23]

Later, it turns out, of course, that he has been hopelessly optimistic.

---

1 His younger brother.
2 Friends from India.

My balance at Cox[1] was a blow to me as I thought I had about £150 there. There must be about £50 due to me for allowances – we are having great trouble about them. I expect some have been paid in by this time. Do not bother about the bills till you want no more money yourself. Send for my passbook at the end of each month and spend the balance in hand. It should be about £25 a month. Let me know if allowances are not paid in. My pay is 16/- a day. There should be 4/- a day field allowance since the day we mobilised (Aug 5th about), 4/- a day lodging allowance since November 15th, and 11d a day fuel and light since Nov 15th – and now I ought to get 1/- a day 2nd-in-command allowance. So that my total pay is 25/11 a day. Cox credits the 16/- on the first of each month, and the allowances are paid into Cox by the Base Paymaster in France. We have no check but the passbook that they are paid in. I am most anxious that you should spend as little of your own money as possible.[24]

By mid-March the Cameronians have learnt the fate of their 2nd battalion at the Battle of Neuve Chapelle, the British army's ill-judged attempt at a spring breakthrough south of Armentières. Over 120 killed, including 13 officers; over 300 wounded, including 9 officers. Only one officer emerges unscathed – he had been sent back to brigade HQ with a message. Now Chaplin knows what kind of war this will be: lethal to officers and ranks alike, no hiding. Many of those killed are men he knew well. Despite the old rivalry between 1st and 2nd battalions, drawn as they were from different regiments on amalgamation in 1881,[25] younger officers had served in both units.

The effects on the 1st battalion are immediate, with his friend RO – Major Richard Oakley – and machine-gun officer Captain Robert Money[26] transferred to the 2nd to help replenish officer numbers. Major Vandeleur is summoned from Scotland to head it.

The casualties send a tremor through the regiment. Chaplin receives confirmation of the names from Oakley, forwarded by Brigadier General

---

1 The army's bank.

Gordon, commander of the 19th, who attaches a hand-written note stating
that the country 'will never forget how the 90th 27 fought and fell at Neuve
Chapelle'. After signing it, Gordon then adds, 'I cannot express how very
deeply I feel for these abnormal losses among your brother officers and
those of the men.'

Chaplin is promoted to Robertson's number two, and the weekly round
of in-trench / out-of-trench continues, but with a new fear – what if the
men leading this army really don't know how to win the war?

Extracts from the battalion War Diary,
April 1915,

Kept by Colonel Philip Robertson

```
Trenches near Bois-Grenier
21 April - One man slightly wounded in D Company.

22 April - GOC VI Div, Sir John Keir, and GOC 19th IB came
round trenches. Enemy shelled while they were up. 2nd Lt
Ansell, CSM Ansell, Sgt Corbett, Pte Morton all wounded. Enemy
also shelled at night.

23 April - Gen Paget CRA VI Div came round trenches. Enemy put
in two shells. We replied. Coy Sgt Major Leckie sniped three
Germans. Congratulatory message from Gen Keir.

24 April - Orders received to show activity. Companies opened
fire to time. Enemy replied with 80 shells. 10 men wounded,
one seriously.

25 April - Quiet day. GOC 19th IB came round in morning.
Relieved by Royal Welch at 7.40pm.
```

Billets near Bois-Grenier
26 April - Dull, practising the charge, bayonet fighting, and
instruction of bomb throwers.

27 April - Draft of one officer Lt CD Rooke and 25 other
ranks joined. Lt Bacon also joined. Some officers played in a
rugby football match against the A&S Highlanders.

28 April - The officers played the 72nd Battery at polo.

29 April - 30 yards range and machine gun range allotted to
the Bn. 200 men to baths.

30 April - GOC VI Div went round billets and transport.
Relieved Royal Welch beginning at 7.45pm.

General Note: The trenches are now very good. A long
communication trench called Shaftesbury Avenue 1000 yards long
now runs back to the Bois-Grenier road. It is deep enough to
allow of a man riding a bicycle up and broad enough to walk
three abreast. A second line about 150 yards is being made
continuous by joining up and improving old pivot points. A Bn
laundry has been started and shirts and socks etc are washed
while the Bn is in the trenches. Three sets of pipes were sent
out from friends in Glasgow.

Tuesday, 20 April 1915 [from billets near Bois-Grenier]
My darling Lil,
    I rode over yesterday after lunch to the 2nd Bn with Capt Money and Capt

Hyde-Smith[1] who had been over here to see us. The latter I had not seen since I left India – he used to be my subaltern. He has just come out from home having been sick since January.

Richard[2] was fit and well, but I soon depressed him by telling him about Vandeleur coming out – it depressed them all. Sandy was there posing as 2nd in command. We sat in a field in the sun until tea time. I came home.

Harriette is in the room and sends his love. It has turned very cold today. We are off again in our old trenches tonight.

Wednesday, 21 April 1915 [from trenches near Bois-Grenier]

I received two letters from you today. I was very glad to hear that Jim has gained another oz and that his food was going to be increased. I also had a letter from Mrs MacAllan in which she gave a very good account of you and Jim. Did you see that Major Vandeleur has been promoted? So I expect that it is true that he is going to the 2nd Bn.

We are very pleased that Private May has been awarded the VC – it is the first one that has ever been gained in this battn.

Just fancy it is six months tomorrow that we have been in trenches. I want to write a lot but my head will not work tonight.

Thursday, 22 April 1915 [from trenches near Bois-Grenier]

We had the General[3] commanding the Division round our trenches for the first time. Our own General[4] came too, so that with a few staff officers it was a regular Lord Mayor's show going round. Whilst we were going round a shell in A Coy wounded Ansell – now a 2/Lieutenant who was my company Sergeant-Major when we came out – and also Sergeant-Major Cliff, whose wife wrote to you when Jim was born. They are not badly wounded fortunately, but a very good sergeant was.

---

1 Capt H. C. Hyde-Smith, later to command 2nd battalion Cameronians.
2 Oakley.
3 Major-General Sir John Keir, who was later relieved of his command after a dispute with General Allenby.
4 Commanding the 19th brigade.

I went for a walk down the communication trench with Capt McLellan after tea – he is not looking at all well.

I am afraid, darling, that there is not the slightest chance of leave re-opening at present. There might be if we were taken out[1] for a rest.

Friday, 23 April 1915 [from trenches near Bois-Grenier]

Today has been no more exciting than usual, except that I had a fine hot bath which the doctor got ready for me at the dressing station in the village behind us, which I reached by the communication trench.

I got the sweets safely, for which many thanks. RO's brother sent me two dozen plover's eggs, which was jolly good of him.

We did not have many imposing visitors today – merely the Divisional Artillery General[2] and the Brigade Major. It is much pleasanter seeing some outsiders. It is surprising that we do not all hate one another after being shut up with one another for so long.

Saturday, 24 April 1915 [from trenches near Bois-Grenier]

Yes, you are right, there will be none of the living in the regiment glad that Vandeleur has got the 2nd Bn. I have absolutely no news. Today was exactly the same as yesterday except that I had no bath and I went and saw our 5th Bn.[3] which I have not done before.

Monday, 26 April 1915 [from billets near Bois-Grenier]

I received your parcel with very nice cakes and potted meat. No, dear, I do not want a new glengarry, as mine is quite good enough at present. Most of the men have Kilmarnock bonnets now. I suppose we shall have to take to that form of headgear – I do not think it will suit my peculiar style of beauty.

---

1 Removed from the front line.
2 Brigadier General Wellesley Paget.
3 A Territorial battalion sent to France to join the 19th brigade.

Tuesday, 27 April 1915 [from billets near Bois-Grenier]

I got your topping parcel of apples and bananas – thousands of thanks, I think the ones you send are better than anyone else gets. Yesterday I walked into the big town with Capt Darling. I met a fellow named Cautley in the Shropshires – he was not very complimentary, I had not seen him for some years. He said "By God! You have got old!"

Wednesday, 28 April 1915 [from billets near Bois-Grenier]

Yesterday I rode over to the 2nd Bn – they are not in trenches now and are about 10 miles from us.[1] It was a lovely day and I enjoyed the ride. The blossom is all out on the fruit trees, the grass is all green now and the crops are starting to grow, so the country looks very different to what it did a month ago. I passed some Punjabis belonging to a native mountain battery and spoke to them in Hindustani, and was pleased to find that I had not forgotten it. I said "This is a very good war, isn't it?" and they grinned all over.

I found the 2nd Bn in very comfortable farms, and the Hd Qrs a particularly nice one. Col Vandeleur had just arrived. He greeted me as if I was his dearest friend and was particularly affable to me the whole time.

Thursday, 29 April 1915 [from billets near Bois-Grenier]

We had great fun yesterday. We played the gunners at polo – it was not quite up to Hurlingham form. The ground was very small with a ditch across the middle. Harriette, Hardinge, Sam D and I played for us and we got well beaten. We played our chargers, which have never played before, and the polo sticks were too short. We got plenty of exercise and I felt quite young again and forgot all about the war. Afterwards Sam D and I went into the Gunner billet, which was very comfortable, and had a whisky and soda.

There is great fighting going on[2] but it has not reached us yet.

---

1 At Doulieu.
2 Around Ypres.

Friday, 30 April 1915 [from billets near Bois-Grenier]

RO and Col Vandeleur came over yesterday afternoon. The latter has already started to set everyone by the ears, as we knew he would of course. As I said, a leopard cannot change his spots.

Each regiment is now to be allowed one camera, so we are getting one from Ballantine and he will continue to print them as before.

I am on a court martial this morning – I have not been on one for quite a while. Very hard up for news, so Harriette will continue.

Written by Harry Lee:

Now a bit of news that will interest you more than anything Bull (pardon, Graham) has told you, and that is that he has never looked fitter than he does now, and although he is fussed at times about his hair coming out it's not much, really, he is only putting on his summer coat. I've never known him in better form either. I am so glad John Humphries has put on a little weight and hope all your troubles in that direction are over. Now Graham – I mean Bull – will carry on.

Hoping that Jim is going on well and with all my fondest love and kisses to you both. I could not get to sleep last night for thinking of you.

Saturday, 1 May 1915 [from trenches near Bois-Grenier]

I was disappointed that Jim had not gained anything at his last weighing but perhaps he will make up for it at his next. It is a great thing that he keeps fit in himself.

We came in last night without incident. It is almost as pleasant in the trenches as out of them now that the weather is fine and there are lots of communication trenches and one can get about. Today has been as warm as summer and I have not worn a coat all day. I went up on top of a haystack with glasses and got a good view, but it is extraordinary how the leaves are coming out and giving cover.

Sunday, 2 May 1915 [from trenches near Bois-Grenier]

The pears and pineapple arrived safely – a most welcome arrival. They are awfully good, many thanks, dear.

Monday, 3 May 1915 [from trenches near Bois-Grenier]

Do not worry about what you see in the papers about the fighting – it is usually incorrect.

The weather has become fine again, which makes a difference to people's spirits. Yesterday we were issued with goggles and flannel respirators, so we look pretty good comics when we are arrayed for action.

At present the Germans are a good deal too bobbish. As I write we can hear them cheering in their trenches, which they do when they hear of some of their wonderful victories. They have put up a notice opposite us to say that they have taken 63 British guns. As we know that is a lie it only amuses us.

A little further along the line they greeted one regiment by singing in English "Here we are again",[1] so the English regiment all sang:

"Here we are, here we are, here we are again,

We licked you on the Marne and we licked you on the Aisne,

We chased you from Armentières and here we are again."

I hope to hear tomorrow that Jim has gained. I should think that you want a holiday as well as the nurse. With all my love to you both and heaps of kisses, ever your loving husband, Graham

*   *   *

So from trench to billet, billet to trench, a normality is established, providing you can dodge the artillery shell and the sniper's bullet. Yet the pounding of guns from Ypres to the north signals a different war coming closer. It is only a question of time before the Cameronians are thrown into something far worse than they currently face. Chaplin is torn between wanting real action and wishing to avoid the slaughter that faced the 2nd battalion at Neuve

---

1 The memoir left by Capt P. R. Hardinge notes the Germans not only sang, 'Here we are again', they announced, 'We are the Saxons, are you the Leicesters?'

Chapelle, where poor strategy and inadequate artillery let down the infantry. The casualty figures there – a foretaste of what is to come in this war – have knocked back the regiment, not least because the problem of replacing so many experienced men is already stretching resources.

Billeted in an old farm a mile back from the Bois-Grenier front line, Chaplin is comfortable if wary. Trips can be made into Armentières, but the 'big town', now under artillery fire, is no longer the haven it was. Nothing is safe, and so much is left to chance. On the front line, one shell rips right through Hammy's dugout, but fails to explode. It most likely comes from their own artillery, a shell falling short from a 'terrier battery' manned by the Territorials now adding numbers to the original BEF. For the old sweats like Chaplin, each wave of recruits to this war will bring more surprises: the Territorials, inexperienced and gauche; then Kitchener's volunteers, enthusiastic but ill-prepared; then the conscripts, sullen and unwilling.

Yet he masks his worries for Lil, and buoys her spirits with a determinedly positive outlook. He describes his visits to the 2nd battalion and the 5th – one of the Scottish Rifles' four Territorial battalions – and recounts who he's seen for tea or drinks, and who has sent him fruit and cakes. War is less frequently a topic. The Cameronians fight as if bystanders, not really involved.

By 9 May the expected 'big push' has started further south. The British army pounds the villages of Aubers, Fromelles and Le Maisnil, just a few miles south of Armentières. The aim is to pin down the enemy and stretch its resources, as the French attack at Vimy and in Champagne, and the Russians in the east. But again, at Aubers, it is the 2nd battalion which goes over the top, not the 1st.

'I felt more depressed than I have been the whole campaign because one knew that they were for it the next morning and we should be comparatively safe. It is not so bad if you are going to be in the show yourself.'[28]

Chaplin rises early with Darling to watch the shells dropping on German lines at Aubers – 'yellow shells, black shells, brown shells, and clouds of white shrapnel' – and the brick dust pluming up. That same morning the sinking of the *Lusitania* passenger ship, torpedoed by a German U-boat, appears in newspapers circulated at the front, prompting his own riposte.

'It will be a terrible reckoning when we are topsides of the Germans.'

But there are distractions too. The British army relents on its ban of cameras at the front – already ignored by the Cameronians – and officially allows each battalion one camera to take suitable photographs for posterity. This experiment is all too brief, but the Cameronians, the BEF's keenest amateur photographers, take full advantage.

Chaplin instructs Ballantine, the Glasgow optician which develops films for the battalion and later makes up its memorialising albums, to send photographs to his wife. The images are posed and sterile, cleansed for an audience at home that does not want to see carnage depicted. In one, Chaplin stands with Robertson at the entrance of an impressively constructed new dugout in the support line, a hundred yards from the front, a teapot left decoratively at ease on the trench top, as if awaiting guests.

On another day he poses with Hamilton and Haywood, the 19th brigade's staff captain, in the long communication trench that runs to the front, looking as swept and clean as Edinburgh's Princes Street.

So quiet is their front, there is even time for a visit from a clutch of senior clerics: 'The General came this afternoon and brought five Scotch parsons! They are doing a sort of Cook's tour.'[29]

The Battle of Aubers Ridge becomes another setback for the British army. The German positions are too heavily fortified to breach. The 2nd battalion suffers again too. Chaplin's letter lists the familiar names among the wounded and dead:

We heard tonight that the 2nd Bn had had five officers killed and seven wounded. Richard Oakley was hit in the stomach but we hear that it is not serious but I shall be very anxious until I know for certain that he is alright. Vandeleur was hit above and below the knee, Money in the seat of his trousers, Hunter in the neck and three others whose names we do not know belonging to the 3rd Bn. Sandy is alright. Loder-Symonds and Sim[30] were killed, also Salmon of the 3rd Bn. Carter-Campbell is alright.[31]

Later, he admits to Lil, almost guiltily, that the terrible toll paid by the 2nd battalion means his own promotion to second in command of 1st battalion will be permanent – 'there will be no question now of one going back to a company'. The upside of war is the chance for rapid promotion. With experienced officers at a premium, those who survive can thrive: 'I was offered command of a Terrier battalion but refused it. You see, I have a very good chance of commanding my own regiment if the Colonel should get a Brigade.'[32]

In the meantime, there are the never-ending lists for Lil of what to send: vests and pants, cakes and fruit, paper and envelopes, and the worries over her health, discreetly alluded to – 'I am very sorry that you have your old trouble again' – and the updates on Jim's progress to note and dissect. His nightly dialogue with Lil has become the most important conversation of the day: 'the only thing one has to look forward to'.[33] It is his hold on normality, and the promise of a family and security, if he can return.

He gets Harry Lee to write to Lil and confirm all is well – 'never seen your Graham looking better' – and passes on reports of RO, recuperating in a London hospital, visited from on high by Lord Stamfordham, George V's private secretary. Clearly, Oakley has connections.

Meanwhile, the 19th brigade switches divisions, from the 6th to the 27th, passed along while it stays put, manning the Bois-Grenier trenches. Chaplin complains about 'the monotony of our existence',[34] enlivened only by the occasional invitation – 'Sam D and I dined with the 72nd Battery and they gave us CHAMPAGNE!'[35] Hamilton is given the cushy job of town major in Armentières, liaising with the local authorities.

In short, there is little to worry about. Death by boredom, he pretends, is the biggest threat. Lil wants to believe that is true.

Saturday, 29 May 1915 [from billets near Bois-Grenier]

My darling Lil,

I had quite a pleasant day yesterday. I walked into the town and had lunch with Hammy.[1] He lives in an old-fashioned mansion, very nicely furnished and

---

1 Captain Hamilton.

quite untouched by war – no shells through it and none of the windows broken. I felt quite envious when I was taken up to a bedroom by the orderly – who in private life is a footman – to wash my hands. The bed had clean sheets, the first I have seen in France. We had a very nice lunch with tablecloth and napkins – our tablecloths are always the previous days' papers. Hammy has got another job, Town Major, but whether it is permanent or temporary I do not know. I walked back and was very disappointed to find that there was no letter mail, but I got a very nice parcel of fruit from you, for which many thanks. You get full marks for your parcels.

Sunday, 30 May 1915 [from billets near Bois-Grenier]

I was jolly glad to hear that Jim had put on an oz, and that he is going on so well – it is splendid. I hope that the snapshots of Jim come out well. I should like a real photo of you with Jim. I know that you hate being photographed as much as I do.

I walk as much as possible so as to keep fit. I generally end up at Wood the Quartermaster's to hear the latest rumour, he being the gatherer of all stories and rumours.

Did you read the Moderator's speech at the Assembly in Edinburgh? I do not suppose that you would have, but he mentioned his visit to our trenches.

The new Brigade Major is an ass as far as one can judge with a small experience of him. I could not get the job in any case not being a PSC.[1] I do not want it. There is no news of the Colonel getting a Brigade yet.

Monday, 31 May 1915 [from billets near Bois-Grenier]

I am very glad that you went to the tennis party and saw people. I hope that you are going to get tennis kit and play yourself. I should like to see you as you were in a nice white skirt.

I went for a long ride yesterday with Harriette. It was like English country

---

1 Passed Staff College, denoting Chaplin had not passed through the Staff College, Camberley, which trained future commanders and staff officers (as opposed to Sandhurst Military College, which trained aspiring officers).

lanes. We saw some pretty farms and cottages and lots of horses. We met Mr Devitt of the Gunners who had just come out with Kitchener's Army. He said that he was d . . . d glad to see that Vandeleur was wounded. It is wonderful how universally popular he is!

When we were coming back by the river two French Engineer privates hailed us and beckoned us to come to the punt they were in, so I dismounted and got into the punt and they showed me a cable which they had discovered when fishing – it was laid right along the bed of the river. I told them to report it to the Staff. I shall be interested to hear if it runs into the German lines and is used by spies. There is no artfulness that they are not up to.

With all my love, dearest, ever your loving husband, Graham

A CERTAIN INACTION

'Serious trouble has occurred over an incident in the
regiment . . .'

Allied attacks at Aubers Ridge and Festubert prove disastrous — Canadian and Indian troops take heavy losses — British high command reconsider tactics — attempts to exploit withdrawal of German forces for Russian front fail to provide expected gains — French and British discuss plans for major offensive as summer stalemate holds

By the start of June, Graham Chaplin has reason to be more optimistic. He is number two in the 1st Cameronians, with a colonel likely to be promoted up at any moment, which would leave him commanding the battalion. His own promotion to lieutenant colonel would likely follow, providing no senior officer returns. He has already been recommended for a Distinguished Service Order for gallantry in combat, and mentioned in despatches (31 May 1915), a feat that has received newspaper recognition. Lil has even cut his youthful photograph from the coverage and added it to her growing collection of clippings.

And the war must improve. No one believes they will have to suffer another winter of awful trench endurance like the last one. The persistent sniping and shelling is still a constant menace, and the new horror of gas, already in use by the enemy, an ever-present threat, but the Germans surely cannot continue to fight on two fronts, holding off the armies of France, Britain, Belgium and Russia, without giving way somewhere. And the level of preparation will be better. Next winter, no surprises.

Back home, his son is now putting on weight; his wife is coping well and sending constant updates. Chaplin treasures the first snapshots of Jim: one of him lying in his cot, another of him propped up in a chair, a third of him carried on his nurse's shoulder. Each has a little description on the back, hand-written by Lil, and each will be kept, while every letter is burnt.

Lil is also sorting out the family's financial situation, and Chaplin has no shortage of food, clothes and correspondence being posted to him, making him feel as loved and valued as any officer at the front. And for all the perils of manning the trenches in the Armentières sector, he now knows it is certainly not as dangerous as battle zones to the north and south. News from elsewhere may be fragmentary, but the casualties taken by the regiment at Neuve Chapelle, and the stories filtering back from the fighting at Ypres, show how much worse his position could be.

That sense of security would increase with promotion, even if it is only to a temporary rank, made permanent later – as the army nearly always insists on. Certainly, a battalion commander remains at the front, running his operations from an HQ dugout in or around the support line, daily walking the trenches, inspecting his men, constantly vulnerable to shell, grenade and sniper fire. But he is generally in the second line, not on the fire step, until a major offensive is planned. Only then can he lead his men from the front, armed only with his Webley revolver – that much will be instilled in Chaplin, not least from his memories of the Tirah Campaign, watching Colonel Henry Mathias leading his Gordon Highlanders, pipers playing, in a glorious charge up the murderous Dargai Heights, dispatching the enemy. That earned Mathias the soubriquet 'Hero of Dargai' in British newspapers, and reinforced the standard expected. Only as this war progresses will others see the sense, against a better-armed enemy, in staying back and issuing commands based on observation.

And a temporary colonel is always one step closer to becoming a temporary brigadier, with the concomitant move back to a brigade HQ, further away from danger. In this protracted slog of a war, dug into trenches, wearing the opposition down, every man soon realises that the further back you go, the safer you are.

Besides, to command 1st Cameronians, for anyone steeped in this army that cherishes tradition, would be a fine accomplishment. Chaplin is known in the regiment as a man of temper and bluntness, who struggles to conceal his contempt for those he thinks inept, regardless of rank – his feud with Major Vandeleur bears witness to that. Nor is he a natural army man drawn from a family with a long record of service. As such, rising to colonel in times of peace might have been denied him. But in this war, with the heavy casualties taken by all sides, speed of promotion will escalate, and experienced officers like Chaplin will be valued, for all their inability to keep quiet when they see incompetence around and above them.

Chaplin knows, too, that the Cams have a long and proud history, stretching back to their days first as the Earl of Angus Regiment in 1689, then as the 26th (Cameronians) Regiment of Foot. They fought gloriously under Marlborough at Blenheim, helped suppress the Jacobites at Preston, defended Quebec for the King, battled Napoleon's forces in Egypt, fought gallantly at Corunna, garrisoned Malta and Gibraltar, captured Hong Kong in the first opium war with China and performed repeated postings in India, defending British interests, prior to this war. They may not have the cachet of the Guards or Cavalry, but the Cams have the army's respect.

To lead this body of men is to join a select group that stretches back into history. And to lead a battalion in your own regiment, comfortable with the traditions that have slowly accumulated with each campaign and accomplishment, surrounded by officers who know your ways, is a far more attractive option that being dropped into a brand new battalion – now a very real possibility with Kitchener's Army allocating volunteers to established units – or even moving to a different regiment entirely. That latter option will become increasingly common as the war progresses and the need for experienced officers increases.

For now, as he rises to the top, Chaplin must learn to deal with the demands of those outside the battalion – above him, the brigade, above that, the division, and over that, the corps. He has contact with all of them. Staff officers, foraging for information to feed up to their generals, now make brief visits to the front line, asking for raids to be made so maps can be verified, and prisoners to be taken so enemy regiments can be identified. The paperwork increases too, as the army attempts to bureaucratise the growing force of men it now has to coordinate. In effect, a battalion commander takes on the tasks of a corporate executive running a distant subsidiary: filing returns, requesting supplies, making reports, motivating the workforce, pondering the demands of those who know little about the local terrain. And at the same time, as commanding officer, friendships will change as decisions need to be made that affect everyone.

Extracts from the battalion War Diary,
June 1915,

Kept by Colonel Philip Robertson

Trenches near Bois-Grenier
1 June – GOC came round. Col Reed (GS1)[1] 27th Div round trenches. Enemy shelled behind AB&C. 18 shells. 2nd Lts Wigan and Buckman joined.

2 June – Had practice gas alarm. Enemy relieved opposite our right. A patrol of D Coy distinctly heard female shrieks in enemy's 2nd line.

3 June – one man D Coy Pte Graham shot through head while on sentry at night. Died later. One man A Coy Pte Hutton shot through head while sniping during day.

4 June – Had gas alarm practice. Better. Relieved at 8.45pm by A&S Highlanders.

Billets near Bois-Grenier
5 June – In Brigade reserve. 200 to Baths. Enemy shelled road near Battn HQ.

6 June – Church parades and 200 to Baths. Relieved Middlesex in Rue du Bois in evening. Shelled during relief, no casualties.

---

1 Staff officer.

Trenches near Rue du Bois

7 June – Enemy shelled us for an hour with Jack Johnsons. One man killed Pte Marshall D Coy. One man wounded Pte Anderson D Coy. 1 man wounded Pte Thomson B Coy. CO had a gas alarm practice.

8 June – Quiet Day. Our snipers report two Germans and an officer wounded by them.

9 June – Enemy shelled. No damage. C Coy again report wounded two Germans.

10 June – Heard that Pte Mardell got the DCM for gallant action on patrols.

11 June – Enemy shelled. One man killed by sniper, Pte Raymont D Coy. About 9pm enemy start with rifle grenades and trench mortars, killing one man and wounding seven, two dangerously. We replied with mortars, grenades, 96th RFA and 87th Howitzers. Our snipers during day had again been successful.

12 June – Enemy shelled doing no damage. Relieved by A&S Highlanders beginning at 9pm.

Tuesday, 1 June 1915 [from trenches near Bois-Grenier]
My darling,

We came in last night. The hour of relief is getting very late now, as the days are so long. We dined before we came in for the first time.

The Major commanding the new battery is a fellow I used to know very well, named Harris. He too has married since we last met. They have just come from the north,[1] so they look on this as a haven of rest after what they have been through.

I have got the snapshots of Jim. They are very good but the little chap looks very thin still. However I hope he will soon be fat and strong.

It is extraordinary not hearing of Willie. I cannot understand Beatrice's[2] letters being returned, but as I said before if he had been hit I think she would have had a wire. I do not know where the Highland Division are,[3] or I might have found out about him.

I have taken to a Balmoral[4] – one of the men's – and like it. It is a much better protection to the head. Harriette has had one made by White and is as pleased as a woman with a new bonnet.

We are attached to the 27th Division[5] now, commanded by a poisonous fellow called Snow[6] whom everyone loathes.

Yes, I still take no lunch and feel much better for it. This life is like being on a ship where one eats too much. I got a very nice parcel from you with cakes and sweets. The Colonel says you must spend all your time shopping for me.

Could you send me half a dozen fairly thin socks?

Wednesday, 2 June 1915 [from trenches near Bois-Grenier]

We are going out on the 4th for two days and then into the trenches that we were in a short time ago. We hope eventually to come back to our own trenches. General Gordon was round yesterday morning and in the afternoon the Chief Staff Officer of the 27th Division, Colonel Reed,[7] a VC, who seemed very nice.

---

1 Ypres.

2 William's wife.

3 It had been sent straight to Ypres in May 1915.

4 Wool cap or beret, also known as Kilmarnock bonnet, worn instead of the Cameronians' normal dress cap.

5 Between May and August 1915, reorganisations of the army shift the Cameronians between four divisions: from 6th division, III corps, to 27th division, III corps, then 8th division, III corps, and finally 2nd division, I corps.

6 Major-General Sir Thomas d'Oyly Snow, grandfather of broadcasters Peter Snow and Jon Snow.

7 Hamilton Reed, who won a VC as a captain in the Royal Field Artillery during the Boer War.

Two new boys joined last night by the name Wigan and Buckman,[1] but I have not sampled them yet. Harriette wants to know if you sent him some cakes from Mackies?

Thursday, 3 June 1915 [from trenches near Bois-Grenier]
It is very disappointing Jim losing [weight], but there is nothing to do, as you say, but to be patient. It is funny to think that he is short coated and I have not seen him yet.

Yes, I am afraid, dear, that the war will last a long time yet. There is always a chance that the Germans may break badly – there is no question but that their troops are not fighting so well.

Friday, 4 June 1915 [from trenches near Bois-Grenier]
The doctor came back yesterday. He spent his leave in a motor boat at the Kyles of Bute, but did not forget us, and brought a bottle of whisky, a salmon and matches. We had a great dinner last night in consequence.

I am glad for your mother's sake that Willie is alright. I thought he would not find war as amusing as he seemed to anticipate. Last night one of our patrols heard a woman screaming in the German trenches. Other regiments have heard the same thing opposite them. I suppose the dirty brutes get hold of the French girls and force them to go into the trenches and rape them. At Neuve Chapelle in one of the trenches our people took they found three women. If they had gone there willingly I do not know.

Saturday, 5 June 1915 [from billets near Bois-Grenier]
We came out last night but go into less pleasant trenches tomorrow night. I have been reading *Oliver Twist*, which I have not read for many years. It is the first book I have read since I have been out here. It is a change from talking of war. Having talked of nothing else for ten months the subject begins to pall.

---

1 2nd Lts Wigan and Buckman.

Sunday, 6 June 1915 [from billets near Bois-Grenier]

Yesterday I went for a ride by myself in the morning. I intended to look for the DCLI[1] who are in this Division, as I know the fellow who commands them, but there was so much traffic and dust that I decided to just ride back through the town. I did not see anyone I knew, but I saw a woman whom I have heard people talking about. She is dressed in a dress entirely made of Gordon tartan and on the sleeves she has a Major's badge.

It is six months now since I last saw you. I think that it is high time they gave us leave again. I have a great longing to see you and the boy.

Monday, 7 June 1915 [from trenches near Rue du Bois]

We came in last night and did not finish the relief till midnight. It is the only night that I have known when the Germans evidently knew the relief was on, as they shelled and fired hard, but no-one was hit.

There has been a lot of work done since we were here last time. I got up early and wandered all round. On the hedge by our dugout are hundreds of wild roses.

I do not suppose Col Vandeleur will come back to the war. We all sincerely trust not.

Tuesday, 8 June 1915 [from trenches near Rue du Bois]

There is nothing to report today. We are much closer to the Germans here – consequently he is a more disagreeable neighbour. The Colonel and I sleep in one dugout. We are not so well off for accommodation as in our own trenches. I received two parcels from yesterday – cakes and sweets. We have been without cakes for some days, so they are much appreciated.

Thursday, 10 June 1915 [from trenches near Rue du Bois]

Yesterday and last night it rained heavily, but it is still very close and muggy. The General came round this morning at 7am. There is no news here, good or bad.

---

1 Duke of Cornwall's Light Infantry; its 2nd Bn had shipped to Britain from Hong Kong in 1914 and was in the 27th division.

Friday, 11 June 1915 [from trenches near Rue du Bois]

It has rained a good deal the last few days and it is much cooler now. We visited our next door neighbours and I walked down to the supporting line and saw Capt Forbes of the 91[st1] who, surrounded by a strong posse of young subalterns, was building himself a place to live in.

I should like a pipe for my birthday present. I am getting fearfully old. You could not make me any happier than I was whilst we were together. If we can only be together again I shall be quite content.

Saturday, 12 June 1915 [FSPC]

I am quite well.

Sunday, 13 June 1915 [from billets near Bois-Grenier]

I am sorry I did not write yesterday. My watch stopped and I thought it was still early when the orderly came for the letters and so I had not time to write anything more than that interesting pc. We got out last night, or rather early this morning, without incident, but we did not get to bed until 2.30am, when it was getting light. We had a pretty uncomfortable six days and a good many casualties, but we were lucky compared to the number of projectiles and missiles of various sorts that they lumped into us.

Well, we have had a great stir in our small world. Yesterday after the Colonel had left the trenches we got a telephone message from the Brigade to say that General Gordon[2] had got a division at home and that the Colonel had got command of the 19th Brigade – so he is now a Brigadier General. So I shall now command the regiment till RO returns. I suppose that he will come to this battalion, but I do not suppose that he will be back for some time. Capt Riddell-Webster is going to get a better staff job, so he will be leaving the Brigade.

Our men are going on six days' leave, but they will not give leave to officers.

---

1 1st Bn Argyll & Sutherland Highlanders, previously known as the 91st (Argyllshire Highlanders) Regiment of Foot.

2 Commander of the 19th brigade.

We are hoping that the Colonel – now that he is a Brigadier – will represent it. I am just mad to come home and see you again.

Monday, 14 June 1915 [FSPC]
I am quite well.

Tuesday, 15 June 1915 [from trenches in La Vese, near Bois-Grenier]
I could not write yesterday as General Gordon came early and went round the companies to say goodbye. I had then to take orderly room and then go to a court martial of which I was president, which lasted most of the day. The Colonel left in the afternoon and so for the present I am the local King.

I heard from RO written by his wife. He is at his own home and has leave until July 25th. I do not know if he will be sent back to this Bn or not. If he is not I shall be a temporary Lt. Colonel.

Wednesday, 16 June 1915 [from trenches in La Vese]
I wrote to Connie about the money. If she does not want paying immediately I would prefer to pay off the bills. I will let you know as soon as I hear. I hope for every reason that I shall remain in command of the Bn but also I shall get 11/- extra a day, which will help.

These trenches are very nice so long as things are quiet. It is lovely weather. The new General[1] is coming round and I am off to meet him as soon as I finish this. We have a cat at Bn HQ which seems very homely. Mr Rooke is out here with us.

I was surprised at Capt Drew's marriage. I should not think it was very good for a dilated heart.[2]

Thursday, 17 June 1915 [from trenches in La Vese]
The Highland Division have been fighting. I hope for your mother's sake that

---

1 Robertson.
2 Drew was sent down sick in September 1914. See letter of 19 September.

Willie is alright. The Calomel has had the desired effect and I feel alright again. I have been very cross the last few days.

Friday, 18 June 1915 [from trenches in La Vese]
Today being the centenary of Waterloo I hope that we shall get some good news. You never mention whether your old trouble is quite gone or not. I hope so.

Saturday, 19 June 1915 [from trenches in La Vese]
I was glad to hear that Jim had gained a little and not lost as you expected.

No, the Colonel being made a Brigadier General does not cause a vacancy and Hammy will not be promoted.

There is absolutely no news. We have not even had a visitor to break the monotony. One of the Forward Observing Officers of the battery supporting us is a United Free[1] minister at St Boswells in private life, which strikes one as comic.

Monday, 21 June 1915 [from billets near Bois-Grenier]
I did not write yesterday at all – I could not. You will be very sorry to hear that Mr Rooke was killed on patrol the night before last. He was shot through the heart.[2] Mr Gray,[3] a very nice subaltern, went out and most gallantly brought in the body, which was only 100 yards from their trench and quite close to the Germans. I was finding out all about it in the morning and then had to go in to the Brigade Office to arrange about the relief. I lunched there with the General and at 3 o'c went with him and RW to the funeral of Mr Rooke, who was buried with the other officers we have lost here. It was very sad.

I returned to the Brigade office where my horses met me and I rode over

---

1 The United Free Church was formed in 1900 by the union of the United Presbyterian Church of Scotland and the Free Church of Scotland, both of which had seceded from the mainstream Church of Scotland in the 1840s.
2 In later years, other officers would tell a different tale about Rooke's death – that a faulty grenade had exploded in his hand. Chaplin, however, had insisted on writing to the family that he was shot through the heart, and he stuck to that version of events in his letter to his wife.
3 2nd Lt M. N. Gray.

to the Quartermaster and got your letter. I then returned and had tea with the General and went to the service with him and afterwards according to my promise to you I attended communion, the first time since I have been in the Army. As soon as I left the service I was met by an orderly with a message to say that Mr Gray had been sniped. He died, poor chap, during the night and we are burying him today.

A lot of letters are being opened by the Censor.

I forgot to say that Capt McLellan has gone home on seven days' leave as he was not well and is going to see you if he can.

Tuesday, 22 June 1915 [from billets near Bois-Grenier]
After I finished my letter to you yesterday I took orderly room and spent the remainder of the morning writing to Mrs Rooke and Mrs Gray about their sons' deaths – a sad job.

Do not worry about Mrs Vandeleur or anything she writes. She is quite mad, poor soul – not that it makes it any less annoying for her to write impertinent letters. If I were you I should only help 1st Bn prisoners. There are very few of them – I will enclose a list with this. You could probably get their addresses from OC Records, Hamilton.[1]

Wednesday, 23 June 1915 [from billets near Bois-Grenier]
They have opened leave for us, one at a time. The probability is that I shall arrive in London at 3pm on Sunday 27th, but of course as you know it is no good counting on it for certain.

I should like you to meet me in London (with my clothes). As there is no time to make any arrangements I will go straight to Mrs Harriette's where I hope that you will be and that you will have arranged for us to sleep in some hotel that night. We will go to Edinburgh next day and see Jim and then I should like to go to Turnberry and play golf with you and forget about the war for a few days. My leave will be for seven days. If you agree, will you get my golf clubs and kit from Brentham? I should like to see your mother

---

1 In Lanarkshire, where the Cameronians kept their home base.

and father and Edith and also see Connie in town. Is Mabel still at Turnberry?

Of course if you cannot come to town you will write a letter to me at Mrs Lee's, or to 96 Piccadilly[1] where I will call to see if there is any letter from you in case Mrs Lee should be away. I am tremendously excited at the prospect of seeing you both so soon, I hope.

Thursday, 24 June 1915 [from trenches near Bois-Grenier]
I could not sleep for excitement last night at the idea of seeing you.

Hammy and I were mentioned in the *Gazette* of June 22nd.

Friday, 25 June 1915 [from trenches near Bois-Grenier]
I am not to get away on Sunday after all. I do not know which day my leave will commence. I will wire to you as soon as I know. It will be one day next week if all is well.

You will see that I have got the DSO. I am awfully pleased and I know that you will be.

Saturday, 26 June 1915 [from trenches near Bois-Grenier]
Another disappointment! I shall probably not be able to get leave until about July 5th – of course one cannot count on it then, in fact until one is on the train one cannot be certain of going.

There will be time now for you to let me know exactly your programme, in case I do really get home.

Yes, Mr Skipwith[2] was killed. We were all very sorry. Your brother's division[3] is joining this Corps, so they will be somewhere new.

Sunday, 27 June 1915 [from trenches near Bois-Grenier]
No more news about the leave. I wish they would hurry up – it is most harassing, this putting off.

---

1 The Army and Navy Club.
2 Granville Skipwith, a forward observing officer for the artillery whom Chaplin had mentioned in a letter dated 13 April 1915.
3 51st Highland Division, including 6th Black Watch, was withdrawn from Ypres.

Billy Croft came to see us yesterday – he says that his wife told him that she could not be bothered to read the *Gazette*, but the cook told her that he was mentioned, which amused me greatly.

Monday, 28 June 1915 [FSPC]
I am quite well.

Tuesday, 29 June 1915 [from trenches near Bois-Grenier]
No further news of leave yet, but I am hoping to get away about the 5th or 6th. I will wire to you when I start.

Yesterday I felt too seedy to write. I got a chill in my waistcoat but took a good dose of castor oil and am alright today. We are not allowed to say now when we are in or out of trenches.

I shall have a lot of writing to do. I have received already 20 letters of congratulation, including Mrs MacAllan, Mrs Riddell-Webster, Mrs Northey, RO, Reggie,[1] Isa.[2] The ribbon of the DSO is crimson with narrow blue edges. I do not know when I shall get it. I could have it presented by the King when I am at home by writing to the War Office, but I don't want to unless you want me to.

Thursday, 1 July [telegram from Hazebrouck]
Arrive Victoria 3pm Friday 2nd July Graham Chaplin

Friday, 2 July [telegram from Hazebrouck]
Leave postponed Graham Chaplin

Friday, 2 July 1915 [from billets near Bois-Grenier]
I am so fed up at being stopped going home at the last moment that I am not able to write much. Serious trouble has occurred over an incident in the

---

1 Reginald Swalwell, a noted cricketer who played for Worcestershire and the MCC, was married to Lily's sister, Mabel.

2 Lily's sister, Isa, married to Tom Mackay.

regiment – nothing to do with me, but as I am commanding until it is settled, I cannot go on leave.

I am afraid that you will have started for London before you got my wire. I am awfully sorry for you, darling. With all my fondest love, ever your loving husband, Graham

*   *   *

Graham Chaplin faces the first test of his leadership. Something happens in the A Company trenches midway through 29 June that – seven days later – causes him to arrest his friend, thirty-one-year-old Captain Tom McLellan. The two are already close, having run A Company together since the start of the war. They had shared meals, rooms, beds, floors, long games of bridge and assorted hardships, both on the retreat from Mons and on the advance back to Ypres, through the battle at La Boutillerie and in the trenches of Houplines. Yet on that warm Tuesday in June, just hours before the Royal Welch relieve the Cameronians in the Bois-Grenier front line, an incident occurs that causes Chaplin to cancel his own leave and spend a week investigating.

The arrest of McLellan is an action that has far-reaching consequences for both men. A number of soldiers in the Cameronians have already faced courts martial[36] for a range of offences, usually involving theft, drunkenness or disobedience, and been sentenced with prison or standard field punishments. But McLellan is the first officer in the Cameronians to be tried before a court martial since the battalion embarked for France. Even if exonerated, it would be a black mark on his army career, and it is likely to have caused some disquiet among the fellow officers that Chaplin has to lead.

Just what McLellan did is not clear. The battalion War Diary on 6 July simply notes, 'Capt T R McLellan arrested for certain inaction on 29 June', suggesting he refused to respond to a command. The War Diary for 29 June notes, 'Enemy tried to make advances on our right. Relieved in the evening by the R Welch Fusiliers.' No memoir or letter cites the incident, but for Chaplin it is plainly a crisis, which effects not just the reputation of the regiment but also how his own leadership will be seen. His letters home become tense and terse, refusing to tell his wife what has happened, but setting out plainly the repercussions. He spends a week investigating the incident and on 13 July McLellan is brought before a court martial. The War Diary for that day simply reads, 'Capt T R McLellan tried on two charges and acquitted on both.' No more is written; no more is said.

That doesn't tell the full story. The amount of German shelling had increased steadily that month, and rumours were circling of guns being brought into the Armentières sector in preparation for a major enemy attack.[37] Anxieties were running high. Perhaps McLellan, unwell and going on leave according to Chaplin's letter of 21 June, had returned emotionally unprepared for the fighting that took place on 29 June, when the Germans raided the Cameronian trenches.

Or perhaps his leave had been cancelled, as the battalion War Diary at the end of June notes that 'leave has also been opened for officers but none have gone yet'. The term 'certain inaction' could include anything from refusing to send his men into battle to collapsing from nervous exhaustion. It is also not clear who reported the 'inaction', but presumably it was visible and dangerous enough to necessitate a trial to take place, involving officers of other regiments sitting in judgement, and Chaplin to spend a week preparing the case. Prior to this, other Cameronian officers who had experienced nervous collapses had been allowed to slip away home with unspecified illness, whatever the reaction from fellow soldiers.[38] McLellan, however, was held to account.

All details of the incident are now expunged from the record. Only those involved know what happened, and the secret is taken to their graves. But at some stage later that month, McLellan leaves the battalion, returning 'to UK sick'. He reappears in France, to Chaplin's surprise,[39] in February 1917, rejoining the battalion, still a captain. It seems, from then, normal relations are resumed.[40]

Extracts from the battalion War Diary,
June / July 1915,

Kept by Major Graham Chaplin

Trenches near Bois-Grenier
29 June - Enemy tried to make advances on our right. Relieved
in evening by R Welch Fusiliers.

Billets near Bois-Grenier
30 June - Ordinary routine.

1 July - Ordinary routine. CO inspected companies. C Coy
particularly well turned out.

2 July - Machine Gun in practice range with reserves.

3 July - Inspection transport.

4 July - Church parades. Relieved RWF at night.

Trenches near Bois-Grenier
5 July - Enemy shelled behind D Coy.

6 July - Capt T R McLellan placed under arrest for certain
inaction on 29 June. GOC came round trenches. Lt Foster went
on leave by order of AG [Adjutant General] though refused 10
days earlier by CO. CO objected to 27th Div.

7 July - Germans shelled a little. Capt Hill put seven rifle
grenades in enemy's trenches, going out in front to get range.
The enemy can get our trenches from his own.

Saturday, 3 July 1915 [from billets near Bois-Grenier]
My darling Lil,

I am pleased about Jim – it is something to cheer one up in very depressing circumstances. I am not sure when I shall get leave now. If I do I think I had better come straight to Edinburgh. I am awfully busy.

Sunday, 4 July 1915 [from billets near Bois-Grenier]
I have not had time since July 1st to write any letter. I have been carrying out an investigation and practically writing all day since then. I have been greatly worried.

I only hope and trust I shall get home soon and see you, but I do not expect at the best to get away for a fortnight, if then.

Monday, 5 July 1915 [from trenches near Bois-Grenier]
My darling Lil,

I was quite glad to get in after an unpleasant week of nothing but worry and writing. I have no idea when I shall get away. With all my fondest love to you both. I hope that Jim continues to flourish.

Tuesday, 6 July 1915 [from trenches near Bois-Grenier]
I have been seedy with my interior economy since I caught a chill but am alright today. I have been worried out of my life by the incident which was the cause of my leave being stopped, which did not make one feel better, and the weather has been horrible, very hot and sultry.

Wednesday, 7 July 1915 [FSPC]
I am quite well.

Thursday, 8 July 1915 [from trenches near Bois-Grenier]
I was sorry that I was too busy and worried to write yesterday. No, I cannot say in a letter what the incident was. I am afraid it will be some time before I can get home. We have absolutely no news.

Friday, 9 July 1915 [FSPC]

I am quite well.

Saturday, 10 July 1915 [from billets near Bois-Grenier]

I am most awfully pleased to hear that Jim continues to do so well. I quite enjoyed myself yesterday. I went to the Brigade Office and then went with Col Williams[1] of the R Welch Fusiliers and had lunch in town – quite a long time since I have had a civilised meal and I enjoyed it.

I received all the things you sent and got another parcel of fruit yesterday – thank you so much for everything. I have been too busy or worried to write much or think of my own affairs.

Sunday, 11 July 1915 [from billets near Bois-Grenier]

Yes, I think that we shall get away on leave soon, within a fortnight unless anything unforeseen happens. I went for our usual ride with Sam D. In the evening the General came to see me and we had a long talk.

I get Lt Col's pay from the 13th of last month, provided I have been a month in command which I shall have been tomorrow.

Monday, 12 July 1915 [from billets near Bois-Grenier]

Don't think that I am ill – I am very well but have been very busy. Sam D and I rode over to the 2nd Bn yesterday and saw Carter Campbell and Sandy – the latter goes home on leave today. No news – everything very quiet.

Tuesday, 13 July 1915 [from billets near Bois-Grenier]

Leave has opened again for us and I hope to get away within a week or so. I will wire when leave is granted and also when I start. The boats are altered and I shall arrive in London at 5am and will go straight to the Curzon Hotel – it will be too early for you to meet me.

---

1 Col O. de L. Williams, described in his regimental obituary as 'normally grim, withdrawn, almost forbidding' but with 'a quizzical humour and charm which turned the lasting admiration of his officers and men into something akin to real affection' [source: *The War the Infantry Knew* by Captain J. C. Dunn].

No, commanding is no strain to me, but this incident has worried me because it reflects on the regiment. I will tell you what it was when we meet.

Wednesday, 14 July 1915 [from billets near Bois-Grenier]

I expect to get leave in a few days. If you are not at the Curzon Hotel I will go to 96 Piccadilly for a letter from you. I am very well but have no time to write. With all my love to you both, ever your loving husband, Graham

Thursday, 15 July 1915 [from trenches near Bois-Grenier]

All our troubles have come to an end and I have more time to write than I have had for the last fortnight and I have also more inclination to do so.

I hope to get home in a very few days but cannot of course say when until I get the orders. I shall have to go to a dentist – I have had a lot of trouble with a tooth.

I became a temporary Lt Colonel yesterday and get Lt Col's pay from that date. You might ask Anderson to put the Lt Colonel's badges on my new coat. It is time I had some new clothes as I look very shabby.

As I shall arrive in London at 5am I shall probably have had no sleep that night, so I should like a bath and to go straight to bed.

I have really scored by being delayed as I shall get nine days' leave instead of seven.

Friday, 16 July 1915 [from trenches near Bois-Grenier]

No news yet about my leave. I am going to try and answer the remainder of my congratulation letters today. The weather is fine again after heavy rain. Capt RW has become Quartermaster General of a Division. I am very glad. With my fondest love, darling, and heaps of kisses to you both, ever your loving husband, Graham

Friday, 16 July 1915 [telegram from Hazebrouck (8pm)]

Arrive Victoria 5am Sunday 18th Chaplin

Tuesday, 20 July 1915 [from Sam Darling to J. G. Chaplin, in Edinburgh]

My dear Colonel,

We are back just now and 2 Battns go into trenches on night 23/24. We will not. We go into trenches where 2 Batts lately were[1] when we used to ride down to see them, not in the ones we dug. The leave train still goes from and to Steenwerck.

Old Harry[2] is the thickest-headed old fusser I've ever met. He has a note-book which he writes everything down in and has now been cross-examining Wood[3] for ¾ of an hour with the same questions, and everything goes down in the book, then he has a "good two hours' think" and gives his opinion very slowly and in a loud voice and it's too painful arguing. Wood and I wink and take no notice.

Hope you are having a good time and will not be sorry to see you back again (for my peace of mind!). Yours ever, John CSD

---

1 Rue Bacarot, near Laventie.

2 Lee.

3 'Tubby' Wood, the Cameronians' quartermaster.

LOOS

'We have had a very trying time – a time of great anxiety for me.'

Allied forces plan coordinated assault on German line north of Arras — British attack at Loos with six divisions — artillery fails to cut German wire — British use of chlorine gas proves ineffective — high casualties and low gains draw criticism — French forces fail to achieve planned breakthrough further south

August 1915 brings movement. Hauled out of trenches near Laventie, the Cameronians find the 19th brigade reallocated to the 2nd division, with a new web of commanders and staff to salute, and facing orders to march south closer to Béthune, where rumours of a new offensive fill every bar and café. The old town, prosperous from the many mining pits that gouge the landscape beyond its southern edge, sits just a few miles from the front; yet, in 1915, it is still unscathed by shelling and far busier than Armentières. Its red-brick suburbs echo to the shouts of quartermasters and transport teams, and its main square, ringed with quaintly narrow houses and dominated by a medieval belfry, provides strolling soldiers with a singular sight, unlike anything built in the mining counties of Lanarkshire, Yorkshire or Northumberland.

Here, among the narrow streets that radiate from the old *mairie*, British combatants bustle through shops still conducting a prosperous trade. The Café du Globe in the old square sells officers champagne cocktails at one franc (ten pennies) a time. But every drinker knows that the slow gathering of battalions can only mean one thing: that this southernmost end of the British line has been targeted for an autumn push.

Graham Chaplin reveals little of that to Lil. He returns from eight days' leave on 27 July to find his battalion in new billets, near Sailly, with new trenches to fill at Rue Bacarot, near Laventie, before the move to Béthune and the promise of rest. By then he has been jolted by another surprise: Lil, recognising the signs of morning sickness, writes that she may be pregnant again, less than a month after his visit. Such leave-babies will become an increasingly common phenomenon. But for now, as he writes to Lil, Chaplin is anxious: 'I know, darling, that it is you who suffer. I blame myself if you do not blame me. You have had such a lot to put up with, with all Jim's illness and the anxiety of the war. It is very hard to write exactly what one feels as one knows the letters may be opened, but you must know that all my thoughts are with you.'[41]

Within days, her mood picks up, and his too. Writing to her at Palmerston Place, Edinburgh, where the family keep an apartment, he ponders gender and plumps for girl: 'I think I should like a little Doreen – she would be more of a companion for you.'[42]

And his letters return to their normal mix of chitchat, health reports and droll observation. Even before Lil's announcement, he had been offering updates on his teeth, an abscess in his lower jaw sending him to the doctor. His solution is characteristically pragmatic: 'I . . . got him to stick a knife in.'[43]

The result is equally predictable. He must book to see an army dentist, who treats him two days later, pulling out stumps and injecting his abscess with cocaine. His face swells, his head pounds and he retires to bed with two aspirins. Days later, on a return visit to the same army dentist in Armentières, he treats himself to a hotel lunch where he is puzzled by a group of Scots in civilian clothes huddled in the corner of the dining room. He finds they are a miners' delegation sent out from Lanarkshire to visit the Scottish regiments. He invites them to the front to see the Cameronians. They never come.

Meanwhile, the usual band predominate – Harry Lee, Sam Darling, Captain Hammy, Billy Croft of the 5th, regulars throughout Chaplin's army career – and the gossip continues: RO's recovery, Robin Money's posting to a staff job in London, James Cotton Minchin's transfer to the Royal Flying Corps, officers from India popping up on their way through. Despite the daily death and maiming Chaplin witnesses in the trenches, he spares his wife the detail, as if this other world of social chitchat can happily eclipse his working worries.

Just occasionally the determination to keep in good spirits slips. The year of war, with the same bunch of men living on top of each other, is starting to take its toll. After Lee is posted temporarily to brigade HQ and others take their turn home on leave, Chaplin finds his enforced proximity to forty-year-old Hamilton in battalion HQ begins to grate: 'His loud and discordant voice making futile remarks would try a saint from Heaven and he is such a fool that he is a hindrance rather than a help . . .'[44]

Lil, already adapting to her new role as wife of the battalion CO – staying in touch with other spouses, creating a network of support, coordinating the parcels sent to the front – sees the other side of Hamilton. While her husband is railing, Lil is sending Hammy's wife flowers as she recovers from appendicitis, receiving a letter of fulsome thanks from the Major:

> Dear Mrs Chaplin,
>
>   I meant to have written to you before leaving London to say how nice we both felt it was of you to have sent Anita those carnations when she was at the nursing home . . . I am glad your youngster seems to be doing so well. The CO says he feels slack but I think he seems very bright and cheery now.

The promise of rest for the battalion proves a false one. From Béthune the Cameronians are sent to man trenches outside Cuinchy, an old village east of Béthune, now shattered by shelling. The 900-yard length of front line, bisected by canal to the north and main road to the south, weaves through a brickfield, around stacks eighteen feet high, which sit surreal and menacing, offering excellent protection for British and German alike, creating dugouts beneath, but preventing the construction of a logical, holdable line. Between the brickfields, no-man's land is pockmarked with mine craters as both sides tunnel voraciously to set off explosives, adding a new layer of nervous tension to the usual five-day trench tour. Anxiety at the advantages that can be gained from a well-blown crater will make this part of the front a difficult posting, every sound underground, every new sign of enemy earth-shifting, a portent of something terrible.

At least, for the most part, the trenches are deeper and drier – hence the mining – than they knew before in Bois-Grenier. Chaplin's HQ is kept in a part-demolished, fortified house near the village, where he takes reports from his company officers, overseeing the paperwork coming in and out, briefing his adjutant, the officer appointed to run the battalion's HQ bureaucracy. Communication with the line is haphazard. Part of the front, known as the 'cabbage patch', is studded with breastworks, called 'grouse butts' – the ground there the only part too sodden in winter for deep trenches. The German line, by contrast, is higher, chosen with care, with better lines of observation, and must be watched constantly. Both sides know any offensive will be preceded by a large-scale massing of men, hard to conceal, and prolonged bombardment. There are few secrets here.

The Cameronians will understand all this in time, as the 2nd division takes on a two-mile-long section of this front, stretching from Givenchy in the north to Cambrin in the south, each part with its own characteristics. The division rotates its three brigades in and out of the front line, in reserve, in rest.

For now, though, Chaplin seems buoyant at the new challenge and the change in scene. He is even duck-shooting in fields away from the front line – one of his old pastimes in India's Cawnpore, where the Cams were the only British regiment for miles, and duck shoots and polo were the younger officers' main leisure pursuits. His humour is lifted, too, at the thought of another addition to the family at home. It won't be long, however, before the war takes another turn.

Monday, 23 August 1915 [from billets in Béthune]
My darling Lil,

A year ago tonight we started to retreat from the Mons Canal!

This morning I went to see our new line[1] and spent all morning there. I

---

1 Trenches in Cuinchy.

was quite pleased with it. Our promised rest has not come off – we have been disappointed so often that we hardly expect it will ever come off.

It is a most lovely moonlit night tonight and if it was not for the distant bursting of shells it would be hard to imagine that there is a war at all.

It is good news the Russians sinking so many German vessels. I wish they were equally successful on land.

Tuesday, 24 August 1915 [from trenches in Cuinchy, east of Béthune]

We are very comfortable here. I have a splendid dugout – we have a house to dine and live in by day. It has a great picture gallery of lovely ladies from the *Sketch* and kindred papers.

Harriette is back in the fold. Could you please send me some carbolic tooth powder?

Wednesday, 25 August 1915 [from trenches in Cuinchy]

We are having splendid weather – really too hot as we live underground a great deal here.

I am very worried about your continued sickness and hope that you will see a doctor.

Thursday, 26 August 1915 [from trenches in Cuinchy]

The anniversary of Le Cateau. I never expected to see another sun rise this day last year.

The War Office is going to make all officers of over 15 years Majors, so practically everyone you knew before the war will be a Major – Sandy, Harriette, Hamilton. Unfortunately for me Sam D also and he will have to give up the Adjutancy. I am going to make Wright Adjutant.

With all my fondest love and heaps of kisses to you both. I pray that the mal-de-mer is better.

Saturday, 28 August 1915 [FSPC]

I am quite well.

Saturday, 28 August 1915 [from trenches in Cuinchy]

The General turned up this morning when I usually write my letter to you so I was only able to send one of those interesting pcs, which was just as well as there is nothing to write about, but I hate missing a day all the same.

We have a gun for use so yesterday I took Harriette for a walk where there are some marshes. I thought I might see some duck, but there was not a sign of one. The sun was setting and it made quite a pretty picture.

The weather is very hot and I feel very slack. This afternoon Harriette brought in Godfrey Fowler. I had never met him before. He did not impress me much and is not a patch on his sister. He stayed to tea.

Then Col Usher who used to command the 90th[1] came in to tea also. He is an uncle of Mr Salmonson.[2] He asked me about him and I gave my opinion quite candidly.

Monday, 30 August 1915 [from trenches in Cuinchy]

I did not write yesterday – I had been on the move all day and was too tired to write at night and this morning I had not time before the post left. The tooth powder and galantine arrived safely – many thanks, dear. I have not tried the latter but it looks very good.

The General came this morning and also some Staff people from home. It is iniquitous Capt Newman[3] getting a Staff job.

Tuesday, 31 August 1915 [from trenches in Cuinchy]

The galantine was uncommonly good! There is absolutely no news – we have seen no-one and heard no news of the outside world.

I am very glad that you are feeling better. I am very sorry to hear that your father is so seedy. It is an awful shame that he has not someone to help him.

---

1 2nd battalion Scottish Rifles had been the 90th Perthshire Light Infantry before the 1881 amalgamation with 26th Cameronian Regiment of Foot.

2 Lt H. S. R. Critchley-Salmonson, joined B Coy, 1st Bn, in September 1914 – not mentioned in War Diary from January 1915.

3 Lt E. W. P. Newman, sent home sick from B Coy on 30 October 1914, after what Chaplin reports is a nervous breakdown.

I can never write the letters I ought to – I am always hoping for a sort of slack time but it never comes. With all my fondest love and heaps of kisses to you both, ever your loving husband, Graham

Extracts from the battalion War Diary, September 1915,

Kept by Colonel Graham Chaplin

Trenches, Cuinchy
1 September – About midnight enemy opened rapid fire and threw trench mortars, our casualties were Piper Robertson and Pte Miles, D Coy, killed, Pte Jones wounded. At 10am 5th Scottish Rifles relieved the Battn which went back to billets near Beuvry.

Billets, Beuvry
2 September – Rifle and boot inspections, also smoke helmets. One Coy (A) at Maison Rouge in support under Bde HQ.

3 September – Companies route marching etc.

4 September – The battn went back to billets just outside Béthune in the cemetery area.

Billets, Béthune
5 September – Companies at Baths. Smoke helmet, boot and rifle inspections. Church Parades. GOC 2nd Div attended Church of Scotland service.

6 September – Ordinary billet routine.

7 September - Ordinary billet routine. Concerts for the men in the town.

8 September - Baths etc.

9 September - Ordinary routine - drill, charging etc.

10 September - Drill etc. Training - fire discipline etc.

11 September - Ditto.

12 September - Church parades.

Trenches, Givenchy

13 September - Relieved 2nd HLI at 3pm. Three casualties from rifle grenades and trench mortars viz L/C Prichard, Ptes Holye and Bankes. Lt Wayett, Battn Grenade Officer, took a party of grenadiers out to the new crater and had a brief fight with the enemy, with good results and quite gaining the ascendancy over them.

14 September - Enemy quiet but still a good deal of rifle-grenading and bombing going on, our artillery retaliated. Eight saps are being pushed out as hard as possible as it is thought enemy is coming towards us south of the Ducks Bill with a mine. Casualties as follows. Wounded: Pte Murphy, Pte Rashley, Pte Abbot, Pte Buchan, Cpl Robb, L/C Hill, L/C Costello, Pte Craig.

Wednesday, 1 September 1915 [from billets near Beuvry, outside Béthune]

My darling Lil,

No shooting partridge today! However we are in quite nice billets[1] – my house is right on a canal. I am very thankful not to be in a dugout and to get fresh air once more.

We met the 9th Bn and saw Col Northey[2] and Major Townshend – the latter had a bullet graze on the head but is alright again.

Billy Croft came back today – he is full of the original Expeditionary Force going home for three months.

Friday, 3 September 1915 [FSPC]

I am quite well.

Friday, 3 September 1915 [from billets near Beuvry]

You must be having a jolly bad time[3] – I wish now for your sake that I had never had leave!

I could not write last night. My eyes were so tired and I had left my glasses in my bedroom, which is a fair way from where we live during the day.

I got two bottles of port today. I think they must be from RO as they are the same bottles he used to get, but there was nothing with them to show who they were from. I got a parcel of fruit from you with some excellent pears – many thanks, darling!

Saturday, 4 September 1915 [from billets in cemetery area, Béthune]

We came today to our old chateau. It seemed quite pleasant and peace-like getting into the town and seeing all the shops. The regiment was all split up for various reasons and I rode in alone with Sam D. We had a cocktail in a café (!) after we deposited our horses, and felt quite dissipated.

---

1 In Beuvry, a small coal-mining town south-west of Béthune.
2 Col Arthur Northey, commanding officer of 9th Bn.
3 Lil is suffering from morning sickness.

We have got an RC[1] padre living with us temporarily – quite a nice fellow and a man of the world.

I only wish that you could feel well – perhaps now the unpleasant part will stop. I can imagine that it will be an awful business moving to Brentham[2] – I wish I could be there to help.

Sunday, 5 September 1915 [from billets in Béthune]

I had a letter from Col Wilson today. He does not give a very cheery account of India – there is a good deal of unrest apparently.

I got up late this morning and then went to the Church of Scotland service. It was held in a cinematograph theatre. They had the divisional band, which added considerably to the service.

Monday, 6 September 1915 [from billets in Béthune]

It was a glorious day today. I got up rather late and wrote one letter – to RO – after all. I went for a ride with Sam D in the afternoon and walked into the town after tea. In the intervals I have sent plenty of reports.

Everybody is now a Major. I am very sorry that it means parting with Sam D and I shall be very lonely and have no congenial spirit to talk to, or what is more important not to talk to. Harriette is very excited at being a major.

Tuesday, 7 September 1915 [from billets in Béthune]

I was very glad to get your letter saying that you felt so much better. There is absolutely no news here. I spent the morning at the Brigade office and went for a ride in the afternoon.

---

1 Roman Catholic – despite its Presbyterian roots, the Cameronians had many Catholic soldiers. The RC padre staying with Chaplin is James H. McShane who goes on to become a renowned figure, decorated for bravery and sketched in Robert Graves' *Goodbye to All That* as Father McCabe. McShane's brother, Vincent, died fighting with the Northumberland Fusiliers in the Dardanelles in August 1915. Chaplin habitually misspells McShane as MacShane in his letters.
2 The Alexander family home in Stirling.

It is splendid that Jim is doing so well. I got the passbook. It is alright except that allowances have not been paid for July and August.

Wednesday, 8 September 1915 [from billets in Béthune]

Yesterday I did exactly the same as the day before so there is nothing to report. The General came to see us and the RC Chaplain has gone home on leave.

Friday, 10 September 1915 [from billets in Béthune]

I did not write yesterday as I had bad toothache and rode over to the dentist instead. It is about nine miles from here and would have been a delightful ride had one been feeling it. I went to the same dentist as before.

I am glad you are settled down and comfortable again. I am tremendously pleased about Jim being so well and getting so heavy.

I wish, my darling, that I could be with you. I am beginning to feel that I want a rest. It will be 13 months by the time this reaches you.

Sunday, 12 September 1915 [from billets in Béthune]

These Zeppelin raids[1] make me furious and I am glad you are not in London.

I went to the Presbyterian service this morning but the parson chose all hymns I had never heard of and as I had toothache I was altogether rather annoyed.

Monday, 13 September 1915 [FSPC]

I am quite well.

Tuesday, 14 September 1915 [from trenches in Givenchy, outside Béthune]

I could only write a card for yesterday's post. I am very busy these days and am either too much interrupted to sit down and write or am so tired that I think I will write in the morning and something prevents me.

I got your parcel and also the lemon squash, for which thousands of thanks.

---

1 The Germans started making infrequent Zeppelin raids on London from May 1915.

I only wish I could be with you. I have never longed for you more than I do now, and I wish I could see Jim and all his teeth.

Wednesday, 15 September 1915 [from trenches in Givenchy]

The news from Russia looks more cheerful – I hope that they really are making some progress. I have had the usual day, round the trenches in the morning and also tonight. The General came today and was very well. I saw Billy Croft tonight. He has cut his hair like a convict. I told him his wife would probably divorce him.

Thursday, 16 September 1915 [from trenches in Givenchy]

I had no letter from you today, but Harriette had so I hope that you are alright but it was a disappointment. I got a parcel of fruit which was very welcome.

We are out tomorrow, back to our old chateau. I shall not be sorry. It has been very hot and muggy but I do not suppose that the heat will last much longer.

Saturday, 18 September 1915 [from billets in Béthune]

We are back in our old quarters – we did not get back till pretty late. I was jolly glad to get your letter as I had not one the day before, but I quite understand that you did not feel like writing – I am very sorry for the cause.

I have got to go off to see the General. They are to send a car for me, so I must close.

Sunday, 19 September 1915 [from billets in Béthune]

There was no post yesterday for us.

I went to dinner last night with Col Wolfe-Murray and had a great dinner – about seven courses, champagne, port, liqueurs. I played bridge afterwards, the first game since the war started. I won all three rubbers and came home with 10 francs and very pleased with myself. I missed a good dinner at home, as the RC padre brought out from leave oysters and partridges.

With all my love, dear, and heaps of kisses to you both.

Monday, 20 September 1915 [from billets in Béthune]

I did not go to the Kirk yesterday. I went out to see the Brigadier.

I am very pleased about Doreen. It is only for what you have to suffer that I am distressed about her. I am glad that you are no longer depressed.

Col CC has got a Brigade and gone home. I am very glad – it shows that merit is sometimes recognised. Sandy is commanding the 2nd Bn. I do not know if they will leave him in command, if RO does not come out, or if they will send H[1] there. I wish they would for my personal sake, but not for the 2nd Bn.

Tuesday, 21 September 1915 [FSPC]

I am quite well.

Thursday, 23 September 1915 [FSPC]

I am quite well.

Friday, 24 September 1915 [FSPC]

I am quite well.

Friday, 24 September 1915 [from billets in Béthune]

You will have guessed from my irregular correspondence that we have been pretty busy. We are out for one day in our old chateau. It is highly probable that I shall not be able to write much, if at all, for some time – so do not be anxious.

I am very sorry that your father is so poorly and hope the change to Turnberry will do him good. I am awfully pleased that Jim is getting on so well – it is splendid. I am very sorry, darling, that you are having such a rotten time.

With all my fondest love to you both and heaps of kisses, ever your loving husband, Graham

*   *   *

---

1 Hamilton.

The last letter he would ever write? Graham Chaplin would likely reckon so. By now he has known for some time that the Cameronians are 'going over the bags'[45] at Loos, in the large-scale offensive that all see coming.

The old British Expeditionary Force, supplemented by Kitchener's recruits, now fills two armies, the First, based around Béthune, and the Second, further north at Ypres. The plan, agreed over the summer of 1915 by Field Marshal Sir John French, commander of British forces, is for a push to be made from the southern part of the British line, beside French allies. The aim is to overwhelm the German defenders with weight of numbers before the enemy can call back reinforcements from the eastern front.

The British First Army, under General Sir Douglas Haig, targets the German-held town of Lens and its suburb Loos, just beyond the Cambrin front line which the Cameronians already occupy. It is not a battle-ground of British choosing. Haig knows the terrain is too flat – desolate mining country dotted with enemy-held slagheaps – offering the Germans too many advantages. But maintaining good relations with the French means refusal is impossible. With the Russians attacking in the east, the British and French have to tie down as many German divisions as possible.

Some of this Chaplin would have been told, but not all. The Cameronians are one of five battalions in the 19th brigade (with the 2nd Royal Welch, 1st Middlesex, 2nd Argyll & Sutherland Highlanders and 5th Scottish Rifles), which itself is one of three brigades (with the 5th and 6th) in the 2nd division. It is one of four divisions (also the 7th, 9th and 28th) in I Corps, which itself is one of three corps (also IV and XI) in the First Army. That puts five levels of staff, each with their own headquarters and bureaucracy, between Chaplin, a battalion commander, and Sir John French. Gossip and rumour filter down slowly, factual analysis more slowly still. Chaplin does, however, have one advantage – the man he reports to, Brigadier General Philip Robertson, is an old friend, a former commander of the Cameronians who had relied heavily on Chaplin's experience during the retreat from Mons, the battles at La Boutillerie and the manning of trenches around Armentières. Robertson, son of a general, is a popular CO, but one who had seen little real action before the outbreak of World War One. His trust in Chaplin will prove to be crucial in the days which follow.

By Friday, 24 September, Chaplin knows how difficult a task his battalion faces. The Cams are in the front line until the evening of 23 September, then march five miles back to billets. The next evening they make the return journey in the rain, ready for the jump off on 25 September. They are already tired troops. And as the lengthy, detailed orders come down from the top, each layer of command taking its assigned objectives and breaking them into smaller, detailed, subsidiary tasks, the Cameronians' role becomes clear. As part of a wider push towards Lens, the 2nd division will attack the German line either side of the La Bassée Canal, the 5th brigade to the north, the 6th and 19th to the south, familiar territory with its brickstacks and mine craters. Chief target for the 19th brigade will be the heavily defended village of Auchy. Its frontal assault is intended as a diversion, to pin down defending forces, for the German position appears too strong to be breached head-on. The real target is the large mound, known as Fosse 8, further south, and the village of Haisnes beyond, to be attacked by 9th division. Take that, and the forces opposite the Cams can be encircled.

But it puts the 19th in a precarious position. A prolonged bombardment will hopefully shatter German defences before the battalions storm across – the order of battle then agreed by Robertson with his divisional commander, Major-General Henry Horne, places the 2nd Argyll & Sutherland Highlanders and the Middlesex in the first wave, with the Cameronians and Royal Welch following on, consolidating gains and pushing beyond the first attackers.

Was Robertson protecting his own by holding back the Cams?[46] Or saving them for the defining action once the first trenches had been stormed? It is hard not to believe that he knew exactly how deadly the terrain was, with raised German positions on both flanks. Everything depends on actions to left and right succeeding simultaneously as the 19th attacks. A successful bombardment will soften the enemy defences, then two large mines will be blown on their front line. Then over the top they will go.

Chaplin also now knows that the First Army has one secret weapon up its sleeve: chlorine gas. Since the Germans' first use of poison gas at Ypres earlier in the year, the decision had been taken to respond in kind. But only one factory in Britain can make the gas, toiling through the summer to stockpile enough for effective use in battle. Under conditions of secrecy, 5,000 cylinders (each six feet high, weighing 150 lb) have been wheeled into specially dug recesses along the front-line trenches. After a four-day bombardment, before the first wave of troops rises from the trenches, there will be a forty-minute release of gas – code-named 'the accessory' – which, it is hoped, will be carried by wind into the enemy trenches.

Everything hangs on the direction of the wind. And that is just one variable. Different scenarios have to be considered. How should an attack continue if successful? Where to stop? What to do if disaster strikes? For Chaplin, the flurry of maps and paperwork grows, with written orders detailing each option, the success of each target depending on the parallel success of brigades attacking along a two-mile front, the coordination crucial. Systems of signage and signalling are worked over to convey back position and status, tasks and targets allocated to company commanders inside the battalion, missions explained, an overview laid out, liaison discussed with the medical officer and his team over stretcher bearing and aid posts.

Chaplin knows too that he will have to be in the front-line trenches with his men, following them over so he can make decisions rapidly as they advance. Even behind the chosen front line in battalion HQ, a handful of dugouts along the reserve line, he is a sitting target, as the enemy's aerial reconnaissance would have pinpointed any cluster as an obvious command post. But he would have wanted to lead from the front. Inside the regiment, the 2nd battalion – which had a tetchy rivalry[47] with the 1st stretching back to the days of the 1881 amalgamation[48] – has already distinguished itself in two offensives, at Neuve Chapelle and Aubers Ridge. It has also paid a terrible price. At Neuve Chapelle, it lost over 600 men, including 30 officers, killed or wounded. At Aubers Ridge, 168 men were killed, including 12 officers.

At Neuve Chapelle, the 2nd Scottish Rifles – they refused to be called Cameronians – were led by an old 1st battalion man, Colonel W. M. Bliss, a former company commander whose promotion from lieutenant to adjutant in 1894 created the vacancy which brought Chaplin into the regiment. His gallant death at the head of so many men did much to bring officers of the two fractious battalions together. Old regiments pride themselves on the price paid in such gallant lives. Chaplin can have no illusions as to what is expected of him now.

Extracts from the battalion War Diary,
September 1915,

Kept by Colonel Graham Chaplin

```
Near Cambrin
24 September - Paraded at 11.15pm and marched off to take up
position in support of 2/A&S Highlanders.


25 September
4.40am - Received a message from Bde Hd Qrs that operations
would take place according to timetable and that hour 0.00
would be 4.40am. The wind was not favourable for the accessory[1]
but it was used and blew up the lines of ours and enemy's
trenches.


6.30am - The Argylls and Middlesex attacked but could make
no headway. Three companies of A&S Highlanders went, and all
the Middlesex and two Coys of RWFus[2] who were supporting them.
All lost heavily. On the left, the confusion was great, the
```

---

1 Gas – first British use of.
2 Royal Welch Fusiliers.

trenches being very narrow, communication was difficult. The
Cameronians were close up ready to support the A&S
Highlanders.

8.32am – Message received from Bde HQ that there would be a
further bombardment of half an hour, that RWFus would move up
to front line on right, Middlesex going back and Cameronians
would replace A&S Highlanders. The Bde asked if we would be
ready to attack at 9.30am but replied it was impossible. CO
represented to Bde HQ that he was ready to attack but he did
not see how it could be successful.

10.30am – Message received from Bde that 2nd Div reported
the attack on our right was progressing favourably and that
no further attacks would at present be made by 6th and 19th
Infantry Brigades, but would be ready to attack on receipt of
further orders.

11.30am – Message received that 28th Infantry Brigade on our
right has been pushed back and that we are to hold line
as originally – A&S Highlanders went back 500 yards to the
sidings in support and the Middlesex did the same on our
immediate right.

12.50pm – Message received that IV have taken Hulluch and
enemy are retiring hurriedly, also that French in Champagne
have done well.

3.54pm – Received message 1st Corps have captured 10 officers
452 men. Our casualties today are Major Lee wounded, Lt Wyatt
wounded. Killed seven, wounded 18, gassed three. The A&S
Highlanders reported to have lost about 15 officers and 400

men. The Middlesex also lost heavily and the RWFus about 6
officers and 150 OR.[1]

11pm - Enemy shelled with asphyxiating shells, which were very
unpleasant. Lt Wigan gassed badly and went back. Our fighting
strength 17 officers, 640 OR.

26 September - Held line as usual. Generally quiet on our
front.

27 September - Received orders that an attack will take place
under cover of gas at 4.30pm. The Cameronians to attack if
gas has been effective, if we attack so will RWFus. The 2/A&S
Highlanders to move up in support of us on the left and
the Middlesex to support the RWFus. The battalion was to go
forward on the same narrow front the A&S Highlanders tried
to get through on the 25th. This time all our four companies
were up in the fire trench, the two centre Coys being opposite
the gap between the craters where the line was cut. C was on
the right then D next, A&B on the left. The scheme was that
bombers of A and D should go forward to the left and right
craters on each side of the gap and ascertain if gas had taken
effect. If so A&D would advance and B&C could close in and
take up A&D's positions then advance.

4pm - The gas started at 4pm and continued till 4.25pm. The
enemy as on the 25th were fully prepared and at once lit fires
all along the line.

4.30pm - The bombers advanced. 50 went. They were at once
fired at and though a few reached the right crater 20 were

---

1 Other ranks.

killed or wounded. The bombers advanced most gallantly. Lt
Wyatt the grenadier officer was killed and, out of 40, 32 were
killed or wounded or missing, probably killed.

Where all did well, the following were specifically selected
by their companions - 9217 Pte W Stephens, 5997 Pte W Tinsley,
10919 Pte Andrews.

The following were bombers who were killed and showed great
gallantry. 8410 Pte F Lawrence, 10049 L/C McDougall, 5245 Pte
H Pollack, 18743 Pte Burnett, 7483 Pte W Coyle missing, 11098
Pte J Carmichael, 11160 Pte Farrell, 8917 Sgt Sangster.

Pte Stevens got back with a message that German trenches
were fully manned and that gas had had no effect. The enemy
had four machine guns covering the small gap of about 80
yards. The attack was not gone on with.

The enemy opposite us were evidently picked troops of great
coolness and gallantry. They never fired unless necessary.
Our machine guns who were covering the advance of the bombers
claimed to have done damage.

28 September - Enemy on the alert. A lot of our wounded
crawled in during the night and Capt Moncrieff Wright and SM
Grant went out to enemy wire to try and bring in a man. This
required great gallantry as the enemy were very much on the
alert.

Day generally quiet.

29 September - Day quiet, troops busy clearing trenches of
dead and material.

30 September - The 2/A&S Highlanders relieved the Battn which
went into billets in Cambrin. Men were very tired and had one
night's rest.

1 Oct - 4.30am: Orders received to move into support trenches between Cambrin and Vermelles.

2 Oct - Still in support trenches, two men wounded by falling bullets fired at an aeroplane.

3 Oct - 2pm: Battn went back as well as all the Brigade to billets round about Béthune. Total casualties since Sept 25: one officer killed, two wounded, one gassed, other ranks 103 killed or wounded.

Sunday, 26 September 1915 [FSPC]
I am quite well.

Tuesday, 28 September 1915 [FSPC]
I am quite well.

Wednesday, 29 September 1915 [FSPC]
I am quite well.

*   *   *

It is a bloodbath. The Germans have sat out the bombardment in deep dugouts, and when they emerge to see the gas cloud rising, they light fires on their front line to push up the air. The wind is feeble anyway, and swirls much of the gas back into British lines. Even so, British commanders decide the attack must be followed through – too much is at stake, too much has been planned, for a postponement to be considered. Two mines are then blown in no-man's land, signalling the start. The explosions simply make the ground more hazardous to cross, squeezing troops into a narrow funnel between the craters. The Cameronians wait in their gas masks as the Argylls and Middlesex go over the top, replacing them, company by company, in the front-line trenches, but fully cognisant of the murderous fire that is now sweeping no-man's land. The wounded start to crawl back, filling the trench, and the enemy steps up its artillery barrage of the lines, sensing the mass of troops waiting. All is confusion, screams, explosions, torn flesh and cacophony. To put your head above the trench to gauge progress risks certain wounding, likely death. So no one knows how far the Argylls and Middlesex have got; telephones lines are severed, contact with brigade HQ can only be made by runner, shells rain down. The survivors recount how the sodden fuses in the new hand grenades have made them unusable. Chaplin's orders are to follow the Argylls – B Company first, while D Company waits to take its place. When B Company is shot to pieces, he orders D Company to wait by the ladders and provide covering fire so the wounded can return. He checks his orders with brigade, pointing out that he is losing men so fast he will need more time to bring the rest of the battalion up to the jumping-off point before making another attack. Lieutenant Patrick Hardinge, in D Company, later describes the division's plan of attack in his memoir[49] as a 'neck or nothing assault'. The odds are on nothing.

And in the chaos of war, Chaplin keeps waiting. What happens next is unclear, but has a profound effect on his army career. Forty-one years later, Brigadier General Jack – Captain James Jack, in 1914 – writes that Chaplin's decision to delay a full attack by all four companies of his battalion saves many lives, but brings immediate complaint from staff officers who insist he must follow orders, regardless of the battle's progress. Chaplin, says Jack, belligerently responds that his battalion was only meant to attack 'provided that the units alongside his were successful in their advance'. As the Middlesex had been decimated and the Argylls shredded, he stood fast.[50] Other versions of the incident have Chaplin insisting, presumably via runners, that divisional staff officers immediately attend the front and see the situation for themselves, if they want the attack to continue. The War Diary written by Chaplin says only that the 'CO represented to Bde HQ that he was ready to attack but he did not see how it could be successful'. Robertson, his old friend, agrees, and by 9 a.m. has cancelled further attacks, instructing his battalions to bring back wounded and simply hold the line.[51] But some at divisional HQ are unhappy. Chaplin's card is marked.

The 5th and 6th brigades, on the 19th's left, initially fare better, winning German trenches, before being driven out. Major gains are made further south by the 9th division, capturing – temporarily – Fosse 8, while Loos and Hulluch are also taken. Other battalions storm trenches, hold redoubts and capture prisoners. But opposite the 19th brigade, it is deadlock. The strategy of throwing tired troops at an impregnable position with poor planning and inadequate communication is proven worthless, and Chaplin for one will not forget the lessons learnt.

Two days pass. The Cams hold the trenches. Then the battalion is told to prepare for a second assault. As fierce fighting continues to the south, it is imperative to pin down the enemy. The men wait in incessant rain until the afternoon of 27 September. Attack is planned for 4.30 p.m., again with a gas release. This time the Cameronians and the Royal Welch will lead the assault. Chaplin and Owen, commander of the Royal Welch,[52] have both argued for a careful approach. A small party of bomb throwers will go first, to see if the gas has had a tangible effect. At 4 p.m., chlorine gas starts to puff into no-man's land via the five-feet-long tubes attached at right angles to the 'accessory' canisters. Thirty minutes later, the bombers crawl out.

But the Germans are ready, barely affected by the gas, and launch a murderous wave of machine-gun and rifle fire. Of the fifty bombers who leave, thirty-two are killed, wounded or captured. Again, the full assault is indefinitely postponed. For Chaplin and the Cameronians it is inglorious. The price paid around them has been high. The Middlesex takes 445 casualties on 25 September, the Argylls, 330; even the Royal Welch, which sends two companies over with the Middlesex, suffers 120 casualties. The Cams lose rather less, but saving one's men for better battles is not yet a strategy to receive approval.

Thursday, 30 September 1915 [from trenches near Cambrin]
My darling Lil,

Just a line to say that I am very well. I am very sorry about your father and hope that he is better now. I got the photos of Jim – he looks splendid. Harriette was wounded in the arm and the Dr in the leg.

Saturday, 2 October 1915 [FSPC]
I am quite well.

Sunday, 3 October 1915 [FSPC]
I am quite well.

Tuesday, 5 October 1915 [from billets in Béthune]
We have had a very trying time – a time of great anxiety for me. We have been very lucky compared to the other regiments of the Brigade.

We are back in our old billets, but I do not know for how long. We shall probably be a few days with any luck.

I am very well, but my eyes have been inflamed from stink shells.

You are always in my thoughts.

Wednesday, 6 October 1915 [from billets in Béthune]
We had a peaceful day in billets yesterday. It rained all day, but Sam D and I went for a ride just for exercise. Last night we dined with Capt RW who is very flourishing. I envied him his comfortable home.

Friday, 8 October 1915 [from billets in Béthune]
We are still in billets. I have absolutely no news.

With all my fondest love, darling, and heaps of kisses to you both, ever your loving husband, Graham

SUCH IS OUR LIFE

'I wish, darling, I was back in room 232.'

**British army reorganises in reaction to 60,000 casualties at Loos —
new commander-in-chief appointed — volunteer and 'old sweat'
battalions mixed for first time to improve professionalism — stalemate
holds as all sides focus on improving defences — Allies prepare
for renewed offensives in spring 1916**

Lil Chaplin is not a woman to panic. She can follow the war's progress in the papers. The news around Loos leaks out slowly. By early October, *The Times* is publishing censored, jingoistic reports. 'The story of the Battle of Loos is one glowing epic of the heroism of the British Army . . .'[53] The thriller writer John Buchan is also walking the support lines, writing paeans of praise to the British artillery, detailing the damaged debris of a German redoubt 'ploughed up and mangled like a sand castle which a child has demolished in a fit of temper'.[54] The reports paint a vivid picture of gallant British heroes overcoming heavily fortified positions and driving the fleeing Germans before them.

What isn't revealed is quite how little was gained at what cost. The fighting splutters on into November, but the losses at Loos and in other subsidiary attacks rise to over 60,000 men. The gain in territory, a small bulge in the line below Béthune, is hardly the wholesale advance that had been hoped for. That breakthrough was denied because the reserve divisions to follow up successes simply weren't available – a fact resented by Sir Douglas Haig and which eventually costs Sir John French his command. For professional soldiers like Chaplin, relentlessly exposed to the flawed planning of senior staff, Loos is a moment of realisation that nothing about this war is in line with expectations. For readers at home like Lil, those realities are still misted in optimism. Graham will have explained some of what goes on, during his periods of leave, but mostly soldiers are happy to forget what they must return to.

By 2 November, *The Times* is publishing the whole of Sir John French's latest despatch from the war, summarising the army's actions at Loos. Behind the scenes, French and Haig are trying to deflect blame on to each other, as the British government realises that, far from being a resounding success, Loos has been a disaster. In the published despatch, French claims that the 21st and 24th divisions, held in reserve on 25 September, were available. They were not. By January, Sir John French has gone, replaced by Haig as commander-in-chief, with the British public and most of the British army none the wiser as to what has happened. For those at the front, experiencing a surge in manpower as an ever-increasing number of Kitchener's volunteers join the fray, there is little free time left to assess anything.

Lil too has enough at home to distract her. She is pregnant again, and with a ten-month-old son who has only just started to put on weight. Then, shortly after the Battle of Loos, her father is taken ill. On 9 October, Thomas Alexander dies, aged seventy-seven, in Stirling. Lil's brother, Willie, returns home to put in order the Alexander business interests. Those interests, vested in Charles Tennant & Co and beyond, stretching from chemicals to mining and explosives, intertwine with the government's drive to produce more armaments. Harold Tennant, great-grandson of the firm's founder and Liberal MP for Berwickshire, is instrumental in calling Willie back. He is both a director of the firm and Under-Secretary for War, under his brother-in-law, Herbert Asquith, Prime Minister.

And so Lil watches with her four sisters as Willie takes charge – younger brother, Tom, is serving in Africa. Chaplin's letters from his billets in Béthune convey his respect for her father – 'As you know I had the greatest admiration for your father – he was all that I like in a man. All my thoughts are with you'[55] – but also his concerns over the will and inevitable tensions. There are hints that the family is already fractured: 'Yes, I sincerely hope that there will occur no more troubles from your father's will. I have the greatest horror of all quarrelling.'[56]

The Cameronians, after a week in support trenches until 3 October, remain in Béthune, as if marooned, unwanted. Chaplin may be anxious as to how the regiment is judged, but he does not articulate those worries in his letters. Instead, only his unease is palpable: 'It is really hard to write a letter nowadays – there is simply nothing to write about. We spend the whole day waiting for orders.'[57]

So he entertains her with trivia. Cakes, buns, puddings, weather, calomel pills, an update on Harry Lee – shot in the arm as his company rose from the trenches at Loos, now out of the war for two months – and teeth, always his teeth: 'Absolutely no news, except that I have lost another tooth. One of my bottom gold crowned ones broke away – if I lose many more I shall have none left. I have lost four during the war.'[58]

Then there are Béthune's billets to describe: 'Sam D and I sleep in one room and beds too small to lie in at full length, which are let into the wall. We have to have our baths coram populo as there are no windows to speak of and we are in front on the ground floor on the main street. However our feelings have become blunted and so have the feelings of the populace.'[59]

By 21 October the Cams are back in the same trenches they filled on 25 September, outside Cambrin, almost as if in punishment. Chaplin's War Diary notes that the German regiment opposite has changed. 'Two enemy seen near Vesuvius[60] wearing caps with red bands. This is not the same regt. who were opposite us on 25 September. Enemy tried to shout to our men, but got no answer except bullets.'

The Cams fire mortars too on the German trenches. The enemy retaliates with bursts of machine-gun fire, then heavy shells, killing two, wounding three, in a bout of mutual molestation that soon becomes the standard.[61] Chaplin's mood is worsened by news that Sam Darling may now be promoted away, and by his dislike of the Cams' new medical officer: 'I am afraid I shall not have Major D much longer, which will be a great loss to me as I shall have no companion left then. We have a most poisonous doctor. I am going to see if I can't exchange him or give him away.'[62]

The battalion is back in billets by 26 October, relieved in the trenches by the Argylls, sporting the first steel helmets issued to troops – a month too late for the battle. Chaplin is then told to scrub up his men for inspection by King George V on 28 October, south of Béthune. One battalion from each brigade attends. Chaplin details the Cams who are fit and able for parade: 16 officers, 5 sergeant majors, 52 sergeants, 19 pipers and buglers, and 615 other ranks. Later that day, the King is thrown from his horse and seriously injured.

Lil is getting other letters too, from old admirers.

1 November 1915 [from Major Audley Pratt,
9th Royal Irish Fusiliers]

My dear Lil,

Just to show you how very much and how very often I think of you I now proceed to send you a few lines. How are you, old dear, I suppose it isn't wrong to ask a married woman how she is, is it? Anyway I'm very well and have been in La Belle France since the beginning of last month. We are back in billets at the "back of the front" – we were in trenches last week[63] – good trenches too they were, fine and dry when we were there but I expect they'll be very moist and muddy "the noo" – stinking weather these last few days. The front is a marvellous place, all ranks living like a lot of rabbits although it must be noted that the numbers only increase by drafts and not in the ordinary rabbit way. Anyway firing is more or less continuous night and day but the trenches being good, it takes the very devil of a lot of lead to kill a man – and what is a good thing is that we feel ourselves top dog over the Hun. These Ulstermen are a hearty lot and take to fighting like ducks to water. Now they are in billets they pay much attention to the French lassies and though they find some difficulty in expressing themselves their advances are very kindly met.

Do write me a line. You know you have only to put 9th Bn Royal Irish Fusiliers and BEF on the letter.

Best love, yours ever Audley Pratt[64]

But, with impeccable timing, Graham's next bout of leave is imminent. His letters promise his arrival on 12 November, and delight in his family's new-found financial buoyancy: 'It is splendid your having paid off so many bills.'[65]

Every cloud has a silver lining. The second week of November finds him pacing the trenches, bemoaning the promotion of his favourite officers away – Hardinge to the 10th Scottish Rifles – and counting off the hours before he can go home, with the promise of a long week in a London hotel with Lil.

Sunday, 7 November 1915 [from trenches in Cuinchy]
My darling,

I could not write yesterday – I was too tired. I was on the move all day and did not get back till 1am. It is nearly 2am now but I am not so tired, and must write.

I have got a lift in a motor and if all is well shall arrive at Victoria at 4.30pm on the 11th. I will write tomorrow but afterwards it would be no use as I hope to be home before the letter would arrive.

Monday, 8 November 1915 [from trenches in Cuinchy]
I am sending this to London as you will not get it before I arrive if all goes well. We have got a grand cellar to live in[1] but the stove is a desperate failure – all the smoke refuses to go out of the chimney.

Monday, 8 November 1915 [from POW R. Beats, Scottish Rifles]
Dear Madam,

I have great pleasure in acknowledging the receipt of your most welcome parcels, which I receive every fortnight, the contents were in splendid order, and first class, and most acceptable to one under the circumstances, also the socks, and I thank you very much for your kindness to me.

I am yours faithfully, R Beats

---

1 In trenches near Cuinchy.

Tuesday, 9 November 1915 [from trenches in Cuinchy]

Just a line to confirm my wire – I cannot get a car till the 13th, but to make up for the disappointment I am getting 10 days' instead of 8 days' leave.

I got no letter today from you. I hope that there is nothing wrong and that it is only the post being delayed. It is raining like mischief but we come out soon.

Wednesday, 10 November 1915 [from trenches in Cuinchy]

I am too tired to write more than a line. I think one of your letters must have gone astray, as I thought you were going to 18 Bentinck St and have addressed two letters there. However I know where you are going now, and will go straight to the Kensington Palace Hotel if anything should go wrong about our meeting.

With all my love, darling, and heaps of kisses to you both – I am very pleased at Jim having defeated the scales. Ever your loving husband, Graham

Friday, 12 November 1915 [from Major Audley Pratt, 9th Royal Irish Fusiliers]

My dear Lil,

Thank you kindly for your letter of the 31st. Curious we both selected the same moment to write, so of course our letters crossed. We are billeted in a nice little country village at the moment but go up to the trenches on Monday, a fact that will probably cause alarm and consternation among Kaiser Bill's troops . . . Thank you very much for offering to make me a muffler etc but at the moment I have everything of that sort.

Best love, yours ever, Audley Pratt

Monday, 22 November 1915 [from Captain Patrick Hardinge, 10th Scottish Rifles]

Dear Mrs Chaplin,

Thank you so very much – it was so very kind of you to write and tell me about poor Major Lee. I was so very distressed to hear about him, as I believed him to be getting on so well, and imagined him to be having the splendid time he so thoroughly deserved.

It was so kind of you to write and I feel it is bothering you a lot, but I should be so grateful if you could let me have any further news of him, some time, as I am so very anxious to hear.

We are having very cold weather just at present. I am afraid I hate the 10th battn and everything to do with it – and shall never be happy till I get back to the 1st battn.

Yrs sincerely, Patrick Hardinge

*   *   *

Chaplin arrives back from Britain to find his battalion not just in new billets – in Busnettes, an unremarkable village five miles west of Béthune, surrounded by flat farmers' fields, still in working order – but in a whole new army, as battalions of volunteers raised under the banner of old regiments are now pushed into longstanding brigades. The aim is to mix professional units with those of recent recruits, in the hope that the veterans' experience will rub off.

So the brigades of the 2nd and 33rd divisions – a New Army division – are shuffled and, inside the 19th brigade, the Argylls and Middlesex are replaced by the 20th battalion Royal Fusiliers. The new-look 19th brigade joins the 33rd division in full knowledge of its previous reputation as a hopelessly miscast assortment, one whole brigade made up of university and public-school men accustomed, as one Royal Welch observer puts it, 'to being waited on, with not a soul to show them an active soldier's chief job – rough casual labour'.[66] The 20th Royal Fusiliers, new companions to the Cameronians and Royal Welch, are swiftly dubbed 'the chocolate soldiers', so great is the amount of confectionary they receive from home. Their habit of stepping around puddles when they march is duly noted. For the army as a whole, the blending of old and new is a shock to all.

For regular soldiers like Chaplin it is not a happy union, almost a demotion following the brigade's failure at Loos. He worries the move will sap morale and offer a threat to the established way of doing things. Little wonder the old sweats become even terser in their reaction to the bloodshed and mayhem in the trenches. Their role now is to show the new soldiers how to endure stoically, how not to complain. But every change throws up new problems. The decision to switch experienced officers into inexperienced battalions – in order to instil good habits – means surviving regulars are now earmarked for redistribution. The upshot for Chaplin is a revolving door of new officers. Added to which, he faces a double load of paperwork, as a bigger army needs bigger resources, and newer battalions need constant oversight, so an even larger bureaucracy is installed to monitor and control everything which is issued, checking who has what where. Messages now arrive at all times of day and night requesting confirmation of stores. The only things that aren't requested, notice older officers, are suggestions on how to improve operational efficiency on the battlefield. Every old sweat has an opinion, but no one is asking.

Chaplin has one other difficulty too. As part of the dwindling band who have fought the war from the beginning, he is now returning from his third stint of leave. The problem of reacclimatising is not getting easier. It is getting worse.

Lil's reaction is typically pragmatic. He must get himself promoted to brigadier, out of the firing line.[67] It is as simple as that.

Wednesday, 24 November 1915 [from billets in Busnettes, near Béthune]

My darling Lil,

It was very hard parting. I hope Mrs Harriette turned up to keep you company. I got to Folkestone without adventure. I knew no-one travelling except General Corbeau.

When we arrived at Boulogne the gentleman with the megaphone shouted out that people on leave would remain at Boulogne until the next day. As I only had about 12 Francs I was wondering what I should do to pay the hotel bill. I thought the best way of settling the matter was to dine at once. I would then be in a more suitable frame of mind to tackle the question, especially as I had had no lunch. So I had a big dinner and was told by an officer that a train left for my destination at 7.30 – I went and found a corner seat and travelled in comfort, but could not sleep thinking of you and Jim. I arrived at 12.30 in the morning and saw no sign of Wardrop with the horses, walked to the hotel where I had told him to be, and after great difficulty succeeded in waking a man who said he had not been there. You can imagine how pleased I was. There was no-one astir in the town – I was determined to reach the regiment[1] last night. My difficulty was that I did not know where the Brigade was, much less the regiment.

So I started to walk to Béthune, hoping that I would find an ambulance or lorry to give me a lift. I had walked about two miles when I was overtaken by a car, which I stopped. Unfortunately it was not going to Béthune but the fellow in it gave me a lift of several miles, going out of his way to do so. I walked on and came to the Hd Qrs of a Division. I tried to get on by telephone to my Brigade or Division but they were not in communication so I had to trudge on about four or five miles to my Divisional Hd Qrs, being very nearly arrested by a post who found it difficult to believe I was a Colonel who did not know where his Brigade was, walking about at 3.30am. I reached the Division, woke a Staff Officer and found that the regiment was five miles away. He wanted me to stay till morning, but having made up my mind that I would be back I refused and walked off. I got a lift for about two miles in a lorry, eventually getting here at 5.15am. The tragic part was that I missed my way in the village and walked about a mile out of my way. I got a whisky and soda and jumped into bed and slept till 8.30. I had walked 10 or 12 miles with that heavy coat and mackintosh and my haversack was no light weight. I was busy till 12. I retired to sleep but only slept an hour. I rode over then to Brigade Hd Qrs which is two or three miles away but found the General was out and came back. The General came to see me and we had a long talk about our leaves and all the changes. We now belong to the 33rd Division. All COs and the Brigade Staff are dining with our old Division[2] tonight – they are sending cars to pick us up. As soon as I finish this I am going to wash.

---

1 By 'regiment' he means battalion.
2 2nd Division.

We remain here[1] for the time I expected. Our mess is the local village general store. I sleep over the way – quite nice but the bed is very short.

The electric lamp arrived today, also a pie from Edith.[2]

This is a very nice place and miles from the enemy – in fact safer than London, as there are no taxis.

Thursday, 25 November 1915 [from billets in Busnettes]

Before I forget can you send me a pencil? At present I am reduced to borrowing every time I write.

We had a great dinner last night with our old Division – we were very late as the chauffeur lost his way. It was like a mess dinner at home. The divisional band played. I sat next to the Chief Staff Officer and a very nice fellow in the Guards, who is some sort of Staff Officer. We sat at table till we left at about 11 o'c.

This morning I inspected the billets, which took all the morning. I afterwards had all my kit laid out and threw away everything I did not want – one collects a lot of rubbish.

This afternoon I went for a ride and finished at Brigade Hd Qrs where I had tea and rode home in the dark. It was so dark that I could see nothing and had to depend entirely on my mare to bring me home. The new Divisional General[3] was there and all his staff.

I am very anxious to hear how you have got on about the house in Sunningdale. Could you send Graham Shepard[4] some tin soldiers for me – I forgot about it.

I feel now that I have never been away from here. I wish, darling, that I was back in Room 232.

---

1 In Busnettes, west of Béthune.
2 One of Lil's four sisters.
3 Major-General Herman Landon, veteran of campaigns in Sudan and South Africa, who had been in charge of 9th division up to the Battle of Loos, before being retired sick.
4 Son of his sister, Florence, who had married Ernest Shepard, the illustrator.

Friday, 26 November 1915 [from billets in Busnettes]
I had hoped that I should get a letter from you today but I suppose it is too soon.

This morning we went for a route march. It was a beautiful day when we started but a snow-storm came on but it did not last long. I had to leave the regiment and ride on ahead to meet the new GOC Division. He was very pleasant.

This afternoon I walked over to the Brigade Hd Qrs. I first went to see Col Williams, whom I found in bed with a bad cold. I sat and talked to him a long time, then had tea with the General and afterwards went to a soldiers' concert – one of the best I have ever heard and the divisional band played. I dined with the General and then walked home.

I suppose that you are now settled down again. I miss you more than I have ever done.

Saturday, 27 November 1915 [from billets in Busnettes]
I was delighted to get a letter from you today and to know that you were well. I also got one from Mrs Lee and was very pleased that Harriette was so much better and that the medicos hope that the tumour will be dispersed by medicines.

The worst has happened – Sam Darling has been ordered to take command of an English K[1] regiment. I am not only sorry because he is a great loss as adjutant but also to me personally as a companion.

It has turned very cold and it is freezing hard – which is better than rain.

Sunday, 28 November 1915 [from billets in Busnettes]
I am distressed to hear that you have got such a bad cold and hope that it does not mean you will have to postpone your journey.

We had to go to the trenches today. We went in a motor – very early start, as we had to ride to Bde Hd Qrs. Billy Croft and I walked back the whole way to Bde Hd Qrs – about 10 miles – and the General gave me a lift home.

They have cancelled the order about Major D, I am glad to say, but it is only a temporary escape, I am afraid, as he is bound to go sooner or later.

---

1 Kitchener – i.e. one of the battalions raised from volunteers. In fact, Darling is given command of the 9th battalion Highland Light Infantry (Glasgow Highlanders).

I feel very lonely now.

It is freezing hard and we shall soon be able to skate over to the Germans.

Monday, 29 November 1915 [from billets in Béthune]

We came into our old town[1] today – raining and very cold. I went to Capt RW[2] – Major H and I dined with him tonight. He had no particular news.

I was jolly glad to hear that your cold was better. I hope that Jim's photos will turn out better than you expect. With all my fondest love, darling, and heaps of kisses to you both, for ever your loving husband, Graham

PS: Forgive the shortness but I am simply dropping from want of sleep

Extracts from the battalion War Diary, September 1915,

Kept by Colonel Graham Chaplin

Trenches, centre section north of canal[3] outside Béthune

1 December - Moved into trenches relieving battn Yorkshire Regt 7th Div. The 5th Bn went in on our right and the 18th Royal Fusiliers on our left. Trenches in most awful state. Everything had been allowed to go. No cover or shelter for half the men. No stores handed over properly. About 6pm enemy had a gas alarm, whistles were blown and one fire was lit.

2 December - Enemy quiet except for a little shelling. All companies busy getting trenches opened up. Major Selby Lowndes attached and a Lt from 15 Hussars.

---

1 Béthune.

2 Riddell-Webster.

3 The La Bassée Canal, in the Cuinchy sector, where the Cameronians fought the battle of Loos.

3 December – Enemy quiet. Our grenadiers have upper hand in craters. Three men slightly wounded (two at duty) by our own trench mortar.

4 December – Enemy shelled support trenches. Very wet and trenches falling in everywhere. All companies doing a lot of work. A few men troubled with their feet which is accounted for by there being no dugouts, and therefore it is practically impossible for them to get their gum boots taken off. The trenches are just as bad as they were last year, which need not have been the case. Pte Bell killed and Timkins wounded.

5 December – Enemy much more active. All support trenches shelled and Windy Corner. One man killed Pte Clark, and Pte Martin wounded. Very wet and trenches falling in as quickly as built up. A lot of work done. The 2nd line is now getting done and is passable.

6 December – Relieved by R Welch Fus at 10.30am and battn went into very dirty billets in Quesnoy. During period in trenches the 5th Bn Scottish Rifles were on our right and the 18th Royal Fus were on our left. The latter are Kitchener's Army and have not yet learnt to find their way about by night.

Thursday, 2 December 1915 [from trenches east of Béthune]
My darling Lil,

I was very glad to hear that you have arrived safely at Stirling, but very sorry that you have such a bad cold and shall not be happy till I hear that you are better.

Could you send me a pair of oilskin leggings – they are like trousers which just reach below the knee.

I shall write to Mrs Newman tomorrow if I get time – I never seem to have any.

Friday, 3 December 1915 [from trenches east of Béthune]

I received my blanket and muffler and cigarettes safely. Yes, I wish Jim's proofs would come quickly – I am very anxious to see them. I wish that you could get rid of your cold – I do not like it lasting so long.

A fellow named Wallis who used to be in the regiment is apparently 2nd in command of the 2nd Bn as I heard from him today. Billy Croft went off this morning to command a Bn of K's.[1]

The weather is very wet as usual. I do not believe that it will ever stop raining.

Sunday, 5 December 1915 [FSPC]

I am quite well.

Tuesday, 7 December 1915 [from billets in Le Quesnoy, east of Béthune]

I could not write last night – I was too tired. I meant to write in the early morning but woke too late for the post.

I do not expect myself that I shall get what you want me to[2] for a long time, if at all, although Capt RW and the Padre have both bet me £5 that I shall get it before April and the CSO[3] of our old Division wanted to bet me that I should within two months.

We have had a pretty rough time – the weather is so bad. We expect to go a long way back soon and spend Christmas in some quiet spot.

With all my fondest love and heaps of kisses to you both – and all my thoughts, darling, ever your loving husband, Graham

---

1 11th Bn of the Royal Scots, the oldest regiment of the line in the British army.
2 Promotion out of the front line to brigadier.
3 Chief Signals Officer.

RAIN AND SHELLS

'What I feel now is the want of a companion – it is an awfully lonely life.'

Steel helmets, lighter machine guns and improved hand grenades among new equipment as British army overhauls tactics — increased artillery strength is prioritised — France, Britain, Russia, Italy and Serbia meet at Chantilly to draw up plans for a coordinated offensive in 1916 — German army uses phosgene gas in assault at Ypres for first time

December marches on with harsh rain and freezing winds, but the surge in manpower means that many of the battalions from the original BEF can now be given a prolonged rest. The Cameronians are marched back to the quiet country village of Ham-en-Artois, north-west of Béthune. Chaplin has new friends to make:

> This is quite different from the sordid and squalid villages in which we usually rest. I have a very nice bedroom with sheets and everything, and generally we are very comfortable. The landlady is a very funny round little fat woman, who hastened to inform me that she had been a servant in the German Embassy in Paris and had waited on the Emperor Frederick[68] – married to the Queen of England's daughter.[69]

His spirits pick up further when an officer attached to the Cams for training turns out to be master of the Whaddon Chase, a well-known hunt in Buckinghamshire: 'He said that he hoped I would fish and shoot with him after the war if we both survived . . .'[70]

The list of letters he must write, however, gets ever longer: to Lil's sister, Edith, saying thank you for port, pies and puddings, to his sister, Connie, a loyal lender when he was short of cash, and to assorted regimental wives. The list of friends torn away never shortens, either. The departure of Sam Darling is confirmed: 'I only wish it had been Major H'.[71] Later, he consoles himself with their regrets. Hardinge and Darling both write to tell him how much they miss the old battalion, and how much they would like to return. Chaplin confides how much he would like to return to the old 2nd division:[72] 'We are all fed up with this crowd – lots of paper and nothing else.'[73]

He worries about his men's feet – too much trench life – and his regimental birthday: twenty-one years in the Cameronians on 12 December. He rides eleven miles into Béthune to see Robertson, and together the two friends go shopping, trying fruitlessly to find a present for Jim's first birthday.

His letters extol the quiet life. He gets his hair cut, lunches other officers, recommends *Punch*'s article on rest out of trenches, and promises Lil he will organise 'the best Christmas dinner we can get for the men.'[74] She, in return, sends him in advance some of Jim's birthday cake so he can celebrate on 13 December: 'To think that we have a son a year old! I tasted his cake set out with the candle and it was very good.'[75]

Lil also reports on the difficulties she is having with Mrs Newman, whose son, Lieutenant E. W. P. Newman, was sent home after breaking down in late October 1914. Later, Newman is promoted to a staff position – much to Chaplin's disapproval: 'I hear that Newman is now a temporary Major. What an iniquitous shame! It is a strange Army ours which rewards the cowards and incompetents!'[76]

Mrs Newman, it seems, is still determined to send parcels for the officers and men in her son's battalion, and needs Lil's approval, as the colonel's wife. Chaplin, however, does not want them: 'I would much rather she had nothing to do with sending things to the regiment and I would rather that the things were sent to some shop in Glasgow if it could be arranged.'[77]

And it becomes a topic that won't go away: 'I am annoyed that Mrs Newman should worry you but amused at her tantrums. Of course she cannot give our comforts away – I told the General and he said she might use them to try and keep dear Edward's feet warm.'[78]

Meanwhile, tensions increase over Thomas Alexander's will. Lil stands to inherit a substantial sum, though quite how much is never detailed: 'You will be a vastly wealthy young woman if you are to have all you expect, but as I told you except for your own comfort and the kids I do not care if you have 1d or £1,000,000 as I just love you for yourself, as you know full well.'

Yet is Lil's brother, Willie, keener on keeping money in the business, rather than distributing it? By the third week of December, there are references to 'Willie's schemes' and Chaplin's tone has turned to acid: 'He seems to spend a lot of time at home.'[79] And again the next day: 'I should not worry about Willie and his schemes – he cannot surely do anything without the consent of the other trustees.'[80]

As Christmas approaches, Lil is receiving thank-you letters from the men for her role as poster-in-chief. Her husband has other worries: he has no number two and no quartermaster, as Wood is recovering in hospital from an accident. Worse still, he has heard that, before New Year, the Cams must return to defend the same strip of trench-locked land they know so well, weaving between Cambrin, Cuinchy and German-held Auchy. It is that part of the line which never moved on 25 September – just south of their original positions, just north of the fearsome Hohenzollern Redoubt, a fortified, cratered mining heap that has already claimed thousands of lives as both sides still fight to claim it. Loos is a battle he is not allowed to forget.

Friday, 24 December 1915 [FSPC]

I am quite well.

A Merry Christmas and a Happy New Year.

Saturday, Christmas Day 1915 [from billets in Ham-en-Artois]

My darling Lil,

I started to write last night but I had such a headache and made so many mistakes that I tore up the letter and sent a pc. I was very glad to get two letters from you today.

I did not go to church today as it was early and I wanted to sleep. The men had quite good dinners. I rode round all the companies and saw them. I wish that I could have been at home with you. It somehow all makes me feel very sad and depressed.

I am glad that you think you are big enough – I was getting rather anxious. It is strange that you should feel anxious this time and not last, but it is like being wounded – you know what it is.

Sunday, 26 December 1915 [from billets in Ham-en-Artois]
Although we have had a longer and more complete rest than we have ever had before I have not enjoyed it a bit really – I have had too much paper worry.

Do not worry, dear, about Willie – the chances of his being able to do anything are surely very small, besides having to come out here again.

If all is well I think I may get home at the end of next month.

Wednesday, 29 December 1915 [from trenches in Cambrin, outside Annequin, east of Béthune]
I have missed two posts by putting off writing till the morning then not getting up in time. You will have guessed we were on the move.

Major H went off today to take command of one of the New Army battalions[1] in the same brigade as Col D. I felt no regret at his going – he does not care a bit about the regiment and I shall not miss him. I am now absolutely the only officer left who sailed with the regiment.

We have a headquarters underground which I hate – I would much rather chance the shells and be above ground. The atmosphere is so horrid.

I was delighted to get a letter from you tonight, having had none for three days. The posts are now all over the place, but it is wonderful how regular they have been on the whole.

I have been interrupted half a dozen times whilst writing this although past midnight – such is our life.

Thursday, 30 December 1915 [from trenches in Cambrin]
I received three letters from you today to make up for the scarcity lately.

---

1 24th Royal Fusiliers.

I cannot write a long letter – our lamp has failed us and I have so much writing to do including everything else.

Poor Mr Reynolds[1] was, I am afraid, mortally wounded today. He was a colour sergeant in the 3rd Bn when I was adjutant. He was commanding my old company. A very good man and stout hearted.

Thursday, 30 December 1915 [from Major Reggie Swalwell,[2] 15th Rifle Brigade]

My dear Lil,

It was so nice of you to send the stocking and the cake. Both are greatly appreciated, also your letter and kind wishes – the same to you! I am not far from the place where you say Graham is. We move up in a short time, then I shall be nearer to him. I shall of course go to see him the first chance. I presume he is with his old regiment but in a new Division. So sorry he does not like it. I think as he has been out here so long that he should have some home appointment in the way of a rest, but I suspect the War Office want all the best men at the Front. I thought of you on Xmas Eve (and on many other times of course) and wondered what you were all doing. I hope your mother is feeling better, although it has been a trying time for her, in fact for all. I have a terribly responsible job here for having such short training but thank God I have got on well so far – touch wood! Give my love to your mother, Edith, Isa, Jessie and of course your dear self. I hope you can read this – I am writing with the aid of a dirty candle in a barn so the conditions are somewhat trying. It is a rough life but I wouldn't like to have missed it. Again many thanks for cake etc. Best love and wishes for 1916. Yours ever, Reggie

---

1 2nd Lieut J. J. Reynolds.

2 Swalwell, married to Lil's sister, Mabel, had been rapidly promoted from temporary lieutenant to temporary major during six months in a Kitchener battalion.

Friday, 31 December 1915 [from trenches in Cambrin]

I got Jim's photos – they are splendid. I will keep one of the mounted ones and return the others in three days' time.

My time is so fully occupied now that I really have not time to write except to say that I am well. Every day official correspondence increases and I have now to think of everything – I have no quartermaster[1] and of course the adjutant has to learn his work, so I am po-bal.

With all my fondest love and every hope that we shall be together permanently in the New Year and every happiness to you both in 1916. Ever your loving husband, Graham

Extracts from the battalion War Diary, January 1916,

Kept by Colonel Graham Chaplin

Trenches outside Annequin, north of the Hohenzollern Redoubt

1 January – The work in progress chiefly consisted of clearing communications trenches which had apparently been left untouched since 25th September. RE material was very hard to obtain. Pte Neilson wounded and Pte Speight wounded.

2 January – Enemy fairly quiet. Our snipers did a considerable amount of work, wounding a German and hitting a periscope.

3 January – We fired rifle grenades at intervals during the

1 Quartermaster 'Tubby' Wood has been in hospital since late October after being run over by a transport lorry during shelling. He is eventually invalided home to recover before returning to the front. See papers filed in the National Archive relating to Wood's requests for reinstatement of his pension after his later dismissal from the army for drunkenness in 1919.

night to which the enemy made a feeble reply. Sgt Irvine
wounded.

4 January - Battalion relieved by 5th Scottish Rifles. Billets
in Annequin Fosse. A great deal of work was done in the
trenches but no footboards and very little barbed wire could
be obtained. The battalion received 10,750 sandbags, 22 sheets
of corrugated iron, 170 pickets, 20 Chevaux de Frise, 10
coils of barbed wire, 30 lengths of quartering, 250 feet of
planking. Far more than this could have been disposed of. This
was the first time we had Lewis guns in the trenches and they
seemed to give the men a great deal of confidence. The weather
was good.

Billets in Annequin
5 January - Six platoons working on communication trenches.
Enemy shelled billets slightly with field guns.

6 January - Eight platoons working in communications trenches.

7 January - The same working parties are found. C Company were
inlying piquet.

8 January - The Battn moved into billets in the Rue D'Aire,
Béthune. The billets were the same that the Btn was in before.
They have been much improved by the erection by RE of proper
latrines and washing places - the floors being cemented and
the water drained off. The only wonder is that this had not
been done before.

Billets in Béthune
9 January - Sunday. Divine Service held.

```
10 January - Companies carried out drill under company
arrangements. Running drill, smoke helmet drill and fire
control. Bomb and Lewis Guns training was also carried out.
Capt Hill rejoined the Btn from hospital on this date.
```

Saturday, 1 January 1916 [FSPC]

I am quite well.

Sunday, 2 January 1916 [from trenches in Cambrin]

My darling Lil,

I find nowadays that it is very difficult to write – I get so little time. But I am sure you would rather I did my duty than spend it in letter writing.

I have simply no news, everything pretty unpleasant, rain and lots of shells to vary the monotony.

I had a telephone call from the General to say that Harriette, Wright, Wood and myself were mentioned in despatches – but you will have seen it.

I am glad you are nice and big – I should certainly not laugh. I have got all your parcels and the men's sweets. I thought I had acknowledged them.

I will try to write a long letter in two days if all is well – at present my brain is asleep. I am off to a very uncomfortable but welcome bed.

Tuesday, 4 January 1916 [from billets in Annequin]

This is the first chance I have had to sit down in any degree of comfort to write to you. You can understand that with no-one to help me I do not get much spare time and I am always so tired by midnight, which has been the only time lately that I have been able to write.

Whilst I remember it, there are orders that no regiment is to appeal for comforts for the men. As a matter of fact now that the laundries are in working order there is no necessity for shirts and socks – it is not like last year when they could not get anything washed.

Connie has asked me to repay her £10 which she lent me some years ago. I do not remember it but am sending her a cheque.

I see that Sandy and Willie were both mentioned in the Despatches also. I am afraid Mrs O will be furious that RO was not. Yes, I hope Harriette gets something.

The General had a narrow squeak – he had his house knocked down.[1]

I want to write a lot of letters – to Edith to thank her for all her parcels, to Mrs RW, she sent some books and a card, and I have never answered all the letters for my DSO. I hope no-one will write and congratulate me for the mention, it would be more than I could bear.

Wednesday, 5 January 1916 [from billets in Annequin]

I have had no letter from you today which was a great disappointment. The only letter I got was from Mrs Lee. She says that Harriette is much better and coming out of hospital – I am very glad. She wrote to congratulate me on the mention – I hope no-one else will.

Mr Gordon has gone off on leave tonight, so I have no adjutant – no-one else could be the slightest use.

I have been busy all day and seen many Generals. I am beginning to feel that I could do with a rest but I do not see how I shall ever get one. The Quartermaster has been invalided home, so that there is no chance of getting him back for some months.

With all my love, darling, to you both, and hoping that some good fortune will bring us together soon.

Thursday, 6 January 1916 [from billets in Annequin]

After today I am going to write my daily letter by day because I find that even with glasses the light is so bad that it bothers me to write and also I am so tired that it is difficult to think.

I do not see any chance of leave until they send someone who can command.

---

1 A shell landed on General Robertson's headquarters.

I am feeling very lonely now. I have absolutely no companion and I combine the duties of CO, Adjutant, 2nd in command and Quartermaster.

I received two letters from you today. I was greatly relieved. I get in an awful state if I do not get a letter every day, although one knows the post must go wrong sometimes.

Friday, 7 January 1916 [from billets in Annequin]

I wrote an immense amount of letters today. I think by tomorrow I shall have written most of those I owe. I find that this is the most peaceful time as regards official correspondence.

I had a letter from Harriette saying that he was alright, but it would be madness to let him come out here again. I hope that he will not be allowed to.

It is no good, dear, setting your heart on my getting a Brigade, as I do not even know that I have been recommended for one. I am not anxious for one – just as everything comes I take it. I should certainly not care to have one by pulling strings, which is absolutely wrong in my opinion and I think that I have been extremely lucky.

Willie seems to do himself well in the way of leave.

Saturday, 8 January 1916 [from billets in Béthune]

We are back in our old billets in the big town[1] – where the landlady was so solicitous of my health and whose daughter is extremely garrulous.

I am jolly glad to be back and to sleep in a comfy bed, with a pretty good certainty of not being aroused.

Capt Hill[2] came to see me. I think he is returning to the regiment when he leaves hospital, where he expects to be only a day or two longer.

Your letters are never dull, dear – I love to hear all what you are doing and how you feel and what Master Jim does.

---

1 In Rue d'Aire, Béthune.

2 Capt Jacobus Hill, who had sailed to France with the Cameronians as a 2nd Lieutenant in C Coy, had left the regiment to work as an instructor in late 1915.

Sunday, 9 January 1916 [from billets in Béthune]

I went to church this morning – the first Sunday for a long time. I went to the Church of Scotland service. I asked the padre to come to lunch – the CofE parson came to see me and the RC chaplain lives with us, so I entertained all the Churches at one time.

I went for a ride this afternoon with Mr McShane the RC padre.

Capt Hill has come back, so he is doing 2nd in command for the time being. I am glad as he is amusing and can help me. It was really getting a bit too much.

Monday, 10 January 1916 [from billets in Béthune]

I have not been able to go out all day, which was a nuisance as it has been a beautiful day.

I cannot think what to advise you if you cannot get a house at Sunningdale – it is very worrying for you. If the worst comes to the worst, if your mother does not mind Jim could remain at Brentham and you could go to the home in Glasgow, although I can understand you would rather have your own house.

I spoke to the General about my leave. He will let me go now that Capt Hill has come back after our next turn of the trenches, so I ought with luck to get away at the end of the month if all is well. I should come straight to Brentham unless you have secured a house before. I should like to do nothing, as I am really feeling that I am a bit worn out.

Tuesday, 11 January 1916 [from billets in Béthune]

I had quite a holiday today. I rode out about five miles to see Col Darling, but when I got to the place I found that he was not there, but about eight miles further on. That was too far for me to go so I turned back. I met Capt Brodie[1] and rode part of the way with him. He is on the staff at present. He told me that Ronnie Forbes[2] was commanding a K[3] Bn.

This evening I went to a soldiers' concert. It was pretty good.

---

1 Of the Highland Light Infantry.
2 Forbes was a Scottish officer who had married and divorced Sita Torr, later to become famous as a travel writer.
3 Kitchener.

Yes, dear, I wish that this separation could be over. No-one will be more glad than I shall when it is all over but as long as the war goes on I do not want to go home.

Wednesday, 12 January 1916 [FSPC]
I am quite well.

Thursday, 13 January 1916 [from billets in Béthune]
Seventeen months since we left Glasgow. What an eternity it seems!

I had no letter from you for two days which makes me feel quite depressed but I am sure that it is the post.

Yesterday I went quite a long way back in a motor bus to hear a lecture – it was very pleasant getting out of the war area.

Today I was away all the morning, and this afternoon I went to buy you a shell filled with chocolates which I hope you will get safely.

We are all fed up with the new Division and wish we were back with any of our former ones.

If all goes well I think I ought to be home for our wedding day.[1] Unless I hear to the contrary I shall go straight to Brentham. I do not suppose that it would be good for you to travel now.

What I feel now is the want of a companion – it is an awfully lonely life.

Saturday, 15 January 1916 [from trenches in Cuinchy]
I was jolly glad to get two letters from you yesterday and to hear that you were alright. I was beginning to be nervous.

I did not get to bed last night till 3am, hence I could not write and the mail was gone before I woke.

I got all your parcels for which many thanks darling – the haddocks and sausages are splendid and came at a very opportune moment. I also got Edith's pie which was most welcome.

---

1 31st January – by 'wedding day' Chaplin means anniversary.

Tuesday, 18 January 1916 [from trenches in Cuinchy]

If all goes well I may get leave on the 22nd, so if I do I should be home the day after you get this letter. Do not count on it too much – you know by this time how chancy getting away is.

If I do I shall come straight to Brentham and will wire from London.

I cannot tell you how delighted I shall be to see you both again. With all my fondest love, darling, and heaps of kisses to you both, for ever your loving husband, Graham

Friday, 21 January 1916 [telegram]

Arrive Stirling 8am tomorrow Graham

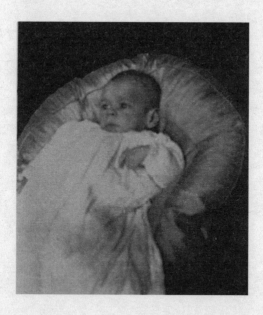

CAMBRIN,
CUINCHY,
AUCHY

'The local paper says "These are the words . . . of his commanding officer, a soldier inured to the horrors of war" – which somehow does not sound complimentary.'

German forces mass heavy artillery at Verdun prior to opening major offensive on French positions — British front extended by twenty miles to relieve French army — German U-boats begin unrestricted submarine warfare on all shipping — fighting persists around Ypres as British and German forces attempt to improve positions

Eight days in Scotland at the end of January – for Chaplin, any chance to be with his pregnant wife and one-year-old son must be cherished, however cold the weather, however demoralising the fast-ticking clock. The travelling north from the battlefield and south in return will gobble up precious days, but better some leave than none, even if each return becomes that much harder, however accustomed he has become to a life that encompasses days under shellfire in the front line, days in support, supervising works, days in Béthune or its suburbs grinding through paperwork, overseeing men, lunching friends, exchanging gossip.

Changes in command are the only constant. By now Sir John French has been replaced by Sir Douglas Haig at the top of the British army – both are cavalry men, likely to garner little more than a shrug from the infantry who are rather more impressed by the famous whisky distillery in their new commander's family. The footsloggers already know that this is not a cavalry war, however often cavalrymen take the top roles. Even their corps commander, General Hubert Gough, one of Haig's favourites, is a cavalryman.

East of Béthune, the Germans are ticklish; activity has been heightened while Chaplin is away, the enemy blowing mines to gain better observation points, and joining saps – the long, listening trenches pushed out into no-man's land – to bring their own front line closer to the British defences. Something is up.

At Cuinchy,[81] where the steel Pont Fixe bridge spans the La Bassée canal and the communication trench, Harley Street, carves its way down to the south, the enemy has installed a giant *minenwerfer* mortar, nestled behind a brickstack, capable of hurling three-feet-long bombs straight up and over, into the British trenches. It takes a terrible toll on unwary troops, so soldiers are assigned to watch for its firing, blowing whistles to alert everyone to gauge its ponderous trajectory before moving rapidly out of the way. The Cams spend January here, running battalion HQ from the cellar of 'Kingsclere', a ruined house, its ground-floor windows sandbagged, those on the upper stuffed with mattresses. Down in the cellar, Chaplin can sleep the sleep of the restless, woken continually, before setting off every morning to walk the lines, checking his men, assessing yet more new work to be done.

At Cambrin, where the Cams spend early February, the trenches are deep and narrow, offering better protection but impeded mobility. Forces are concentrated at two strong points, Sim's and Arthur's Keeps, named after the engineers who built them, while platoons take turns at repairing the trench walls from daily shell damage. All the routes now carry English names to help soldiers find their way – Wimpole Street, High Street – and the War Diary details the continual work necessary to facilitate passage and protection. Chaplin is tetchy, as usual, peeved at the lack of application from the Kitchener battalions, noting 'many very useful dugouts in High Street had, for some reason, been allowed to fall into disrepair'.[82] His eighteen months at war, and forced alliance with volunteer soldiers, now make him intolerant of the failings of others. He details his men to dig new, deeper dugouts in the front line – akin to those that protected the Germans at the battle five months earlier. With each return from leave, he throws himself more assiduously into such work.

Tuesday, 1 February 1916 [from billets in Béthune]

My darling Lil,

General R was at the station alright with his wife. Harriette also turned up to see me off. I felt more sad at leaving you than I have ever done. I had a seat with the General in the Pullman – we had a very good lunch. The boat was crowded. I met General Kays[1] who has the Territorial Brigade at Edinburgh – he used to command the HLI.

We had an extraordinarily smooth passage and got to Boulogne about 6pm. The car met us alright. We had dinner at the Louvre Hotel and started at 7pm. It was very cold and I was thankful for your gloves. The front of the motor was broken so it was like being in an open motor. We are in the same old town and back tomorrow to where we spent Christmas.[2] We got to our Hd Qrs at about 10pm. The regiment are all well – they had very heavy shelling one day but no harm done. I had a whisky and water and went to bed and slept soundly.

I wonder if Jim knows that his daddy is no longer in the house – do you think that he does? I cannot tell you how much I miss you both. I cannot get you out of my head.

Wednesday, 2 February 1916 [from billets in Béthune]

The mystery of your shell[3] is explained – it arrived back here yesterday re-addressed by Edith to me. I suppose she mistook it as a parcel for me. I have sent it off again to you. I hope it will reach you this time safely, but I expect the sweets will not be much use.

Manser[4] came back last night. I was glad to see him.

Col Darling has put in an application to come back to the regiment as his regiment has been sent right back. I only hope that they will allow it.

I suppose I shall get used to being back but I miss you both horribly.

Thursday, 3 February 1916 [from billets in Béthune]

Last night I went with the General to a soldiers' concert. They had a cinematograph which gave *Bootles Baby*[5] – it was extraordinarily good.

---

1 Brigadier General G. F. Kays.
2 Ham-en-Artois.
3 Full of chocolates, posted as a present.
4 His 'servant'.
5 A four-reel British film released in 1915 by American director Harold Shaw about a deserted mother and child.

Our proposed rest has vanished and we go back to the line instead.

I received the cake and buns from Edith and the sausages and haddocks from you – for which many thanks, darling.

This afternoon I went for a long ride by myself, which was not very exciting, and in the evening went for a short walk with Capt Drew.[1]

It is very lonely without any letter from you but I hope that I shall get one tomorrow. With all my fondest love and heaps of kisses to you both – I would willingly take Jim from 5.30 to 6.30 alone.

Friday, 4 February 1916 [from billets in Béthune]

I was jolly glad to get your letter today – it somehow makes one feel not so lonely. I understood quite well, dear, why you left so abruptly and did not say anything – I think it is the best way.

I got a cake and buns from Skinners[2] today – I suppose it was from you. I forgot to order refills for my lamp from Smith's – could you drop them a pc?

I have had a very easy time since I returned – the correspondence seems to have died down. I suppose it is only momentarily.

Saturday, 5 February 1916 [from billets in Béthune]

We are still in the old town – our move having been postponed.

We had the sausages for breakfast this morning – they were excellent.

I went up to the trenches today and then found that we remained here.

The light is very bad so I will end this uninteresting epistle.

Sunday, 6 February 1916 [FSPC]

I am quite well.

Monday, 7 February 1916 [FSPC]

I am quite well.

---

1 Lieutenant C. F. Drew sailed with the 1st Cameronians to France, then was invalided sick in September 1914. He rejoined as captain in January 1916.
2 Baker in Stirling.

Tuesday, 8 February 1916 [FSPC]

I am quite well.

Wednesday, 9 February 1916 [from trenches in Cambrin, east of Béthune]

I have sent three of those interesting postcards for the last three days, but you will not have expected much more. I shall not be able to write any decent letters for quite another week, if not more. The circumstances are not favourable – principally want of light.

I heard from RO – he has got command of the 10th Queens at Aldershot.

I also heard from Sam Darling – he is off home on leave.

I had a letter from Sandy[1] – he expects to get leave at the end of the month. Wallis[2] is invalided so Capt Jack is 2nd in command again.

Do not worry about anything you see in the papers – it is mostly untrue.

Thursday, 10 February 1916 [FSPC]

I am quite well.

Friday, 11 February 1916 [FSPC]

I am quite well.

Sunday, 13 February 1916 [from 19th brigade HQ, behind the trenches in Cambrin]

Eighteen months today since we left Glasgow.

My letters have been poor in quality lately but we have had a roughish time.

I am out commanding the Brigade for a week – so it is a rest for me and I am not sorry.

---

1 Commander, 2nd Scottish Rifles.
2 Capt Braithwaite Wallis.

Yes, I sincerely hope you can keep on Coval Court[1] until Doreen's arrival. I trust she will not make an early appearance.

I do not know how much you have in Levers.[2] I should certainly remove part of it, if it is a large amount. You know that I am not a financier but I believe in having your eggs in lots of different baskets.

Monday, 14 February 1916 [from 19th brigade HQ, behind the trenches in Cambrin]

I went for a ride yesterday, which was very pleasant. There is of course absolutely nothing to write about.

I should like to have seen Harriette being decorated.

I am glad Jim remains so fit and lively.

Tuesday, 15 February 1916 [FSPC]

I am quite well.

Wednesday, 16 February 1916 [from 19th brigade HQ, behind the trenches in Cambrin]

Owing to my laziness in getting up I had not time to write a letter this morning. This is a regular rest cure after commanding a battn. I go for a ride every day and get a good night's rest, so I am feeling very fit. I was feeling pretty seedy before I came here.

You must not worry about me, dear. Things have been a bit lively lately but nothing more. I shall be here till the regiment comes out, so I shall not be in again for another fortnight.

Thursday, 17 February 1916 [from behind the trenches in Cambrin]

---

1 A house in Sunningdale, built in the early twentieth century and designed in arts-and-crafts style by architect M. H. Baillie Scott, rented by the Alexander family – it is now a Grade II listed building.

2 Lever Brothers' soap business had bought into Ogston & Tennant – a rival soap firm in Aberdeen, part-owned by Charles Tennant & Co – in 1911. The shares may have been used as part of the deal, and been inherited by Thomas Alexander's children.

I had a very quiet day. I rather expected the Corps Commander,[1] so hung about in the morning. In the afternoon, although there was a howling gale blowing I went for a ride alone, but met Capt Wright[2] on the road in a car. He was coming over to see me, so I came back in the car with him. He then went on to the 10th Bn. to see Capt Hardinge. He was much the same.

We are to have sailors with us to see the show – so they ought to be amusing. I wish I could see Jim in his new suit.

Saturday, 19 February 1916 [from billets in Annequin]

I am back with the Regt. I was lucky to get a week's comparative rest.

I would be very pleased if Ronnie M[3] could be exchanged.

Mrs Van[4] wrote to me too – a mad sort of letter. I am sorry that his leg has broken out again.

It becomes harder and harder to think of anything to write about.

Capt Wright motored up to see us – he was very fit and well. I chaffed him and called him the embusque.[5]

Sunday, 20 February 1916 [from billets in Annequin]

I am afraid that I am very little use to you. I have no suggestions if you cannot get a house except to take rooms for Jim and nurse and go to a nursing home for the event – if the worst comes to the worst – but I expect a house will turn up alright.

Col Darling came to the Brigade and lunched today with Col Heywood who was Brigade Major – they came in a car from GHQ. I have never seen Col D look so well – he is very optimistic about the end of the war. He enquired after you and asked particularly after Jim. I told him that Jim was a tiger now.

---

1 General Hubert Gough.
2 Douglas Moncrieff Wright left the Cameronians to train as an instructor in November 1915.
3 Captain Ronnie MacAllan, held as a prisoner of war since September 1914.
4 Vandeleur.
5 'Shirker', can also mean 'ambusher'.

Monday, 21 February 1916 [from billets in Oblinghem]

We are back beyond the old town in comfortable farm houses[1] and I am going to wear my pyjamas for the first time in the war.

I got my cleaned coat and also the Findon haddocks and sausages, for which many thanks, darling. I got no letter tonight, but they come very irregularly now.

I think Reggie must be quite close to us and I am going to try and find him. I also want to go and see the 2nd Bn – as a matter of fact it is generally difficult to get away.

Everything has been very quiet lately. I am extraordinarily well but very sleepy – and will do better tomorrow. With all my fondest love and heaps of kisses to you both, for ever your loving husband, Graham

                    *   *   *

The Cameronians move to softer billets north-west of Béthune, into farm-houses in Oblinghem – flat, featureless pastureland swept by freezing February winds. Chaplin writes to Lil that he has a bed, and sheets, and can wear pyjamas: small tokens of a regular life. All he needs is sleep. It is the one stress that wears him down after eighteen months of war: the need for constant alertness in the trenches, being woken often hourly with reports and worries. The week spent filling in for Robertson as brigadier – while his old friend is on leave – gives him some respite, but liaising with divisional HQ, conveying wishes down, pushing paper up, holding his tongue, is another trial. He is already nervously exhausted. He rarely mentions his terrors and sleepwalking after Mons, but his attempts to regain lost slumber obsess him.

He still writes nightly to Lil as if to lose himself in her world. She is weeks away from giving birth to their second child, moving south to Surrey – like many officer wives, to be closer to a husband on leave every quarter – and assailed by her own worries as to where to live, where to have the baby, how to organise her finances now she has inherited a substantial share portfolio. Graham chips in with characteristically wary financial advice:

---

1 In Oblinghem, on the north-west outskirts of Béthune.

'Yes, I should think that War Loan was as good as anything you could put your money in, but I should split it up and not put everything in it – at least that is my idea.'[83]

His father's misfortune, losing everything in a roll of the dice at Lloyd's, underpins all his counsel. Likewise: 'I think you are doing very wisely about the shares, but I should split it up as much as possible and not have more than £1000 in any one stock.'[84]

He also gently reassures her about Jim, who had been sporting a head wound in photographs at the end of the year: 'I expect Jim will fall on his head many times if he is like his father. I do not expect it will do him any harm.'[85]

With or without advice, Lil seems more than capable, a single parent by force of war, but working in an efficient triangle with nurse and cook, preparing for 'Doreen', moving between Alexander households, mothering Jim but also keeping an eye on her mother, and continuing the process of posting to Graham his needs – sausages, haddock and cake sent weekly; clothes, toilet paper, writing pads, pencils and photographs sent monthly. Then there are the regimental wives to coordinate.

She has a wedding to arrange too, as her sister, Bee, is rushing to marry Graham's friend, Sandy – Vincent Sandilands, commander of 2nd Scottish Rifles. Imagine that, they can joke, both girls have bagged a colonel, both in the same regiment. It will be a quick affair, a wedding in Surrey while Sandy is on leave, the war necessitating no time is wasted. Lil has a lunch to organise, guests to sort out, her mother's arrival from Scotland to plan for. Graham, riding his horse through the snow in and out of Béthune, tries to keep up with the gossip: 'By Jove, things are moving if Sandy and Baby are going to be married at once – we shall have to give them a good present. Give them my love and blessing.'[86]

And as the day approaches, his yearning to be there is palpable as he scours newspapers for announcements: 'I see in the *Morning Post* that Baby is to be married on Tuesday at Windlesham,[87] so I suppose it will be from Coval Court – tell them I wish them jolly good luck.'[88]

In recompense, he falls back on getting things done, ordering permanent

latrines to be dug and cook houses to be built and wire beds to be made
for the barns in the new billeting area of Oblinghem.[89] And he relies on
the companionship of Robertson, Darling and Williams, the CO of the
2nd Royal Welch – 'We are . . . the only two of the same service in the
Brigade.'[90]

His letters are now peppered with references to his own singularity, his
isolation and his apartness. The loneliness of command, of survival in war,
of life away from your wife, away from your children, never sleeping, never
knowing when you will see family or friends again, is abrading him. To
cope, he simply shuts his humanity down: 'I hope the Germans will attack
everywhere – it is much easier to kill them if they will.'[91]

But of course, the Germans never do.

Wednesday, 1 March 1916 [from trenches in Cuinchy]
This is one of those 2am letters again.

If you spent about half the £17 on cigarettes for the men and kept the
remainder I will let you know if there is anything we want when we go back.

I got three cakes tonight, and also sausages and Findon haddocks, which
have come at a most appropriate time as all our eggs were smashed by the
fatigue party. Many thanks, darling, for all the parcels.

How is Jim getting on with his walking?

Thursday, 2 March 1916 [from trenches in Cuinchy]
Just a line to say that I am very fit and well. It is very late and I am very
tired. We are having a very quiet time, I suppose in consequence of Verdun.[1]

Friday, 3 March 1916 [from trenches in Cuinchy]
It was awfully bad luck Baby getting ill and a great upset for you. I have
not got your letter describing the wedding but I had one from Mrs Harriette.

---

1 The Battle of Verdun started on 21 February when German forces attacked the French,
and lasted throughout 1916.

She said that you were looking extremely well and that Jim was admired by everyone and that everything went off splendidly.

I had a letter from RO saying that he was at Aldershot. His wife and the children are there now. He said that they were going to see you as soon as the roads were passable.

We are having a very quiet time at present. The rain has started again, which is a nuisance.

Sunday, 5 March 1916 [from trenches in Cuinchy]

I am very sorry that I did not write last night, but I did not get back till 2.30am – it was very bad weather and I was very tired.

I was jolly glad to get your letter tonight and to know that you were better. My hands are so dirty that I am trying to keep them from touching the paper, which makes writing difficult.

We had one officer killed today – a Mr MacDonald.[1]

Tuesday, 7 March 1916 [from billets in Annequin North]

I am desperately sorry that I did not write yesterday but we got out very late. All of us in Hd Qrs went to poor MacDonald's funeral. It was a typical soldier's funeral, a little way behind the trenches, the guns were going hard and the flares occasionally lighting up the scene. I hate these things myself and always have, but thought I ought to go. By the time we got to billets and had had dinner and dealt with a mass of correspondence I had a blazing head and thought I would write in the morning, but of course was too late.

I walked to Brigade Hd Qrs after orderly room and had a long talk to the General and a very nice gunner Colonel who has just come.

I am very glad that your mother will be near you for the event and that you have a home to go to if you should not get a house.

There is a rumour that Col Northey has gone home – I wonder if you could find out if it is true?

---

1 2nd Lieutenant A. H. MacDonald was killed by a sniper. A shell also killed Private P. Cairney that day.

I have a great longing to see you but I see no chance yet. I do not see any prospect of a Brigade – Col Williams has not got one. He is senior to me and has had command longer. All these things are greatly a matter of luck – not that I have anything to complain of in that way.

The French seem to be holding their own at Verdun and killing lots of Germans, which is a great thing.

I did not tell you that General Gough[1] asked one of our subalterns which Bn he belonged and when he was told the 1st the General said "I know them well. You should be proud to belong to such a grand regiment."

Wednesday, 8 March 1916 [from billets in Annequin North]

It has been a beautiful day but the snow is thawing, which is bad for the trenches. I was busy all the morning with correspondence – this afternoon I walked down to see the General.

I am very sorry about Col Northey[2] – I suppose he has returned to the store. You did not say what the rumour was, but we hear he has joined at Nigg. He is not a genius, but at least he is a brave man, so I am sorry.

Thursday, 9 March 1916 [from billets in Annequin North]

We have had our tin helmets issued to us and have to wear them this side of the big town. They are not becoming – very like a useful piece of household crockery. I think my appearance in one caused great amusement to the men.

It is pretty hot stuff Crailsham[3] getting a battalion. He is about as much fitted for it as I am to lead a choir.

---

1 General Hubert Gough commanded I corps, in which 1st Cameronians had fought the Battle of Loos.

2 Northey, commander of 9th Bn and a former 2nd Bn officer, was invalided home in early March 1916. A brief and less than flattering portrait of Northey can be found in John Baynes and Hugh MacLean's *A Tale of Two Captains* [Pentland Press]. The reference to Nigg, an army camp, implies he has been given a desk job.

3 Captain, later Major, Harry Rollo Crailsham didn't get a battalion.

Saturday, 11 March 1916 [from trenches in Cuinchy]

I missed a post again yesterday – I am very sorry but I was beastly tired and got up too late to catch it. I shall have to take to writing in the afternoon again. We have just got in[1] and it is 1 o'c in the morning.

The weather is much better, if it will remain so – last time we were in, one was wading up to one's thighs in places.

I saw the General today and also Capt Twiss the Brigade Major who is a very nice fellow and has lots of common sense which I have come to the conclusion is a rare quality – so many people fuss about things that don't matter and leave the things that do.

There is a monster rat making a devil of a noise gnawing the wood over my bed.

Sunday, 12 March 1916 [from trenches in Cuinchy]

Absolutely no news. It has been the best day we have had for ages. The sun actually shone for a bit.

It will be a year tomorrow since we left Glasgow and nine months since I took over command. It seems as though one had never known any other life.

Monday, 13 March 1916 [from trenches in Cuinchy]

Today has been a lovely day and we came out of our cellar and basked in the sun. It makes a lot of difference the sun coming out – it is really quite a pleasant life in contrast to the rain and snow.

I had a letter from Col Darling. He is very discontented at being where he is. He said Sandy stayed the night with him.

I shall not be happy until Doreen has made her appearance. It must be simply unbearable what you have to put up with – I cannot get it out of my mind.

I am most hopeful about Verdun. The report today is that fighting has practically ceased. If it is true, it is very good news as it looks as though the Germans had staked everything on it. Altogether it looks as though the tide has

---

1 Relieving the 2nd Royal Welch Fusiliers in trenches in Cuinchy.

turned. Rats soon leave a sinking ship – and we may see Turkey and Bulgaria soon throw up the sponge.

Tuesday, 14 March 1916 [from billets in Annequin North]

We are out and I am very tired so I am not in good form for writing. It is funny that one feels much more tired when one has just come out although it is only 10 o'c and as a rule I should not be in bed till 1.30am or 2am if I were in and I should not feel tired then.

We have had a new officer, a Mr Ritchie,[1] join today – looks very nice, and small and a gentleman.

If everything goes as we expect, we should not be in again for a month or so.

With all my fondest love and heaps of kisses to you both, for ever your loving husband, Graham

*   *   *

He is wrong. The Cameronians are back in trenches within a fortnight, but compared to others they have an easy March – the weather is foul at first but improving, and casualties are low. The trenches at Cuinchy, a killing ground at the worst of times, require incessant work, but at least they are familiar territory, and that saves lives. Rumours of a planned attack, ordered from I Corps HQ, thankfully come to nothing.[92]

Only the constant mining beneath their feet, deep under the trenches, grates at the nerves – and those below now want more saps[93] dug above, protruding into no-man's land, to deter the Germans from scouring the ground, listening for digging. Even when pulled back to nearby Annequin, where the 19th brigade keeps its base, the battalion must provide working parties to dig and mend. Daily the Germans send over *minenwerfer* bombs and rifle grenades, almost nonchalantly, as if to stop the molestation would disappoint – but few are hurt.

Late March sees the Cameronians back in their billets beyond Béthune in Oblinghem, practising drill and playing football, before manning the

---

1 2nd Lieutenant J. A. Ritchie.

trenches facing Auchy, south of the La Bassée Canal around which much of their work is done. Snow returns. All is quiet.

Chaplin's letters are upbeat. Many believe the new French front at Verdun is the start of the end: 'There is a great wave of optimism over here that the Germans are done.'[94]

There is news of Bee's wedding to pull in, and updates on old friends. Harry Lee has recovered from his injuries at Loos and wants to return. Chaplin is puzzled: 'I think that he would be extremely foolish to return out here. He seems anxious to return as 2nd in command.'[95]

New drafts of men and officers arrive from Scotland to replenish the battalion. None impress him: 'Any amount of new officers but none of any experience.'[96]

And those he knows go sick. Captain Drew is hospitalised first with a temperature then likely pneumonia. Chaplin writes almost with a sigh: 'I am afraid that he is much too delicate for the rough game of war, and will have to be sent home.'[97]

Yet the new spring gives him hope. Lil now has a house in mind, 'Swinley' in Sunningdale, available furnished to rent for three-month periods at four guineas a week. His family will soon be settled, his new child will soon be born, winter is nearly over, primulas and violets are opening in the shell-blasted gardens that dot the front line: everything is looking up. He hears that Lee has taken command of the 12th East Surreys – 'he seems to be pleased with the whole outfit'[98] – and wishes his friend well. Only a small, surprising cloud reappears on the horizon: 'I have just heard that Major Hamilton is being sent back to the regiment. I feel that he has let me down, as I recommended him for a command. I knew that he was not a genius but I thought he would have done alright – I feel very annoyed about it.'

They are old friends reunited, but Chaplin, heading into the Cuinchy trenches at the start of April, is peeved. He had recommended Hamilton for promotion solely to get him out of the battalion, as their pre-war friendship had become strained. Now not only is Hammy back – pending a period of leave he is owed – but Chaplin's judgement may be called into question at divisional level, or higher. What effects will that have on his own chances of promotion?

Sunday, 2 April 1916 [from trenches facing Auchy]

Just a line to say that all is well. Owing to our move[1] I could not write this afternoon – now it is past midnight.

Major H[2] has got his leave and gone off tonight, so Capt Drew has come back to Hd Qrs much to his joy, I think.

Major H's Brigadier outed him as he did not think he was stern enough to manage his crowd.

The Padre has come in with us this time. He paid me his fiver,[3] which I enclose to start Doreen's banking account.

Monday, 3 April 1916 [from trenches facing Auchy]

One of the subalterns showed me a cutting from a local paper of the unveiling of a memorial to Mr Wyatt, who was killed on Sept 25th. The local paper says "These are the words not of a fond parent but of his commanding officer, a soldier inured to the horrors of war and not much given to sentiment" – which somehow does not sound complimentary.

I hope the weather will soon allow a snapshot of Jim.

Wednesday, 5 April 1916 [from trenches facing Auchy]

It has not rained today although it threatens to do so.

Major Draffen is out here. I had a letter from Col Darling – but no news of any interest.

I am so tired, dear, that I cannot write any more. It is long past midnight.

---

1 The battalion moved back into trenches facing Auchy-les-Mines, east of Béthune.
2 Hamilton.
3 Betting he would be a brigadier by now.

Thursday, 6 April 1916 [from billets in Beuvry]

I cannot write a long letter after all as we did not get to our nice billets till very late.

We expect to be in our old billets beyond the Old Town soon for quite a long spell – though the expected seldom happens – this time I hope we shall not be disappointed.

Friday, 7 April 1916 [from billets in Beuvry]

I was jolly glad to get your two letters today and to hear that you were alright and the removal successfully accomplished.

I went to bed as soon as I had written last night and slept like a top.

We have lost our nice Cure's house and are now in a laundry – it is really quite comfortable.

All your parcels have arrived. If I have not said so it is when we are in the trenches and I am generally jolly tired when I write then.

I do not know whether Major H will get another command – he is after a territorial regt – I hope he gets it.

The leaves are beginning to show now.

Sunday, 9 April 1916 [from billets in Beuvry]

I was relieved to get a letter today – I was afraid your time had arrived.

I was busy this morning writing official correspondence so did not either go to church or for a walk. I went for a ride alone in the afternoon.

I am so glad you like the house. If I should get leave, how do I get to Swinley House – what station do I go to?

There is no news about anything the last few days. I wish we could get some good news from Kut.[1]

There is a chance I may get leave any time after the 15th as they are trying to get everyone to attend the Investitures who have decorations to receive.[2] I

---

1 A British–Indian garrison in the town of Kut, one hundred miles south of Baghdad, is besieged by the Ottoman army from 7 December 1915 to 29 April 1916.
2 Chaplin had been awarded the DSO in June 1915.

am simply longing to see you and I hardly like to think about the possibility as every time one seems to be doomed to disappointment.

Monday, 10 April 1916 [from billets in Béthune]

We are back in our old billets where the landlady was so solicitous about my health.[1] I am not really sorry to be back.

I put in an application today to be given 10 days' leave, but I do not know what will happen. There is a chance that I may see you in the next week or so but the odds are that I shall not.

I had a letter from Col Vandeleur about a woman in the regiment who has had three sons in 15 months – not bad going. Also he wrote about Mrs V's prisoners' fund. I shall have to send something as they have about 20 of ours and unless we send something I suppose the prisoners will be badly off.

I am afraid the income tax will hit your income badly,[2] but it is lucky they have not increased it on our pay, so we escape something. The worst of it is I do not see how it will ever be reduced in our time and it may get worse.

With all my fondest love and heaps of kisses to you both. For ever your loving husband, Graham

Friday, 14 April 1916 [telegram from Folkestone]

Two days' leave home at about 4pm Graham

---

1 In Rue D'Aire, Béthune.
2 The UK government is gradually increasing its rate of tax from its previous six-per-cent base.

NEVER BETTER

'I have been very lucky. I am the only officer left out of the whole Brigade who has served continuously and never been away.'

Fierce fighting continues at Verdun between French and German forces — uprising by Irish nationalists in Dublin shakes Britain — German and British fleets meet in North Sea at Battle of Jutland with no conclusive winner — German forces attack at Vimy where British have taken over line from French allies — British secretary of state for war, Lord Kitchener, dies en route to Russia

Graham Chaplin heads home, leaving a battalion feeling better about itself. Battered by German field guns firing at the Cuinchy trenches, and under orders to raid enemy lines for prisoners,[99] the Cameronians have plotted a careful retaliation plan. First Chaplin sends out his most capable lieutenant to check the wiring in front of the German position. Robert Laing is just twenty-three, son of a schoolteacher from Clackmannanshire, near Stirling, and already known as an accomplished athlete. He brings back a section of German wire to test with wire cutters, reporting that divisional HQ's chosen spot for a raid is impenetrable. However, he has noted an unused trench twenty yards from the German line and suggests he take a four-man party out the next night to hide for twenty-four hours, observing enemy movements.

They set off at 3.30 a.m. and return the next evening, only being spotted in the trench at dusk, and bombing their way out of likely capture. Laing's report details the habits of enemy sentries, hours of standing to arms, methods of carrying it out, sniper and machine-gun positions. The army commander and the divisional General send commendations. Laing, who is later killed on the Somme, receives the Military Cross for his exploits. Chaplin is commended too. The ripples of pleasure from Laing's raid continue to roll out over the battalion for weeks.

So Chaplin is in good spirits when he makes the brief trip back to Britain a fortnight later. The extra leave, allotted for investiture, allows him just two nights in Surrey with Lil, but he will take any respite offered. The ceremony at Buckingham Palace is short but illuminating, a band of CMG, DSO and MC winners guided in front of the King. Names are read without citations; pace forward to allow monarch to pin on decoration, shake hands, pace back, bow, right turn and away. Chaplin must entrain back to France before unpacking his haversack.

He returns to a Béthune that is rapidly adapting to the war on its doorstep, its inhabitants prospering from the sheer numbers of men living in or around the town. Black-market trading of British supplies is now a thriving activity, even though security is tight – military police occasionally cordon off the whole town, searching everyone who goes in or out, chasing real and make-believe spies. Rumours abound of messages carried by pigeons and dogs to the enemy, such is the proximity of the German line.

For the soldiers it is a life of routine and occasional amusements – theatre follies, singsongs in estaminets, sporting contests. As the weather warms, the officers play cricket, the ranks football. The 20th Royal Fusiliers is suspected of keeping its team out of trenches, so successful is it in the inter-battalion championship.

From the moment Chaplin leaves London for the return trip back to France, his thoughts are with his pregnant wife, just weeks away from giving birth for the second time. His letters detail the usual list of chance encounters on the way back – old friends from India, a former medic from the Cams – the gossip about Hammy (happy) and Drew (posted to a training school), and the sudden switch to stormy weather on their front. But mostly he thinks about Lil: 'I only wish I could know by some means if you were alright.'[100]

Three days later, he is back in the trenches facing Auchy, doing what he always does, pacing the line with his adjutant, dictating a list of work he wants to see completed, keeping busy. And waiting for news from home.

Extracts from the battalion War Diary,
April 1916,

Kept by Colonel Graham Chaplin

Trenches in Cuinchy, east of Béthune
19 April - Weather stormy and cold. CO round trenches in
morning giving instruction to OC Companies regarding work
required to be done. Trenches appear to be left in good order
by outgoing Regt.

The following were wounded - Capt K Butterfield, Sgt A Watson,
Pte T Johnston, Pte J McNeally. Capt Butterfield's wound was
serious though not dangerous as far as can be seen. Enemy
machine gun fire was responsible.

20 April - Enemy sprung a mine at 4.45am, making a crater
some 30 yards across, its near lip 10 yards from our front
line trench occupied by A Coy and No10 saphead of ours being
destroyed, also part of adjoining sap blown and our trenches
a good deal shaken for some 70 yards round. Work was at once
started clearing saps and other communications. This crater and
adjoining craters being closely overlooked both from the German
and our own observation posts, no good object could be served
by actual occupation of near lip during daylight.

The following were casualties - LCpl W Bloomfield, Pte H
Walker. Wounded - Pte R Adams, Pte A Moultrie, Pte T Warren,
Pte W Smith, LCpl J Winsper, Pte G Rowland, Pte A McLaren.
Above casualties were in connection with mine. Also wounded
by shell fire in communication trench same evening Pte J
Stevenson and Pte M Cullen.

A raid on two enemy saps was carried out at 9.30pm with cooperation of trench mortars and artillery. Lieuts Munro and Percy each led 15 men. The enemy saps were found to have been evacuated with the exception of one man with whom Lieut Percy had an encounter at close quarters, the German unfortunately escaping.

21 April – A considerable amount of sunshine today, but trenches have become very water-logged. Steady work repairing and draining is being put in on them. In the evening a patrol went out from D Coy under Capt Brickman who was accompanied by Lieut Ritchie. A gap in the enemy wire was taken advantage of with the object of nobbling a sentry, but the enemy were alert and a hand grenade thrown at the party went very near Lieut Ritchie. Our patrol then retired after getting soaked to the skin, the weather having again become squally.

22 April – Weather cold and rainy again. Companies worked hard to put trenches into as good order as possible for 20th Royal Fusiliers who relieved us, starting at 7pm. Relief completed in two hours. Most of our casualties during the tour in trenches were the result of the enemy mine explosion. The enemy have refrained from any real retaliation either at the time or on days following the expeditions of our patrols against their trenches. We moved into billets at Le Quesnoy.

Wednesday, 19 April 1916 [from trenches facing Auchy]
My own darling,

I cannot tell you how relieved and pleased I was to get your telegram saying that Doreen had arrived safely and that you were both well. Now that the matter is settled for us I am glad that she is a girl – I should like her to be called Dora.

It is past midnight and therefore not a good hour for writing. After three days I will write decent letters again.

Thursday, 20 April 1916 [from trenches facing Auchy]
I have had a very long and tiring day, being up at 5am and it is now 1 o'clock.

I was awfully pleased to get Edith's letter and to have it in writing that all is well and that the girl weighs 8lbs. I also got a nice letter from Mrs Lee and a letter from RO.

In two days, all being well, I will write a long letter.

Good Friday, 21 April 1916 [from trenches facing Auchy]
Just a line to say all's well.

I cannot tell you how pleased I was to get your letter of Tuesday – to hear that you had not too bad a time and that you are pleased with your daughter. I am really pleased that she proved to be a real Doreen.

The rumour that leave is to be opened still continues so I hope that I shall see you soon. With all my love and all my thoughts and heaps of kisses to you all.

Saturday, 22 April 1916 [from billets in Le Quesnoy, near the front line]
No letter from you tonight but I suppose you will not be able to write. We are in billets but I am very tired and just off to bed. I will write a long letter tomorrow.

Easter Sunday, 23 April 1916 [from billets in Le Quesnoy]
I am still very sleepy and do not feel my brain very active for letter writing. I have had a pretty strenuous time. I am off to bed as soon as I finish this.

I have had no letter from you today, which makes me feel so anxious. If the nurse just dropped a line to say you are alright it would allay my fears.

I hope to get leave very soon, if all is well probably about the 1st.

I am very anxious to see you all.

Monday, 24 April 1916 [from billets in Le Quesnoy]

I had a real good sleep last night and so feel more in form for writing. I did not get much sleep in the last few nights.

I was jolly glad to get two letters today, not having had one for two days. I began to be nervous about you.

I am terribly sorry, dear, that you should have had such a rotten time and hope that you will very soon be fit and well. I hope that I shall very soon get leave and see you all.

We have a good billet here, an old chateau but hardly any furniture, but I have a bed with sheets.

I am going to dine out tonight – an unusual event – with a fellow named Ionides[1] whom I used to meet at the Jackson Russells, now 2nd in command of a Pioneer Battalion.

With all my fondest love and heaps of kisses to you all.

Tuesday, 25 April 1916 [from billets in Le Quesnoy]

I was very pleased to get another letter from you today and to hear that the doctor thought so well of you both.

It has been a lovely sunny day – these last few days have passed like lightning. I went for a long ride with the padre this afternoon. I walked into the Brigade this morning – the General expects to go on leave tomorrow. I hope that I shall get mine on the 6th, if all is well. I shall not be able to write much for the next four days and then hope to write regularly till I get home.

Wednesday, 26 April 1916 [from billets in Le Quesnoy]

Just a line to say that I am very well.

It has been a topping day, just like summer. I received no letter from you today, but I suppose the post is delayed.

Friday, 28 April 1916 [from 19th brigade HQ, near Annequin]

I could not write last night. I received an unexpected message that I was to

---

1 Major Philip Ionides, 10th Duke of Cornwall's Light Infantry.

command the Brigade whilst the General was on leave so I had dinner and walked down to the Brigade.

If all is well I shall get my leave as soon as the General returns.

I am not sorry to be here – it means one gets much more sleep and we had had a good dose of trenches lately.

Sunday, 30 April 1916 [from 19th brigade HQ]

I received three letters from you today and was very glad that you are all so well.

This is a very comfortable life compared to being with the Regt. I get a lot of exercise and go to bed early and get a lot of sleep.

I heard from Col D but he gave no news – he is going home for his DSO.

The General has put in for an extra day, so I suppose I shall not get away until the 7th.

The Divisional General is just coming so I must close. One sees lots of people here – Generals and staff.

Monday, 1 May 1916 [from 19th brigade HQ]

Capt Drew is going to instruct in a school miles from anything, so he is out of it all now.

This is a grand rest for me and I am enjoying it. The weather is topping. I get enough exercise now and ride usually morning and afternoon.

I am very glad the baby is doing so well. I should not worry about the dairy not playing up.

I like the gunner Colonel who is with us very much – Rochford-Boyd[1] by name. He is a very nice man and an excellent soldier.

I am sorry about Reggie and Mabel.

I cannot make out why Connie[2] has not written to you or me – she has not written to me for months.

---

1 Lieutenant Colonel Henry Rochford-Boyd, Royal Horse Artillery, was killed a year later at Cambrai. J. C. Dunn describes him as 'a pious fire-eater and a most acceptable referee at the boxing-matches at Béthune' [Chap VIII, *The War the Infantry Knew*].
2 His sister, Constance, who was married to a doctor, William Young.

Tuesday, 2 May 1916 [from 19th brigade HQ]

Just a line to say all is well. I cannot get in the way to write by midday.

We are very quiet.

If all is well I hope to come home on the 9th – only a week.

With all my fondest love and heaps of kisses to you all.

For ever your loving husband,

Graham

Wednesday, 3 May 1916 [from 19th brigade HQ]

There is really nothing to write about – each day the same as the last. Yes, it is a bad business about Kut,[1] but it was known for a long time that there was no hope.

I am simply longing to see you all and to be introduced to Dora.

I hate the idea of you having to suffer all this pain and hope this is the end of it.

Thursday, 4 May 1916 [from 19th brigade HQ]

We are going this evening to the Old Town.[2] I believe I have got a splendid bedroom.

I wish the next four days would pass quickly so that I could see you all – however it is the time at home that goes like lightning.

I am glad they shot the Irish rebel leaders[3] without any waste of time. I hope compulsion[4] is passed without more ado and that they will include Ireland.

I have got a small cyst in my eye, but I hope it will clear off – it is a nuisance.

---

1 Kut fell to the Ottoman army on 29 April 1916. Germans in trenches at Cuinchy taunted British soldiers with the news before it was released to the press. See Twiss papers [IWM]: 'about the limit when the first news one gets of it is from them'.

2 Béthune, to billets in the western suburb of Annezin.

3 Following the Easter Rising on 24 April 1916, fourteen leaders of the revolt were executed over nine days in early May.

4 Conscription.

Saturday, 6 May 1916 [from billets in Annezin, western suburb of Béthune]
My eye has got very bad – a bad cyst – so I cannot see to write well. I am trying to get the Dr to lance it. I am afraid you will see me with a very swollen eye, otherwise very fit. With all my fondest love to you all and heaps of kisses. For ever your loving husband, Graham

*   *   *

Less than a month after his last visit, Chaplin is back in Britain on eight days' leave. He arrives in a country still reeling from events in Ireland just a fortnight earlier, when the six-day Easter Rising in Dublin had challenged British rule. Its suppression, and the forthcoming trial of former diplomat Sir Roger Casement – arrested after negotiating for the Germans to supply arms to the Irish rebels – has pushed the war in France out of the main newspaper headlines. Already, for some soldiers returning home, it is as if many in Britain have decided there are bigger things to worry about than a trench war many miles away. Only the ongoing debates over conscription and food prices – up fifty per cent since 1914 – and news photos of the giant Zeppelin that crashed in a Norway fjord, returning from a bombing run on Britain in early May, remind people that the war may soon come closer.

For a proudly Presbyterian regiment like the Cameronians, the conflict in Ireland brings added problems. Just two years earlier, before the war had started, there had been speculation that the 1st battalion would be sent to Ireland to help suppress unrest caused by the Ulster Volunteers, a Protestant armed militia raised in protest to suggested home rule. Given that the Cams' ranks mix many Ulstermen, recruited in Scotland, with Glasgow Catholics, it would have been a fraught mission. There had already been rumours that army officers in Ireland had refused to disarm the Volunteers, so sympathetic were they to their cause.

Chaplin – a commander who prefers to stay in bed on Sundays rather than attend a church service – is not an officer to choose sides in religion. He as often has an 'RC padre' attached to his HQ as one from the Church of Scotland, and is clearly close to Padre McShane, the Catholic priest whose bravery and kindness make him a popular figure within the 19th brigade. The important fact for Chaplin is that any padre should offer good conversation and be 'a man of the world',[101] requirements which Northumberland-born McShane fulfils. But that doesn't alter Chaplin's view that Irish rebel leaders should be put against a wall and shot – as happened. It is a view shared by most in the regular army, who put loyalty to Crown before all else.

Chaplin shares a week at home with Lil, Jim and new daughter Eileen – his choice of Dora as the girl's name has been quickly quashed – and returns to Béthune with a promise of snapshots to follow, as he readies himself for his other life. The crossing is so familiar to him now – 'the sea was like a millpond'[102] – that it barely requires comment. His immediate anxieties are with Lil, left behind with two children: 'I feel very homesick and wish I was with you and the kids. I miss you more than I can say.'[103]

He is also tellingly pragmatic, hoping he has not left her pregnant again: 'I wish I could hear that the K[104] was with you.'[105]

He has missed little while away from his men. They have been out in billets, training, and he returns to find them at Annequin South, behind the lines, furnishing working parties for the front trenches, principally helping the mining teams with their hated tunnels. He wakes the next day in billets to find his face swollen with an abscess: 'I went to see the dentist in the Old Town but he could not get the bridge off without destroying it, so he just painted the place with iodine. I hope it will be alright.'[106]

It is a worsening of the dental problems that have dogged him since the start of the war. His eyes too are hurting, inflamed by clouds of tear gas blown into Annequin from the front. 'It was strong enough to make everyone's eyes water and smart. The goggles in possession are not much use,' he writes morosely in the War Diary. The gas has drifted for miles. Others hope that it will at least knock out the rodents that plague the billets.

By the end of May he is back again in the trenches facing Auchy, dealing with an aggressive enemy, now blowing its own mines and rushing the British trenches – not in any large-scale offensive, but just to raise the stakes of mutual molestation. It has become a tit-for-tat war here, each side retaliating for every slight received, bullet for bullet, shell for shell. Both fear that simply to hold the ground without firing would give their opponent an unthinkable advantage.

Chaplin will know that another British push is coming. The Germans had surprised the French by attacking at Verdun in February, but that had quickly become a stalemate. Haig wants to mount an offensive in the north, to push the Germans away from the coast, but is persuaded to refocus on the sector where the British and French armies meet: the Somme. A summer push would relieve the French defence of Verdun by pulling German forces north. A simultaneous Russian offensive in the east would prevent the enemy moving reserves west.

By late May, Béthune is awash with rumour as to where the 33rd division will move next – up to Vimy, beyond to Ypres, down to the Somme, where British divisions are already taking up the line left by the French, as their allies commit more troops to the ongoing battle at Verdun. For Lil, sitting in her rented home in Surrey with a toddler and babe in arms, it can only have been a period of strained anxiety, as she plans for an unknown future. She must stay in the south, as it is easier to see her husband on leave. But it is not worth buying a house, as her situation will change the moment Graham is killed. She can now read short daily reports of the fighting beyond Béthune, and knows from her husband's own descriptions the danger he faces. He has been lucky so far, but a soldier in war always is, until he isn't.

Two years on the front line have already aged Chaplin a decade. 'I never knew I looked so desperately old before,'[107] he writes, on receiving more snapshots of himself with the children. At times, he not only feels unwell – inflamed eyes, abscessed teeth – but overwhelmed: 'We are getting crowds of new officers – I shall never remember all their names – they are all from the 3rd and 4th Bns.'[108]

Lil cheers him by sending him cakes from Gunter's, the fashionable teashop in London's Berkley Square that bakes for Buckingham Palace, and gossipy stories of people she has met. She recounts the faux pas she made when introduced to a Lady Monro, asking what regiment her husband was in – General Sir Charles Monro had recently masterminded the Allied withdrawal from Gallipoli and now commanded the British First Army around Armentières.[109] Graham is consoling: 'but of course you could not know who she was'.[110]

Good follows bad follows good. Chaplin is awarded a brevet,[111] which confirms his rank as lieutenant colonel. Lil loses her rented house. All is up in the air again. Colonel Williams of the Royal Welch is promoted to brigadier, and given a brigade. That leaves Chaplin as senior colonel in the 19th, which means, should Robertson be promoted, he might stand a chance of replacing him. But would divisional HQ want another Cameronian leading the brigade?

They might, after Chaplin masterminds another successful raid on Sunday, 4 June, sending out a large party from the Cameronians' D Company, covered by artillery and mortars, through the wire and into the German trenches at Auchy. It is a carefully planned operation, with artillery doing some 'not too obtrusive work'[112] cutting the wire in the days before. The raiding party return with one German prisoner, claiming eight killed. Cameronian losses are five wounded and one missing.

Chaplin receives a telegram of congratulation from General Rawlinson, commander of the Fourth Army. The next day he receives a visit from General Landon, commanding 33rd division, to give his thanks in person. The leaders of the raid, Captain Evans and Lieutenant Ritchie, are sent back to Béthune to tell the general staff about their exploits. The raid, writes Chaplin to Lil, 'was not so successful as I had hoped, but the powers that be are pleased'.[113]

By the end of that week, other news takes precedence, as the troops learn of Lord Kitchener's death at sea.[114] It hits the veterans hard. Kitchener of Khartoum epitomised the unbreakable spirit of the old army, and its values of duty, honour and discipline. Chaplin tells Lil of his sorrow but – always careful to bolster her spirits – he adds that at least the raising of new recruits is complete: 'Fortunately for the country he had performed the work of organising the Army, which probably no-one else could have done.'[115]

Kitchener's death does, however, deprive the army of a figurehead of status capable of providing effective liaison with an increasingly beleaguered French army. His absence will soon impact on the British plans for a new offensive. Despite Haig's desire to fight the Germans nearer Ypres, British divisions – many of them untried in battle – are already rolling south to the plain above the Somme river, preparing to attack heavily defended enemy positions, in order to assist the French position further south. For now, the Cameronians are left on the old Loos battlefield, with its sniping, shelling and mining, never quiet.

'I sometimes feel I could do with a change of scenery',[116] Chaplin writes wearily. He will get his wish, but not for a month.

Extracts from the battalion War Diary,
June 1916,

Kept by Colonel Graham Chaplin

Billets, Beuvry
1 June – Practically no working parties today, those required being furnished by the 2/5th Royal Warwicks of the 61st Div just arrived in the country. We loaned them guides and steel helmets.

2 June – The battalion left Beuvry at 7.30pm and moved into trenches, relieving the 20th R Fusiliers in Auchy, left sub-section. Distribution of Companies, front line, right to left, C, B, A – support D. No casualties.

Trenches, Auchy
3 June – A few light mortar bombs and rifle grenades were fired into A Company's trenches and part of B's during day. We had three casualties, Pte D Colman and Pte W McCoombs both

of A Coy, and Pte T Nixon B Coy. Our artillery and mortars
are doing some steady and not too obtrusive work cutting the
German wire opposite Queen's Crater.

4 June – The 121 men of the 6th Scottish Rifles who have
only been with us four days were marched off for return to
their regiment which is not being disbanded as apparently
had been intended. More wire cutting by our artillery and
mortars and brisk retaliation by the enemy. Two artillerymen
in our trenches were casualties from shelling, one killed.
No casualties to us during daylight. At 11pm a raiding party
formed of D Coy augmented with C Coy's bombers crossed
No-Man's Land from Queen's Crater into the German Front Line
trench and returned with one prisoner, having killed eight.
Our advance was covered by artillery and mortars. Capt D Evans
was in command. Lieut R B Ritchie shot two of the Germans
with his revolver and was instrumental in saving the one
prisoner brought in alive. Our casualties were five wounded
and one missing. Wounded: L Cpl J Kerr, L Cpl I McIntosh, Pte
R Crawford, Pte R Needham, all of D Coy, and Pte I Geddes
of C Coy. Telegrams of congratulation were received from Army
Commander, Divisional Commander and GOC Brigade.

5 June – A heavy bombardment of the trenches occupied by our
left Coy and trenches immediately north of us, in retaliation
for last night's raid, between 5am and 6am. We sustained no
casualties. After this a quiet day but usual bomb throwing
after dark when two men were wounded, Pte M Rafferty and Pte A
Kelly, both of A Coy. The GOC Division visited Battalion
Hd Qrs to hear about the raid, as did GOC Brigade. Capt Evans
and Lieut Ritchie were taken back to Béthune to tell the Army
Commander and others of the General Staff about it.

6 June - A normal day in the trenches. We had no casualties.

7 June - A fairly quiet day with occasional bursts of light
artillery and mortars on both sides. We had one man killed
through looking over the top of a crater lip instead of using
the periscope - Pte G Cason, B Coy.

8 June - Same kind of day as the 7th until 4.30pm when an
underground gallery was blown close to Queen's Crater, covered
by fire from our artillery and mortars. Enemy retaliated in kind
causing two casualties in a party from a pioneer battalion.

9 June - A quiet day. The battalion was relieved by the
16th KRR[1] of the 100th Brigade. Our companies marched back to
billets in Annezin, six miles, packs being carried by wagons.

Friday, 9 June 1916 [from billets in Annezin, western suburb of Béthune]

My darling Lil,

I simply could not write last night, I was so tired.

We are back in real billets beyond the old town and I am jolly glad. I feel I want some good nights in bed.

I thought the snapshots very good, especially the one of Jim sitting up.

I am off to bed.

Saturday, 10 June 1916 [from billets in Annezin]

For the first time for a long time I have got leisure to write a long letter. We did not get to billets till 2am last night but I had a very good sleep.

---

1 16th battalion, King's Royal Rifle corps, raised in Buckinghamshire in September 1914 by Field Marshal Lord Grenfell, commandant of the Church Lads' Brigade.

I had just finished orderly room when the General arrived. I went for a ride with him. Everyone is convinced that the situation is never better – the Russians advancing in great style against the Austrians – the German Fleet coming out is looked upon as the best sign that they are desperate. There can be no doubt that the internal state of Germany is getting daily worse. I quite believe now that the war will be over this year.

I am going to try and get a motor to go over and see RO and Harriette.

With all my fondest love and heaps of kisses to Jim and Eileen.

Sunday, 11 June 1916 [from billets in Annezin]

I got up in a furious temper as I had a message that I had to meet the Divisional General early. As Sunday is only a Sunday for us about once in three months I did not appreciate it – however he said some flattering things about the regiment. And I went for a ride.

I had a sleep in the afternoon – about the first I have had in the war. I feel quite fit again now, but my left eye is not quite right.

I think you are quite right to take the house on for a month and it would be splendid if you could get Brabazon Lodge.[1]

There is nothing, dear, that I want for my birthday. I have everything now that I have my pencil and my watch. It is awful to think that I shall be 43. On Tuesday I shall have commanded the regiment for a year and been out a year and 10 months. I have been very lucky. I am the only officer left out of the whole Brigade who has served continuously and never been away.

Monday, 12 June 1916 [from billets in Annezin]

It has been a miserable, cold, rainy day – quite depressing. I rode in to see the General and then went for a ride alone. In the afternoon I went for a walk with the doctor.

We are going to have a concert. I feel very hurt that I have not been asked to sing.

Tell nurse that I think it is time that Jim started to learn some drill.

---

1 A house near Sunningdale.

Tuesday, 13 June 1916 [from billets in Annezin]

A year and ten months since we left Glasgow and a year since I got command today – long time.

Major H went off to command his terrier bn.[1] today. I think he was sorry to go – the war is beginning to tell on him.

I went to a memorial service to Lord Kitchener at 11am. It was very impressive – they finished up with the 'Dead March' in *Saul* and sounded the 'Last Post' on the bugles.

It continues to be miserably wet and cold – quite depressing weather.

Wednesday, 14 June 1916 [from billets in Annezin]

It has rained a little less today. I went for a ride alone this afternoon. This evening our pipes and drums have been playing. Tonight I am dining with the General to celebrate the anniversary of his command of the Brigade.

I heard from RO today. He said he had not seen the honours list before and wrote to congratulate me. His Brigadier has been wounded. He was relieved by Harriette's band of heroes.

No, I see no sign of what we want coming yet.

Thursday, 15 June 1916 [from billets in Annezin]

I hope the rumour that there are to be no posts is not true – our chief pleasure will be done away with.

It has been fine today and very pleasant. I went for a ride with the padre through a very nice wood. I am very pleased Major Hyde-Smith has come to be 2nd in command – it is not settled for certain. I like him very much. He was my subaltern and knows my ways, and those of the regiment.

Tonight we had dinner early as we had a concert. It was quite good but lasted too long.

Saturday, 17 June 1916 [from billets in Annezin]

We were inspected by the Corps Commander today. He was very complimentary

---

1 One of the battalions of the Gloucestershire Regiment.

– said that our raid was a very good show and that the battalion was a very fine one and well turned out. He also said I would get a Brigade very shortly, whatever that means. If I do get one I will wire you a number which will be the number of the Brigade and will mean that I have got a Brigade. You can then address my letters Headquarters, __ Brigade, BEF.

You will be sorry to hear that Major Hardinge has been very badly wounded in the stomach. I saw him in the hospital – the doctors say he has a chance. I am very sorry – he is a splendid soldier.

I am glad you have taken Brabazon Lodge and are settled. I certainly hope that I shall play golf with you soon. I am glad that Jim has taken to Nancy and that Eileen progresses.

We are moving billets today. I like the ones we are going to.

Sunday, 18 June 1916 [from billets in Le Quesnoy, near the front line]

Major Hardinge died from his wounds. I am very sorry. I went to his funeral today with Major Hyde-Smith. You will be sorry to hear that Major Purvis of the 93rd[1] was killed by a chance shot – he was only married a few months ago.

Today is Waterloo day.

I am surprised at Willie resigning and suppose he will go back to his business.

I am very glad to have Major Hyde-Smith back – he is a companion, which Major H never was.

I wish Jim would commence to walk by himself.

Is Eileen's new hair coming in?

Monday, 19 June 1916 [from billets in Le Quesnoy]

I had a ride on business this morning, which passed the whole morning. In the afternoon I rode over to see Col D. The weather has turned cold and threatening again. After tomorrow I shall not be able to write these long and interesting epistles again.

I shall be quite sorry to leave this billet – a large but unfurnished chateau, but the garden is quite nice.

---

1 2nd Argyll & Sutherland Highlanders.

Tuesday, 20 June 1916 [from support trenches in Givenchy-lès-la-Bassée, north of Cuinchy]

We – that is, the Division – had a horseshow today, rather a good show. It goes on tomorrow. My mare is in for the jumping – I wish I could ride her but dare not on account of my riding muscle. We moved out of our nice chateau today.[1]

Wednesday, 21 June 1916 [from support trenches in Givenchy]

I got two letters from you today to make up for two blank days.

My charger won the jumping today, ridden by Capt Leighton.[2] I enclose the rosette. What day do you move to Brabazon Lodge? Or rather take it from?

Thursday, 22 June 1916 [from support trenches in Givenchy]

Just a line to say that all is well. I have been up all last night so cannot write much.

Friday, 23 June 1916 [from support trenches in Givenchy]

We have had a catastrophe with the lamp, so have only a candle to write by.

The letter I should have got yesterday I received today – the posts are very irregular.

No, I like Eileen – not with an H.

I am very sorry that your mother has been ill, and also that Edith will not be able to go south.

I hope Eileen is not getting ill gaining so little – but I suppose she cannot keep up with her former gains. Poor Jim has had a bad time with his teeth. I have no more news of what we both want and have put it out of my mind.

Saturday, 24 June 1916 [from support trenches in Givenchy]

There is no post again today – most days are blank now.

I am very fit and well.

It is impossible to write anything. We are having a very quiet time.

---

1 To trenches in the Givenchy sector.
2 Capt C. D. F. Leighton joined in March 1916 as a lieutenant.

Sunday, 25 June 1916 [from support trenches in Givenchy]

I was delighted to get three letters from you today to make up for the blanks. I am very sorry that you are still having trouble with your eyes – you had better see the Dr.

I am glad also that Jim has started to walk.

Poor Mabel – I wish her operation was safely over.

I had a letter from Connie tonight. She wrote to Ascot but the letter was returned to her. She enclosed the receipt for the £200. She was very anxious to hear about Jim and the baby, which she had not heard about before.

Monday, 26 June 1916 [from front-line trenches on La Bassée canal]

I shall not be able to write much for the next week – it is nearly 2am so I am not in good form for writing.

I had a note from Harriette, who said that he had had a shell through his room, and also a long, rambling letter from Mrs Vandeleur, who threatened to write to you.

Wednesday, 28 June 1916 [from front-line trenches on La Bassée canal]

I could not write last night. We had a disturbed night and I was so tired I went straight to bed. I was glad to get two letters from you today. I hope your eye is better but you do not say so.

We have got splendid roses in the garden and our cellar – which is the best in France – looks very nice.

Thursday, 29 June 1916 [from front-line trenches on La Bassée canal]

I got a letter from you today. I was surprised as I had three yesterday. It is 2am and I am very tired as usual.

We have had a good deal of rain, which makes things unpleasant.

Yes, I hope that I shall be able to see Brabazon Lodge in August, but still more you and the children.

Saturday, 1 July 1916 [from front-line trenches on La Bassée canal]
I have dated this the 1ˢᵗ as it is my birthday – it is now 2am. I should ordinarily
have dated it the 30ᵗʰ so as to keep the sequence of dates.

I got the two pipes – they are just what I like. Thank Jim and Eileen. It
was very good of them to think of pipes.

There is absolutely no news. I should like to sleep for a month.

Sunday, 2 July 1916 [from support trenches in Givenchy]
Just a line to say I am very well but I am very tired and just off to bed. We
have had a fairly trying time.

I had a blackcurrant tart today!

I had a weird letter from Mrs Van addressed to me but apparently intended
for you.

Monday, 3 July 1916 [from support trenches in Givenchy]
I do hope Mabel is better – fainting sounds bad and also the Dr getting another
nurse.

I should love a snapshot of Jim walking by himself. I heard from Lindsay[1]
– he said the children were very flourishing. I think it was very rude of him
to say that you looked haggard, even if he thought so – I hope it is not true.

These are exciting times.[2] We get our news from the papers at home – we
seem to be progressing favourably. I want to see the Russians get busy with
the Germans.

I went straight to bed after I had written last night and slept like a log, but
still feel very sleepy. I reckon that Nature owes me about six months' sleep.

I saw an aeroplane shot down today – the first I have seen in the war. One
of our own, unfortunately. I have seen thousands of rounds fired at them but
never seen one hit before.

---

1 His brother, Lindsay Chaplin.
2 The Somme offensive started at the beginning of July.

Tuesday, 4 July 1916 [from support trenches in Givenchy]

I rode in today to the big town to go to the funeral of Col Douglas. It rained hard and I got very wet. I am very sorry that he was killed – he was a nice man and very cheerful.

The news is still good about our operations.

I hope that Sandy will come through alright.

I want to hear that the Russians are setting about the Germans in the East – also that Romania has come in, which ought to finish Austria.

Thursday, 6 July 1916 [from support trenches in Givenchy]

I could not write last night. I should be able to write a long letter tonight but I am very tired, having had very little sleep last night.

I shall probably not be able to write much after tomorrow for some time.

I am very glad to hear that Mabel is going on alright.

Everything seems to be going on well everywhere.

With all my fondest love and heaps of kisses to the children. For ever your loving husband, Graham

THE SOMME

'It was the losses which remain a blow to me . . .'

Allied forces attack on the Somme in largest assault of the war – British losses top 58,000 on first day – German commander-in-chief replaced after reverses – British fight successive actions at Albert, Bazentin Ridge, Fromelles, Delville Wood, Pozières Ridge, Guillemont, Ginchy, Flers and Morval – tanks used for first time by British army

Orders arrive on the evening of 5 July telling Graham Chaplin to ready his battalion for departure in twenty-four hours – destination unknown. He will have a fair idea. The slow build-up of forces and training of troops before 1916's big push has been evident since Easter. The division is awash with gossip as to who is where and what is planned. By 24 June and the beginning of the six-day onslaught of shelling that precedes the British attack on the Somme, everyone knows. Spirits are up, hopes are high, and if this is to be the moment the British army punches through the German lines, every soldier wants to be there.

So much has to be prepared and packed. The battalion – nearly 1,000 strong again after the arrival of new drafts – has been on the Loos front for almost a year. It will now need to pack up and transport cookers, supplies, ammunition, horses and more, fitting in with a detailed logistics plan drawn up by staff officers shifting divisions across clogged railway networks and through exhausted billeting villages. At battalion level, Chaplin has his own team of HQ officers to coordinate the move: a number two – Major Hyde-Smith – to share the planning, an adjutant – Lieutenant Gordon – to work out the detail, a transport officer to organise horses and wagons, a quartermaster and his unit to oversee sourcing of supplies, a medical officer and his orderlies to maintain the health of the men, and HQ clerks to process the paperwork. Most are soldiers he can trust, and they are operating beside familiar battalions in a brigade with many familiar faces, not least his own brigadier, and within a division in which he is already one of the senior colonels. Chaplin is known as a commanding officer who has been at the war since the beginning – and the number of those is beginning to thin rapidly. If there are doubts over his single-mindedness at Loos, the Cams' successes holding the line facing Auchy will have helped to dispel them, and a new fight on a fresh battlefield offers him another opportunity for redemption.

On Friday, 7 July, the Cams are pulled out of the Givenchy line and march to Oblinghem to organise themselves, pulling in supplies and reconnecting with transport and cookers, before marching around Béthune to the railway junction at Fouquereuil. There, they board long trains for the slow journey through undisturbed countryside to beautiful old Amiens, fifty miles to the south, a bustling textile town fattened by trade, departmental capital of the Somme. The train pulls in late on Saturday evening. By now the battle to the east has raged for eight days, but inside Amiens, all is quiet. Without so much as a moment to take in the town's famed thirteenth-century cathedral – its gargoyled walls sandbagged against bombardment – the Cams leave the main station at midnight, wheel right and march north on the long straight boulevard that once marked Amiens' eastern walls. Chaplin rides in front of his men as they step quietly through the empty streets, over the river and out into the countryside. They are heading for Poulainville, a farming village five miles to the north, which offers barely a welcome. 'Very bad billets, but weather luckily fine,' he writes in the War Diary. The region has seen so many men pushed through so many places, as the British army replaces the French in the front line here, that local villages reel under the onslaught of accommodating so many, jamming the roads, churning the fields, digging mass latrines. The fees paid, set by the French government, please neither side.

For Chaplin, heading towards the slaughter of the battlefield, reading Lil's letters as she recounts how she has finally moved into Brabazon Lodge – the Surrey home she has looked to rent for months – there may have been ironies. How she will furnish it, who she will see, what she will do with the children, how she will pay for it all. She is already paying the premiums on the life assurance he took out before marrying. All the major life assurance companies have agreed to waive the exemption for death in war as a patriotic gesture. Alongside the letters that Lil now tucks together in a box, each one maybe the last, are the receipts for premiums paid in Edinburgh on her visits back to the Alexander family home.

They will console Chaplin that he has done his best. Late at night he can see flashes of shellfire light up the summer sky as his battalion nears the Somme front. It will only remind him that he is now even further away from home.

Sunday, 9 July 1916 [from billets in Poulainville, north of Amiens]
My own darling,

I have not been able to write for two days – we have hardly been to bed and have had a hard time.

I was awfully glad to get your letter of the 4th. I wish I could see Brabazon Lodge – the carpets sound very nice. It will be a very tiring journey rushing up to Brentham and back. I am awfully glad that Mabel is getting on alright.

I had a very nice letter from Major Hardinge's father in reply to mine.

We had a long train journey, passing through very pleasant country – all pleased to get a change of scenery. One station we halted at, General C-C[1] and young Stirling were in the train going the other way. They were both very well – it was curious meeting like that.

We are quite close to Sandy.[2] I hope he is alright, if so we may see him.

You must not be anxious – we have always had good luck and it may continue.

Monday, 10 July 1916 [from billets in Poulainville]
I slept till pretty late today. The Brigade staff came this morning and the General came to see me. I rode to our new big town[3] – very pleasant, I rode straight back to find that we were to move at once – but it was only a false alarm.

---

1 Carter-Campbell.
2 Colonel Vincent Sandilands, 2nd Scottish Rifles.
3 Amiens.

We are going to have a tremendous dinner tonight – the padre has bought all sorts of luxuries, including a lobster. Everything seems to be going very well as far as one can hear.

Tuesday, 11 July 1916 [from billets in Daours, east of Amiens]

We had a very pleasant march today – very early. I was awakened at 2.30am. After I got in I had a sleep.

We are very anxious about Sandy's battalion. We can get no news but plenty of rumours. Reggie[1] must be in this part somewhere – I may see him.

I hope to be able to write a letter tomorrow and after that I expect my literary efforts will only be pcs.

Wednesday, 12 July 1916 [from billets in Buire-sur-l'Ancre, outside Albert, east of Amiens]

We had quite a pleasant march today. I am extraordinarily well, but one feels tired with all this hustling.

Our Corps commander is one of our old Divisional commanders[2] – he was awfully nice when we saw him today. We feel we are amongst friends again.

You will be pleased, I know, to know that I am not to go into this show,[3] so there will be nothing for you to worry about.

Thursday, 13 July 1916 [from billets in Buire-sur-l'Ancre]

The General[4] has got a division and left today, so we have a new General.[5]

General Gore and Major RW[6] came to see us today – every day one sees someone.

Everybody is very pleased the way things are going. With all my fondest

---

1 Reginald Swalwell, married to Mabel.

2 General Henry Horne, commander of XV corps, formerly commanded 2nd division.

3 Chaplin is held back as a reserve brigadier, to cover for officer casualties.

4 Brigadier General Philip Robertson, former CO of 1st Cameronians, becomes GOC 17th division.

5 Brigadier General Mayne takes over 19th brigade.

6 Riddell-Webster.

love and heaps of kisses to you and Jim and Eileen. For ever your loving husband, Graham

*   *   *

Everything changes for Chaplin before his men even see battle. Sitting in billets in the tiny village of Buire-sur-l'Ancre, south-west of Albert, ten miles from the front line, he is summoned by Robertson to be told that his old friend is leaving, promoted to command of the 17th division, a New Army division of Kitchener recruits drawn mainly from the north of England. Replacing Robertson as commander of 19th brigade is Brigadier General Charles Mayne, Highland Light Infantry, a veteran of the Egyptian army and, at forty-one, two years younger than Chaplin.

If being passed over for the post hurts, Chaplin does not show it. To promote consecutive Cameronian commanders to take charge of a brigade containing their own battalion would be awkward. Better a fresh start in another place. And Mayne, imposingly tall at over six feet but soft faced and genial, is a hard man to dislike.[117] But if reporting to a younger superior is not bad enough, Chaplin is immediately told he must leave his battalion and join 33rd division HQ for the next week – part of a new policy of holding experienced officers and men in reserve to replace casualties. One lesson from the first fortnight's fighting on the Somme has been quickly learnt. Too often men have been left leaderless and battalions stripped of veterans around which to rebuild their strength after the losses suffered in the initial fighting. So Chaplin is held as reserve brigadier, to replace any of the brigade commanders who might suffer injury, and to oversee the replenishing of the Cameronians when they return. Others are kept back as 'battle surplus'.

For a man proud to lead his own battalion, in which he has served for over two decades, it is agony. However reassured he is by the implied approval that goes with the tag of reserve brigadier, a commander wants to be with his men, not kicking his heels. Instead, he must hand over to Major Hyde-Smith and sit, waiting for reports, while his number two leads the Cams into the fraught battle for High Wood, their first taste of action on the Somme. It is not what he had envisaged.

The Cameronians are joining a battlefield already churned by a fortnight of fighting, with the British army's July push juddering to a halt against the Germans' formidable defences. Now it has become a campaign of slow, bloody struggle, taking a field here, a wood there, trying to amass small gains that, added together, will give a decisive strategic advantage. But at each point along the line, British forces find the Germans too well prepared, with deeper bunkers, widely spaced support lines and well-fortified strongpoints. The British response is to keep throwing men at the problem.

The 33rd division is detailed to relieve the 21st beyond Mametz, perched east of Albert, where a clutch of woods that define the Somme landscape has proved difficult to clear. Surrounded by wide wheat fields, the woods – left for hunting, or wind cover, or simply because farmers had ploughable land enough – squat like fortresses, darkly mysterious and often occupying the highest ground. Beyond Mametz, they offer invaluable protection for defenders in front of a heavily defended German trench called the Switch.

The Cams join the fighting by degrees. On Friday, 14 July, they bivouac outside the village of Méaulte, due south of Albert, already under shellfire. On Saturday, they march in platoons to camp at Mametz Wood. Here, they find a scene that no amount of trench warfare at Cuinchy could have prepared them for: dead bodies pushed beside roads, broken wagons littering the fields, artillery batteries, drawn up in tight ranks, firing continuously, creating constant, ear-splitting noise – both sides remain determined to bombard the other into submission. Sleep is impossible. Men crouch in shell-holes or behind banks of earth – trying not to breathe in the fumes from German tear-gas shells – counting the hours, counting the minutes, with evidence all around of what awaits them.

At 1 a.m. on Sunday, 16 July, the battalion is given orders to take up position manning trenches, hastily dug, two miles to the north-east, in front of High Wood, a twisted square of shell-blasted tree trunks and dense vegetation that rests on a ridge, bounded by open fields, and blocks the advance on the German-held town of Bapaume, a key target. The seventy-five acres of High Wood have already seen fierce fighting and an ill-advised cavalry charge by the British, who took heavy losses. Each time the enemy is driven back towards the north of the chestnut wood, the ground proves impossible to hold, as machine-gun fire and shelling turn the area into a killing zone.

The Cameronians make an uneasy entry, relieving the Glasgow Highlanders who send guides to show them in, promptly leading C Company in front of a German machine-gun post, which mows down forty-nine men – three killed, forty-six wounded. Once in new, shallow trenches, they sit and hold position, waiting for orders. But planning is chaotic as corps and divisional headquarters try to react to a battlefield changing hour by hour, stretched over many miles. By Sunday afternoon, the Cams have been ordered to a new position, in trenches near Bazentin, where they wait till Tuesday, under constant shellfire, losing another sixty-six men killed or wounded, before being moved back to trenches at Mametz Wood on Wednesday, again under continuous fire. At 7 p.m. they are told they will attack High Wood before dawn. They set off at midnight. The War Diary says, simply, 'No sleep.'

They attack at 2 a.m. under cover of a rolling artillery barrage, with the 5th Scottish Rifles attacking on the right and the 20th Royal Fusiliers in support. A true account of the next twenty-four hours is hard to find. The Cameronians' War Diary, written by Hyde-Smith, describes the battalion pinned down by shelling, then reinforced by the 2nd Royal Welch, who help to capture virtually all the wood. Others tell a different story, of loss of officers, panic in the RF ranks, a rush out of the wood by assorted RF, Cameronian and Scottish Rifle ranks who are calmly gathered by Father McShane, the RC padre, and sent back into the battle.[118] The Cameronians take heavy casualties as the German defenders fight hand to hand for each square foot of woodland – the natural dips and dells, the shell-pocked ground, the blasted trunks and scattered trees, all in full leaf, providing easy defensive cover, slowing any advance and disorienting the men. Communication is impossible, groups get stranded, soldiers lose their bearings – unable to tell north from south, friend from foe. Leadership disappears as, one by one, company commanders are killed or wounded. By the time the Cams withdraw, relieved by battalions of the Queen's and the King's Royal Rifle Corps regiments, they have lost 382 men – 57 killed, including 5 officers; 161 missing, including 4 officers; and 164 wounded, including 4 officers. In three days, Chaplin has lost more than a third of his men and more than half his officers – and they were not even under his command.

At first, he sends Lil postcards – 'quite well' – then letters again from the 33rd division HQ. He is rested but worried, 'sick of doing nothing' and 'anxious the whole time about the regiment'. He has seen hundreds of German prisoners, but even before the fighting, his officers are cracking with the strain: 'Poor Mr Gordon[119] the adjutant has broken down. I was afraid he would – he was badly wounded in '14. He has been very plucky sticking it out so long.'[120]

Chaplin has scant idea of how the battle progresses for his men, or more widely, as news filters back to divisional HQ, two miles from the front, so slowly – even 19th brigade HQ cannot actually see the battle. He knows the gains are small, the casualties high, but staff officers remain determined. He can also see at first hand the pressure applied on division from corps, as each link in the chain of command is placed under stress. Above every battalion commander is a stack of top brass, of very different character – Chaplin reports to Mayne (19th brigade), who reports to Major-General Landon (33rd), who reports to Lieutenant General Horne (XV Corps), who reports to General Rawlinson (Fourth Army), who reports to Field Marshal Haig, commander-in-chief. Each tier sits further back from the front, overseeing more men and a wider area of campaign. Each has a point to prove to his superior. Even Haig is answerable to the British government.

And so, as the battle on the Somme sinks into stalemate, blame is allocated. Within XV Corps, Horne has already started removing divisional commanders who have failed to reach objectives. Pressure is pushed downwards to show gains. Chaplin will be fully aware of the orders issued to Mayne to take High Wood at all costs. Landon's senior staff officer (GSO1) sends a message to the 19th-brigade commander before the artillery bombardment that precedes the Cameronian attack: 'The Major-General wishes me to point out again the urgency to press right on in the rear of the barrage, even at the risk of losing a few men from our own fire.'[121]

Those men are Chaplin's soldiers. He can only sit tight and wait, watching the staff officers work. The GSO2 of the same division is a young major – already wounded, recuperated and back in action – from the Royal Warwickshire regiment, called Bernard Montgomery. What he witnesses will influence his military career for the rest of his life.[122]

Chaplin will know some of those already involved in the battle for High Wood. Sam Darling's Glasgow Highlanders have suffered severe losses on the same ground, before the 19th brigade is sent in. But even at divisional level, a full overview is unclear, and without seeing the ground, with its shattered villages in dells and deadly copses on ridges, he can only piece together a fractured narrative: 'We get all our news from the English papers, so we do not know as soon as you do what is going on.'[123]

By 22 July his sojourn at 33rd HQ is over, and the 19th brigade is withdrawn from the front line to recuperate. Landon has told Horne, the XV Corps commander, that the 33rd division will need a fortnight to rebuild strength before returning to the line. It has lost over 5,000 men. Horne is asked to explain why the division failed to take High Wood.

Chaplin returns to his shattered battalion, back in its old billet at Buire-sur-l'Ancre, and prepares himself for the reckoning. There, the surviving Cameronians will parade in front of their seemingly imperturbable colonel while the roll call is read. Those dead and missing are established, witness accounts requested for how they met their end.[124] Officers will later divvy up who writes to which mother, which wife. For any commander, it is a difficult business, when he must show steely resolve to his men, whatever his real feelings, and commend the survivors on their bravery – doubly piquant when he was forcibly pulled away from them before the fight.

In any unit that has seen heavy casualties, the practice is now established of restocking and retraining around the core that remains, so the Cameronians prepare to receive large drafts of new recruits: 129 on Sunday, 23 July; 46 on Monday; 170 on Tuesday. Many come from reserve battalions of other regiments, not always Scottish. Chaplin's War Diary notes morosely, 'no officers'. All four of his company commanders have been killed or declared missing. The war is gobbling up men, with rank no protection in the front line. An estimated 15,000 officers have lost their lives already. He must promote from the non-commissioned ranks, and train the new force relentlessly. He is in a different army now, where discipline is more lax and parade-ground drill a mystery to many new recruits.

For an experienced soldier of the old army, like Chaplin, brought up with a comforting system of rigidly observed hierarchies, prompt saluting, infallible smartness and a variety of punishments inflicted for the slightest step out of line, it is a new world to which he must adapt. Rumour spreads that senior staff now want to break down the demarcation between the old regiments – the esprit de corps that comes with singular traditions and established customs – so that all soldiers fit easily into any unit. The result is many men arriving resentful and demotivated, wishing they had been posted to battalions linked to their home towns or counties. The official War Diary carries Chaplin's concerns: the new drafts are 'very backward, many of them hardly knowing how to handle their arms'; he has only ten officers, stretched between four companies, to oversee it all. The battalion which sailed to France had more than twice that, at least five officers per company of 200 men, and more in HQ.

The old soldiers, especially those who had spent their formative years in India, where the traditions and habits of the British army were most deeply engrained, find it unconscionable that men can be thrown into battle with so little discipline and so little preparation. But the war has reached a new stage, where individuals blur into numbers, where the churn among incomers brutalises the survivors, where all participants build their own emotional defences against the carnage they are witnessing. So reluctant are some of the new drafts to fight that rumours are already circulating of officers in other regiments shooting men in the trenches who refuse to go over the top.

The battalion stays in Buire-sur-l'Ancre for a fortnight, then moves back towards the front, bivouacking at Bécordel. The 19th brigade remains in reserve, behind the 100th and the 98th, working fatigues, training with the bayonet, the bomb and the Lewis gun. Chaplin's letters shorten, and are frequently replaced by postcards. He passes on the gossip: Hammy has lost his leg in the fighting, Robertson likes his division, a new doctor arrives as medical officer – 'a nice little fellow named O'Grady, very Irish'.[125]

By 5 August Chaplin has caught the stomach bug now sweeping the front line – 'I have been very seedy' – as the heat on the unburied corpses in no-man's land attracts clouds of flies that then cover cookware, eating utensils and drinking vessels. Once he recovers, old associates visit – Minchin, one of his lieutenants in A Company, now a pilot, and Hunter, 2nd Scottish Rifles, wounded at Aubers Ridge in 1915. He comments on the weather, he passes on his love to Lil's sister, Mabel, who has been ill too, he admires the photographs of Brabazon Lodge which his wife sends, but the letters are short, his thoughts jotted down as disconnected fragments or terse answers. The pressure of preparing his men for a return to the front is intense.

There is no hint that High Wood has tarnished the battalion's reputation – quite the reverse. 'This business has been a blow to me,' he writes of the losses suffered, but he is adamant 'the regiment did splendidly'.[126] Amid so much chaos, he is determined to press on.

Lil, however, has noticed his letters dropping away, the use of field-service postcards increasing, with their impersonal tick-box messages. She is worried, and lets him know. He responds bluntly.

Wednesday, 9 August 1916 [from billets near Bécordel-Bécourt, five miles east of Buire]

My own darling,

Your letter today rather hurt me. You might be sure that if the circumstances permitted I should always write and I never cease to think of you all. It was the losses which were a blow to me and as we expected to go back any day after four days you can imagine that there was a good deal to do.

Col Jenney,[1] who left the regiment 12 years ago, came to see me. He is

---

1 Lieutenant Colonel A. O. Jenney.

commanding a territorial battalion – I think it is Willie's battalion. He was very fit. I had not seen him for 13 years or so.

It was a blow to me not being in the fight. It was much more anxious work sitting behind.

I do not think I shall have a hair left – it is all coming out. Fortunately my teeth are giving no trouble. I suppose by the time this arrives it will be the second anniversary of leaving Glasgow. What an age it seems. I have never had a single day off yet except leave home.

Perhaps we shall have all this separation made up to us by a good time after the war.

PS: Please send some toilet paper – we cannot get it here.

Thursday, 10 August 1916 [from billets near Bécordel-Bécourt]

Fortunately we have had some rain which has laid the dust and cooled the air. I feel quite fit again and my interior is alright.

I do not know where Reggie has gone to, but I suppose he is out of this.

No, there is no truth of course in my having a Brigade. I would wire to you if I had.

Friday, 11 August 1916 [from billets near Bécordel-Bécourt]

No news. We are still in bivouac. No exercise, which is rather trying, but the weather has been more bearable.

I have played bridge the last two nights with Major HS, the padre and the transport officer.

Sunday, 13 August 1916 [from billets near Bécordel-Bécourt]

Yes – yesterday was the third anniversary of our fortunate meeting – at least it was fortunate for me, but these two years have made it seem years ago.

I wish, dear, that I could send Jim a flag but there is nothing to make one out of in these wilds.

Many happy returns of the 15th. I want to give you an evening gown as a birthday present, so I wish you would go and order one and pay for it out of my account.

Tuesday, 15 August 1916 [from billets near Bécordel-Bécourt]

I hope you have had a happy birthday.

The Russians are getting on splendidly, also the Italians. I should think Austria will soon have the sense to give in.

Col D dined with us last night to commemorate the completion of two years in France.

Major RW also came to see us – he is very flourishing.

I am glad to see that Ronnie MacAllan[1] is in Switzerland, so I suppose that Mrs Ronnie has now joined him.

I had a letter from RO – he is still in the same place.

With all my fondest love and heaps of kisses to you all. For ever your loving husband, Graham

Wednesday, 16 August 1916 [FSPC]

I am quite well.

*   *   *

Nine more field-service postcards follow.

Extracts from the battalion War Diary,
August 1916,

Kept by Colonel Graham Chaplin


```
In bivouac near Bécordel-Bécourt, held as reserve
brigade
15 August - Five second lieutenants arrived from 2nd Bn.

16 August - Large fatigue parties.
```

---

1 Taken prisoner in 1914, released in 1916.

17 August - Five second lieutenants arrive from 10ᵗʰ Bn.

18 August - Bn ordered to be in instant readiness to move
after 2pm in connection with an attack on German line at
2.45pm. Fell in at 7.30pm and marched to Mametz Wood. Only 20
officers went up with Bn, remainder being left with transport
near Fricourt. Casualties: killed 4 OR, wounded 4 OR.

19 August - At 12.30am the Bn moved up to relieve the 4ᵗʰ
King's (98ᵗʰ Brigade) who were believed to have taken part of
Wood Lane from the Germans. The relief was complete by 5am.
It was found on arrival that the 4ᵗʰ Kings were back in their
original trenches. The attack of 98ᵗʰ Brigade appears to have
completely failed but divisions on the right and left are said
to have done well. The 2ⁿᵈ RWF and 5ᵗʰ Scottish Rifles took over
the line on our right and left respectively. At 2pm the Bn was
withdrawn to near Bazentin, their line being taken over by the
5ᵗʰ Scottish Rifles. Casualties: killed 1 OR, wounded 17 OR.

20 August - Remained in support. Casualties: killed 1 OR,
wounded 7 OR.

21 August - Remained in support. Casualties: wounded 6 OR.

High Wood
22 August - At 6am the Bn begins to move up to High Wood by
companies taking over trenches there from the 2ⁿᵈ RWF. The 20ᵗʰ
Royal Fusiliers took over the line on our right. Casualties:
killed 1 OR, wounded 7 OR.

23 August - Heavy shelling of the front trenches otherwise a
comparatively quiet day. Casualties: wounded 2Lt J M Miller,
killed 1 OR, wounded 7 OR.

24 August - An attack was made all along the line at 6pm.
The Bn however remained holding the trenches in High Wood.
The 100th Brigade on our right took some trenches. Casualties:
killed 2Lt J H MacRae, wounded 7 OR.

25 August - Remained in High Wood.

26 August - Moved back to Brigade Support at Crucifix Corner,
Bazentin. Heavy rain storms during the day.

27 August - In the evening moved back to Pommier Redoubt in
support of 98th Brigade. A miserable place, no shelter for
officers or men.

28 August - Fatigue party to front line at night.

29 August - Marched to Fricourt Wood at 7am. An unlucky shell
fell in on trench occupied by the sapping platoon. Casualties:
1 killed, 2 wounded.

30 August - Rain all day, everyone got very wet and miserable.

31 August - At 8am the Bn paraded and marched to Ribemont. The
division being relieved by the 24th Division.

High Wood is not done with the Cameronians yet. For a month, the British
army throws brigade after brigade at the ill-fated woodland on the Bazentin
Ridge. Trenches are dug, strongpoints fortified, routes of supply hacked
through the shell-blasted undergrowth, but still the British cannot shift
their enemy from the final corner where the German trench line defies all
attempts at breaching, at encircling, at bombarding into submission. No

alternative is mooted, no argument is broached; pushing on and through is the only British strategy.

By the evening of 18 August, the Cams are back at Mametz Wood, west of High Wood, ready to support another attack – they lose four men to shelling before they even get near the front line. By midnight they are moving up 'Death Valley' towards the infernal chestnut woodland, where they must relieve the 4th King's in trenches near Wood Lane, the heavily defended country road that runs from the village of Longueval to High Wood's southern corner.

Chaplin will be seeing this for the first time, like the new men who only recently joined his battalion. Yet the area is already unrecognisable to veterans of the fighting just weeks ago. The fields are criss-crossed with diggings, one deep communication trench runs directly to the wood, bodies and debris still remain uncleared and, ahead of them, up on the ridge, the woodland itself has gone, now a smoking ruin of stumps and blown branches, criss-crossed again with more trenches, many with parapets built of mud and corpses. Piling the bodies in front and throwing the dug earth over is the best protection soldiers can find for hasty trenching in a barrage.

For Haig and Rawlinson, studying their maps of the campaign at the Fourth Army's HQ in Queirreu, seventeen miles to the west, plotting the moves of the 400,000 men in the sector, the capture of High Wood has attained a high value – it blocks advance, its occupation offering the enemy unparalleled sight lines over the countryside left and right. But the Germans are so well dug in, so well defended and led, that it seems impossible to push them out, except by repeated, brutal attack.

The 98th brigade – 1st Middlesex, 2nd Argylls, 4th King's and 1/4th Suffolk – are thrown at High Wood, armed with any number of new-fangled devices aimed to give them the upper hand: flame throwers to burn out the enemy, 'pipe pushers' (literally, explosive pushed in a pipe) to explode new saps at right angles to the front line, oil-drum projectors to send over vast, fiery bombs. None proves effective. More are killed in the deadly artillery barrage both sides inflict on the wood. So it goes on. By the time the 19th is sent in to replace the 98th, it is a scene of corpse-strewn devastation with no gains made.

Chaplin's men must sit and hold the position, the 2nd Royal Welch to the right, the 5th Scottish Rifles to the left, waiting for orders. Then, a day later, they are pulled back to sit under shellfire in support, leaving the battalions beside them to fill the gap left. If ever there was a clear indication that high command had run out of ideas, this restless shifting, one day in, one day out, offers a suggestion. Communication with brigade HQ is haphazard, the chaos on the battlefield recurrent. Every battalion in the 19th has noted that the new brigadier is not as often seen in the front line as his predecessor.[127] But then his predecessor was not fighting on the Somme. And the pressure from the top on the 33rd division to show progress can now be felt by those who directly face the enemy – patrols and raids are constantly requested, as if no amount of information is sufficient.

For a veteran like Chaplin, already showing signs of disillusion with the way the army is conducting this campaign, it must have been close to demoralising. As a commander, there are few with whom he can discuss his views – perhaps old friends like Sam Darling, fighting in the same division on the same front with his Glasgow Highlanders. But junior officers must never know. And as his letters are read by censors, so it would be unwise to share his opinions in writing.

He loses more men to shelling while the Cams wait in support, then, on 22 August, they return to the front line at High Wood, replacing the Royal Welch. The 20th Royal Fusiliers take a position on their right, a move which will make the old hands nervous, wondering if the 'chocolate soldiers' will hold their ground should the Germans attack. The 19th brigade's role is simply to stay fast in the wood, while the 100th brigade prepares for a frontal attack on a position to the east. Heavy shelling continues all day on the 23 and 24 August. Then, at 6 p.m., supported by a continuous concentration of machine-gun fire, the 1st Queen's, the 16th King's Royal Rifles and the 2nd Worcesters go over the top, with Sam Darling's Glasgow Highlanders held in support. Their objectives, German trenches to the east of High Wood, are taken. But the enemy still holds the north-east corner of the wood itself, and still proves immovable.

The Cams remain in High Wood until 26 August, when they are ordered back to Bazentin, as the weather breaks and summer storms lash the countryside. Then they are pulled further back, as the 33rd division is replaced by the 24th division, and Chaplin stands in for Mayne, as his brigadier goes on leave, less than two months after taking over the 19th brigade. Perhaps Mayne is still pondering the congratulatory telegram sent by General Rawlinson to the 33rd division, which specifically singled out for praise the 100th's brigadier general, Baird. 'Please convey to the 33rd division and especially to General Baird the Army Commander's congratulations on their performance . . .'[128]

If Rawlinson is happy with the 33rd, he has a strange way of showing it. He relieves Landon of his command, moving him over to the 35th division of 'bantam' – under-height – soldiers, while bringing in its commander, the teetotal, devoutly religious Major-General Reginald Pinney. It is Pinney who Siegfried Sassoon, serving with the Royal Welch, later immortalises in his poem 'The General' as a 'cheery old card' who 'did for' his men with his plan of attack at Arras. But that is to come. It will take the British army another month to clear High Wood. Horne, commander of XV Corps, is later promoted and given command of the First Army.

Chaplin starts writing to Lil again on 29 August, from the 19th brigade HQ near Fricourt, a village now demolished by shelling. He is cheery, clearly upbeat having survived the battering taken by his brigade at High Wood, but conscious that his days alive may be numbered. He has a new plan – to meet Lil in Paris, if she can find a way over: 'I believe the Ritz is the place to stay, so we will meet there. If you know any other better place let me know, but we shall have to decide where to go or we shall miss one another.'[129]

The plan has been borrowed from a new friend, Major Twiss, brigade major at the 19th, who wants to bring over his own wife for a short stay as the division organises three-day leaves for officers. Everything else is up in the air, so the immediate seems compelling: 'We do not know where we go or what is going to happen to us. We have had a very trying time and we deserve a good rest.'[130]

Chaplin appears buoyed at the thought. As the battalion marches out of shelling range, he plasters his wife with requests: send me shirts, send me underclothes, new envelopes, photographs of the children, cigarettes for the men. He rides over to the Glasgow Highlanders to console Sam D., whose father has just died. He welcomes back to the battalion Captain Hunter. He delights in the news that the Germans have changed their chief of staff[131] – 'it shows they are getting rattled.'[132]

Now every letter comes from a different village as the Cams march west and north – Ribemont-sur-Ancre, Molliens-au-Bois, Vacquerie – each note reflecting his relief to be out of the line, his delight to be on the road each day, riding at the head of his marching men, moving away from the Somme, to be outside, under blue sky, without shelling. The landscape they move through reflects his spirits, cottages with hedges, little well-kept gardens, more like the British countryside of sentiment than any they have yet seen in France. And he apologises again for the break in writing: '. . . but when one expects every minute to be hurled into eternity one has not the inclination nor the time to write.'[133]

Lil has her own plan. She uses the news of the death of Sam Darling's father to write to her husband's old friend, offering condolences, and asking for his views on just how Graham is doing. By 8 September she has had her reply. Darling consoles her that Graham is 'well and cheery' but admits they could all 'do with a rest'. He also adds, tellingly: 'I wish they would give him a Brigade. He deserves it and it's a damned (please excuse this) shame they don't. If he would not tell Generals what he thinks of them it would be better really for himself – but don't say I said so!'[134]

He adds that he won't tell her husband that she has written.

The Cameronians must return to the trenches, just when Chaplin thought they would get a break. The 33rd division is detailed to defend the line at Gommecourt, scene of a 'diversion' on the opening day of the Battle of the

Somme, two months earlier, when the Third Army's 46th and 56th divisions had attacked a heavily defended German salient, curling round another infernal wood. The attack had been widely advertised with conspicuous preparation, part of a ruse to draw German troops and guns away from the main British thrust to the south. Even so, the assault went ahead against a well-forewarned enemy. The result was over 7,000 British soldiers killed, wounded or missing and little ground gained.

And yet, despite the purpose being diversionary, it was felt the 46th division had let the army down. Days later, an enquiry is opened into its 'lack of offensive spirit' – the words chosen by VII Corps' Lieutenant General Snow, who Chaplin had met and instantly disliked ('poisonous') earlier in the campaign. Snow eventually removes the commander of the 46th, part of the ongoing pressure on all divisional generals to get results. Despite the pretence to troops at the front that progress is being made, the army's high command knows there is unease in London with the scale of the losses and lack of territory gained. The British government is questioning Haig's strategy.

But Gommecourt, for now, is quiet, both sides happy to hold what they have. The line, running in front of the village of Foncquevillers, is the scene of sporadic shelling but little else. The Cameronians man the trenches so fresher troops are freed for the fighting further south. At some points, no-man's land widens from 250 yards to nearly a mile, allowing the Cams to walk around freely. The trench facilities, originally built by the French, are an upgrade too. Chaplin has a bedstead in his command HQ, and eats lunch in a house – it seems unreal after the destruction around High Wood. The troops aptly rename the village they defend: Funky Villas.

Wednesday, 13 September 1916 [from trenches in Foncquevillers, twelve miles south of Arras]
My darling,

I could not write last night, I was absolutely tired – but I went to bed early and had the first real night's rest that I have had since the middle of June.

We are in the most delightful trenches – I have an iron bedstead, looking-glass, dressing table in my dugout and we mess in a house.

Two years and a month since we left Glasgow and Jim is a year and nine months. There is talk that some of us may get a week's leave, so do not be surprised if you get a wire from me from Folkestone, but do not count on it at all. I should love to see you all. I should like to have a month's leave. I have felt really tired lately – but I am very well. The war is going very well, which is the great thing.

Thursday, 14 September 1916 [from trenches in Foncquevillers]
I was pleased to get the photographs today. I think they are excellent. Yes, Eileen has grown out of all knowledge and looks splendid. I like Jim sitting upright best.

There seems a good chance of getting six days' leave home – I only trust that it will come off.

Saturday, 16 September 1916 [from 19th brigade HQ, behind Foncquevillers]
I could not write yesterday as I was sent for to command the Brigade for a few days and am now in a fine house and comfortable quarters.

We are all very pleased at the way our people are getting on at the Somme.

Monday, 18 September 1916 [from 19th brigade HQ, behind Foncquevillers]
I hope your headache is nothing and that you're not ill. I regret to say that I missed the post yesterday by going to sleep. I am very sorry, although there is nothing to say. I am having a peaceful and restful time, although I feel I should like to sleep for a month.

If the General had not gone on leave I should be with you now – it is very hard luck. Major HS goes off tonight. If nothing unforeseen occurs I should get leave in a week's time, but it is very uncertain owing to the situation. We have been doing splendidly the last few days.

I am simply longing to see you and the children.

Wednesday, 20 September 1916 [from 19th brigade HQ, behind Foncquevillers]

I am still commanding the Brigade and shall till the 25th when I hope to get leave, or on the 26th – unless something unforeseen happens. In these times everything is very uncertain.

I have been going to bed very early trying to make up arrears of sleep, but I still feel very tired.

Thursday, 21 September 1916 [from trenches in Foncquevillers]

I am sorry you have had a fit of the blues – I thought it was the fault of the post that I had no letter. I am very glad that Jim is better. I began to be frightened that he was getting ill.

Absolutely no news to give you. I am only thinking of the possibility of leave on the 26th. If it comes off we must play golf together. Could you find out about joining the club if we can temporarily? I have forgotten how to play golf but I suppose it will come back.

Friday, 22 September 1916 [from trenches in Foncquevillers]

If I get leave – nothing has cropped up yet to stop it – I hope to be at Victoria about 3pm on the 26th.

I do hope Jim is alright again. It must be an awful job with both the children teething.

I had a letter from RO to say that he was in hospital wounded again in the right arm and the back. He says he is not bad – I hope he is right – and expects to be home soon.

The weather has become very fine again after heavy rain.

We are getting a new divisional commander.[1] All these changes are bad for my chance of a Brigade.

---

1 Major-General Pinney, Royal Fusiliers, formerly commanding the 35th division, becomes GOC 33rd Division, replacing Major-General Landon.

Saturday, 23 September 1916 [from trenches in Foncquevillers]

I was jolly glad to hear that Jim is alright again. My leave has been granted from the 26th. If nothing occurs to stop it I shall be at Victoria about 3pm on the 26th.

It is glorious weather again now. There is no news one can write. With all my fondest love and kisses to Jim and Eileen. For ever your loving husband, Graham

*   *   *

Chaplin is home by 26 September, just as England is turning to autumn. These short periods at home are becoming increasingly difficult for him, thrust into family life, almost a stranger to his own children, then after a week returning back to the front line. He is often left bereft, unable to lift his own spirits. He starts writing to Lil again on 6 October, detailing his journey back to France, the chance meetings with various officers at Folkestone and on board the ship that takes him across the Channel. He spends much of the journey locked in conversation with Sir Eric Geddes, the businessman recently appointed to oversee the army's transport needs. Geddes, initially brought into government by David Lloyd George to oversee shell production, had started his business career in India, where he worked on the Rohilkhand and Kumaon railway and crossed paths with Chaplin.[135] Now he has the ear of the Prime Minister and Douglas Haig too. Chaplin has his own views on the conduct of the war to convey: 'He had a cabin and asked me in and I sat and bucked to him all the voyage – he was very interesting.'[136]

Chaplin returns to his battalion to find them out of the fighting, resting in comfortable billets strung around the picturesque village of Lucheux, twenty-odd miles north of Amiens. The rest does not last long. By 8 October they are preparing for another attack on another copse – this time, Rossignol Wood, part of the Gommecourt salient. Behind the lines, brigade HQ has laid out a practice terrain, which fails to impress the older hands. Three days later, the battalion moves in buses to trenches at Hébuterne, near the wood, to await detailed orders. By now they know their assault is to be yet another diversionary action, to prevent the enemy from thinning its line and sending reinforcements south to the Somme. No solider wants to die in a diversion.

First, the division's artillery pounds the German line, attempting to cut its defensive wire. 'Results not very noticeable,' writes Chaplin sardonically in the War Diary. The battalion takes casualties from retaliatory fire before the division suddenly cancels the operation. No reason is given, but word circulates that fighting on the main Somme battlefield is not going well. More units may be needed further south. For officers like Chaplin, commanding large bodies of men but controlling little – and knowing less of the war's progress on a bigger scale – it is just another change in a bewildering process. Every soldier begins to believe that fate and luck determine everything, so little is left to their own decisions.

Out of trenches, Chaplin suddenly receives orders late at night to move his men. Transport is provided to drive them west to Ivergny. From there, they march to Doullens, then take more buses twenty miles south to Amiens and east again to Buire-sur-l'Ancre, moving inexorably back towards the war's epicentre. The 33rd division has been switched to another corps, the XIV, under Lord Cavan, which operates next to the French army. It has been pulled south to add numbers to a series of joint Anglo–French attacks planned on the German lines around Guillemont and Ginchy, two French villages flattened by bombing just beyond Longueval, only a few miles south-east of the High Wood they remember so well, now finally in British hands. The front line, however, has moved barely three miles since the Cameronians went through Bazentin in mid-July, and much of that gain was achieved in one September day with the first use of tanks. Then the Germans dug in and held on.

The terrain the 19th brigade enters is worse even than High Wood's 'Death Valley', churned by more rain, more shelling and more men. Nothing is recognisable. All distinguishing features have been obliterated by three months of war, all roads dissolved into a brown sea of mud, all movement hazardous – farmhouses, villages, woodlands gone. There is just a slipping scrum of men and horses and the occasional lorry moving back and forth, filling and relieving lines, preparing for yet another push. It takes the battalion four hours to march less than five miles to old trenches near Bernafay Wood, south of Longueval, then on the next day to Guillemont, in reserve to the 4th division. It will attack at 2.30 p.m. on Monday, 23 October.

By then, Chaplin has gone. On a churned road outside Corbie on 21 October, his horse loses its footing, slips under him and collapses, crushing Chaplin's thigh and tearing his ligaments. His first serious war injury is inflicted not by the Germans, but by his own horse – an injury that will become increasingly common for officers riding in the Somme's winter mud, where each step can be calamitous. Unable to walk, Chaplin transfers to the mess cart and is wheeled into Bernafay Wood laid flat, yet still with his men – determined not to leave them just before they enter the front line again. But news of his injury reaches Mayne, who sends a runner with orders forbidding him to continue. From a small aid post halfway to Guillemont, Chaplin starts the long journey back, first to the town of Albert, closest to the fighting, then down the doggedly straight Roman road to Amiens, cathedral spire visible for miles, where a hospital awaits. The ambulance carrying him struggles against the mass of men being pushed forward into the war. Chaplin is on his own, heading against the flow, to be beached for at least a week. A commanding officer who cannot move forward with his men is of no use to any division.

BEFORE YOU GO

'I had a letter from Sam Darling's brother in answer to mine
to his mother. He said that his mother had had a sort of
breakdown . . .'

British forces on Somme fight major battles at Le Transloy, Thiepval Ridge, Ancre Heights and the Ancre — bad weather quells fighting from mid-November — German army plots retreat to new defensive line — British politicians query gains made for casualties taken — French and British generals meet at Chantilly to draw up plans for new offensive in 1917 — French army replaces its commander-in-chief

Lil Chaplin knows that her husband is in hospital long before she gets the War Office telegram, forwarded from her parents' home in Stirling to Sunningdale. Graham has written every day from Amiens, and his first letter has reached her before the Whitehall clerk has even licked his pencil, checked the officer casualty lists, consulted the records and picked up the telegram form to scrawl the message that vanishes into the system, postmarked 2 November 1916.

It is the beginning of a warm, damp, stormy month in Britain, when doubts about the war's progress are swirling, and many have already realised that getting out of the front line may be the only way to survive. The rich pull strings to get their sons on staff jobs. The poor self-mutilate to take themselves away from the action – doctors in battalions see an increase in bullets through hands and ankles, knives dropped on feet, and accidents varied. Conscription, introduced for unmarried men in March, had been extended to married men in May. It does not extend to Ireland. Military Service Tribunals now sit in judgement of those who claim exemption. At the highest level, politicians are questioning Haig's tactics. Patriotic fervour for the war is starting to wane.

For most army wives, there is no easy answer. They are proud of their husbands' bravery but would dearly like them home. Lil will know already that her brother, Willie, has found a way out. He was lucky to be withdrawn from the 6th Black Watch long before the 51st division followed the 33rd into High Wood in July 1916. Back in Scotland after his father's death, Willie has spent the summer overseeing Charles Tennant & Co's industrial interests before being summoned to Whitehall by Harold Tennant, Under-Secretary for War. He knows Willie's business talents from years of friendship, and he knows, too, of the Tennant companies' links with Nobel, the Swedish dynamite and armaments manufacturer. Willie is made Director of Administration of National Explosive Factories in 1916 and, a year later, Controller of Aircraft Supply and Production[137] – one of a clutch of businessmen co-opted into the war effort after a national outcry over inefficient arms production. It is a contribution for which Willie wins first the DSO, then the CMG, then a knighthood, as well as promotion from lieutenant colonel to brigadier general. It is also a prelude to a successful business and parliamentary career. In the short term, it saves him from a return to the firing line.

For his brother-in-law, laid out in hospital in Amiens, destined to limp back into the thick of the battle, knowing the likelihood of his own death is high – even from one of Willie's own shells, given the British artillery's predilection for firing short – it will have been a bitter-sweet thought. He is pleased his wife's brother is safe, jealous he cannot match Willie's connections. Lil's letters will plead again and again: why cannot he get promotion to brigadier? Why cannot he be safe? From brigadier he can jump to a division, or a job at home. He must see people, put his case, pull strings if he has to, explain the injustice. Day by day, the number of men who sailed with the original British Expeditionary Force is dwindling – dead, missing, wounded or retired. Each of the original battalions has but a handful left, mainly rankers operating often behind the front line, in transport or HQ. Chaplin is now one of the very few Old Contemptible officers still serving in the front line.

And yet he is a man who has always made his own way without pulling strings. He doesn't have a large circle of friends, he is often blunt, he refuses to be falsely charming, he is wary of sentiment and scheming – all qualities respected in the older, smaller, professional army. Now they make him ill-suited to deal with the desperate politics of the new million-strong force, with pressure for instant, visible success continually being applied, utilising shoddy standards, slapdash planning and obvious tactical incompetence.

So, with his ligaments pulled, his back bruised, his rest in Amiens enforced for a fortnight, he is caught: grateful to be out of it all, wondering how he can get out permanently, yet desperate to return to his men. It is the second time in four months he has been withdrawn from battle shortly before his battalion must make an attack. Neither withdrawal was of his own volition, but if he suspects there are doubts lingering over his and Robertson's refusal to send the Cams over the top at Loos, this can only reinforce them. And yet Robertson has been promoted. The churn of appointments at senior level continues as Haig demands more progress from his generals. Rare is the colonel who serves for more than a year without promotion. Why not him?

Tuesday, 24 October 1916 [from No.1 NZ Stationary Hospital,[1] Amiens]
My darling,

I was brought here yesterday in an ambulance and carried up in a stretcher. I am all black and blue down the inside of my legs and the lower part of my stomach. I seem to have ruptured several muscles. I shall not be out of bed for 10 days. I also have an appalling abscess in my mouth and I shall probably lose the bridge in my mouth.

I feel very depressed at being knocked out like this and leaving the regiment just as they are going into a show. It would not matter any other time.

I feel very cheap.

Wednesday, 25 October 1916 [from No.1 NZ Stationary Hospital, Amiens]
I shall be able to write you a better letter tomorrow as I am going in an

---

1 Sited in the Sainte-Famille convent close to Amiens station, the 350-bed hospital was run by New Zealand military medical staff. It also oversaw another 380 beds for less serious cases in the Sainte-Famille girls' school, overlooking the railway tracks a few blocks away, where Chaplin is likely to have stayed.

ambulance to the dentist this afternoon. He is going to lance the abscess. At present it is pretty painful and gives me a beastly head.

The worst is that I get no letters from you as neither you nor the regiment know where I am at present.

Thursday, 26 October 1916 [from No.1 NZ Stationary Hospital, Amiens]

I went to the dentist yesterday but he did not do anything. In the evening the Dr lanced the abscess, which has been a great relief. Tomorrow I am going again to the dentist – he is going to remove the bridge and pull out all the roots, so I shall have to have a plate – if I get home. It is a great nuisance.

My ruptured muscles do not get much better or not fast enough to please me. I can only walk very slowly and can hardly lift my legs at all. I shall certainly be in bed another week. I was not intended for the role of an invalid. I feel so depressed about being away from the regiment like this in such a rotten way.

Friday, 27 October 1916 [from No.1 NZ Stationary Hospital, Amiens]

I am just off to the dentist to have my bridge removed and the stumps pulled out.

My ruptured muscles are much better and I can move with comparative ease.

I have not heard from you of course since I left the regiment on the 22nd but I hope I shall get a letter direct in a day or two. I do not know anything about what has happened to the regiment. I wish I could hear about Sandy too if he is alright.

I wonder if Jim remembers me now.

Sunday, 29 October 1916 [from No.1 NZ Stationary Hospital, Amiens]

Yesterday they put me under chloroform and pulled out the stumps of my teeth and my face is alright now but I shall have to get a plate – if I get home again.

I have got up today and dressed. I can walk pretty well but I think I shall be here some days yet.

I think about you all day and I wish I was at Brabazon Lodge.

Tuesday, 31 October 1916 [from No.1 NZ Stationary Hospital, Amiens]

I went out yesterday for the first time and forgot to write for the post before going out. It was raining like anything, but I was glad to find I could walk pretty well – although I was stiff afterwards. I expect I shall go back to the regiment in a few days.

I wish they would give me a job at home now for a bit – I really feel that I have done all I can. Perhaps they will soon. My eyes are beginning to trouble me a lot, they are always inflamed now.

Wednesday, 1 November 1916 [from No.1 NZ Stationary Hospital, Amiens]

I have got a cyst in my good eye, so cannot write much.

I got all your letters forwarded from the regiment and was jolly glad to get them. I am sorry you have been troubled with your old complaint but I am glad that you have defeated it.

I hope the regiment have opened the parcels or the chicken etc will be bad. I am fed up with hospital, although everyone is very nice. I want to get back to the regiment.

Thursday, 2 November 1916 [from No.1 NZ Stationary Hospital, Amiens]

I was very glad to get your letters of the 28th, 29th and 30th this morning. I am very sorry that you have been worrying about me because I am very comfortable and have had the best rest for sleep that I have had during the war. I am very sorry that your K is troubling you so.

Capt Minchin[1] came to see me this morning and brought me some cigarettes. He enquired particularly after you.

If my eye goes on alright I expect to leave here in four days' time to rejoin the regt.

Friday, 3 November 1916 [from No.1 NZ Stationary Hospital, Amiens]

I received the books, for which many thanks.

I am disappointed that my eye does not make better progress. All the lower

---

1 Captain James Cotton Minchin was a subaltern in Chaplin's A Company.

lid is very swollen and inflamed, but it does not appear to be forming a cyst.

I have not heard that General C-C had got a Division[1] – are you sure?

I have started playing Bridge as I cannot see to read. It passes the time.

Saturday, 4 November 1916 [from No.1 NZ Stationary Hospital, Amiens]

My eye is a good deal better today.

Capt Minchin came to see me last night. He goes home today and he is going to see you if he can when he gets home.

I got two letters from you today. I am glad the kids are so fit and hope that you are alright again.

It is very extraordinary about Col Jenney.[2] I suppose he must be in some hospital – of course he is too old to be with a battalion.

They have been very nice here. The New Zealanders are very English and have no accent. I only wish you could have come out here. It would have been topping if you could.

I like General P[3] very much and think he is a good man at his job.

This has been a good rest for me – I sleep so well – I was getting absolutely cooked before. I only wish they would give me a job at home for a bit.

Sunday, 5 November 1916 [from No.1 NZ Stationary Hospital, Amiens]

You will be grieved to hear that Sam Darling was killed on the 1st by a sniper. I am very distressed – he was a splendid fellow – and I shall miss him greatly. It always cheered me up to see him.

I heard in a letter from Wood, the Quartermaster. Young Brickman has also

---

1 Brigadier General Carter-Campbell, formerly CO 2nd Scottish Rifles, did not in fact assume command of a division until March 1918, when he became CO of the 51st. Carter-Campbell, born 1869, was commissioned into the Scottish Rifles in 1889, five years before Chaplin.

2 Lieutenant Colonel A. O. Jenney, formerly of the Cameronians, commanded the 6th Black Watch – Willie Alexander's battalion – in June 1916, before leaving to command No.33 Prisoners-of-War Camp in October the same year.

3 Pinney, commander of 33rd division, had become unpopular with the ranks for replacing the regular issue of rum with tea.

been killed – a very brave young fellow – and three other officers missing, probably killed.

My eye continues to improve and I expect to go back in a day or two. I do not feel sure about these ruptured muscles – I think that it is very likely that I shall not be able to stand walking through heavy mud.

I have a great longing to go home to you all. With all my fondest love and heaps of kisses to Jim and Eileen. For ever your loving husband, Graham

Extracts from the battalion War Diary, October 1916,

Kept by Major Herbert Hyde-Smith

Bivouac'd at Guillemont in the Somme
24 October - Remained in reserve to 4th Div at Guillemont. Work done to improve shelters and camp generally.

25 October - Remained in Guillemont.

26 October - Carrying parties for bomb and trench stores to RWFusiliers.

27 October - Orders received to relieve RWFusiliers in trenches east of Lesbœufs-Morval. 2Lt Mackay and four men wounded by shellfire going up. Paraded 4.30pm.

Trenches at Lesbœufs
28 October - Orders received for the Bn to attack Hazy Trench in conjunction with 5th Scottish Rifles on a one company front. Heavy shelling. Six men killed. 14 wounded.

29 October - Attack on Hazy Trench by D Coy at 5.45am. No

preliminary bombardment. Company enfiladed from right by machine gun fire and suffered heavy casualties and were unable to gain their objective. B Coy went forward to support and entrenched themselves 50 yards in front of Boritska Trench. Casualties: Capt Brickman killed, 2Lts Angus, Connison, Boyd missing. 2Lt Dalrymple wounded. Casualties in other ranks: 17 killed, 49 wounded, 33 missing.

30 October - Relieved by 9th HLI 98th Brigade. Bn moved back into shelters at Briqueterie near Bernafay Wood.

Briqueterie
31 October - Men cleaning up.

1 November - Men cleaning up and drying their clothes. Working Party carrying floor boards from Ginchy to Flers Line (200 men).

2 November - Working party 8.15am carrying floor boards from Trônes Wood to Flank Alley. Stretcher bearer party (50 men) to Ginchy dressing station.

Trônes Wood
3 November - 19th Bde relieved 98th Bde, Battalion in reserve. Relieved Argyll & Sutherland Highlanders in Trônes Wood.

4 November - Battalion remained in Trônes Wood.

5 November - Battalion moved at 3am to the Flers Line forming with 5th Scottish Rifles reserve to 33rd Division, who were attacking in conjunction with 17th Div on left and French on right.

6 November - Continuous working parties - one Coy going out at
a time for 3 hours and then relieved by another Coy.

Chaplin finally leaves Amiens on 9 November. The fortnight he is away
proves treacherous for the Cams. In front of the hamlet of Lesbœufs, two
miles beyond Ginchy, they lose nearly a hundred men in an ill-planned
attack on Hazy Trench – aptly named, as it proves too hard to find in the
mud and mist. The 33rd division is close to Bapaume now, fighting side by
side with the French, but across such terrible terrain as makes each yard
gained a miracle. The month ends in freezing storms. Mud, water, cold,
fog and torrential rain pull back every push. Old hands note with alarm
the lack of coordination with their French allies, which often leaves their
flank unprotected. The orders from on high for continual attacks, each
battalion taking a turn, is designed to keep the Germans pinned down,
unable to withdraw divisions to fight elsewhere, and unable to organise
the concerted counter-attack which many believe the Kaiser is demanding.
Had the men a fuller knowledge of the questions being raised at home
over Haig's tactics, they would also have recognised a commander acting
in desperation.

Chaplin uses the enforced rest at Amiens to have his rotten teeth pulled
and his inflamed eye treated. He notes dryly in his letters that his urge to
return to the fighting surprises some of those treating him: 'I told them I
wanted to get back to the regiment as soon as possible – it is not apparently
a universal desire.'[138]

He discusses the mundanity of hospital life, the reactions to the chloroform used in operations, the arrival of cigarettes and roly-poly pudding,
the non-arrival of papers about his income tax, the unlikelihood of him
ever finding his brother-in-law, Ernest Shepard,[139] newly posted to the
front, or Shepard ever finding him. For the moment, the death of his
closest friend, Sam Darling, remains undiscussed. The simple descriptive
line he has already given Lil – 'It always cheered me up to see him' – is
left hanging. It is a loss that will, eventually, affect him deeply.

And then he is packing to leave. Before he gets to Amiens station, he receives three visitors – Scott, his adjutant; Crawshay, commander of the 2nd Royal Welch; and Father McShane, his favourite priest – all of whom have commandeered a motor car and driven into Amiens to pick him up – a kind act to revive his spirits – and take him out to lunch in Amiens' tight streets. They give him welcome news: the 33rd division is being withdrawn from the front.

> They told me that we were to go for a good long rest, so instead of going to the trenches I find myself going backwards. We went together and did some shopping. I sent some flowers to my ward in the hospital and we all dined together in a hotel. It was the best dinner I have had in France – fried sole amongst other things. We all went back in the motor and got to the Bn about 11 o'c.[140]

By Sunday, 12 November, the Cams are billeted in Citerne, another sprawling, red-brick village south of Abbeville, twenty-odd miles west of Amiens, encased in wide farmland and dominated by an exquisite eighteenth-century chateau set in woods turning tawny in the winter winds. The battalion has journeyed there by hellishly slow train, leaving Méaulte, south of Albert, at noon and arriving seven-miles'-march from Citerne in the middle of the night. Méaulte has been an eye-opener for the front-line soldiers – it is the new base for the corps command and rather plusher than what soldiers experienced in the front line. Here, the staff have wind-proofed huts, plentiful stoves, duckboards laid two-deep, hot baths and no mud.

Arriving in Citerne at 5 a.m., Chaplin is billeted with the *Maire*, who rises to greet him and entreats him to eat the dinner that had waited for him since the night before: 'I have got a very nice bedroom with sheets and we have a big room for a mess. Altogether it should be very pleasant here, if they do not worry us too much with inspections.'[141]

But, even out of line, a colonel has duties – restoration of equipment, training of men, paperwork. Chaplin now gets more news of Darling's death – 'shot dead through the brain by a sniper'[142] – and feels his spirits sink as the cold sets in and his plan to lobby Pinney for promotion is put on hold. The general has returned to Britain for a fortnight's leave. Chaplin broods, and misses India: 'I walked round the billets this morning. This afternoon I sat over the fire trying unsuccessfully to keep warm. This cold is too much for me – I do not feel very well. It chills my Indian liver.'[143]

He only cheers up when he hears that those who have spent two winters at the front may be given extended leave for Christmas. He wants to get into Abbeville to buy presents for Jim and Eileen. Even the arrival of snow can't dent his enthusiasm: 'I should love it if I could get leave to be home for Christmas – I should love to have a Christmas tree for the kids.'

By 20 November, Pinney has returned and the subject of promotion has been broached. No promises are made, but hope is given: 'He said he would do all he could for me.'[144]

And just maybe Chaplin will get his leave at Christmas. He will have to see a dentist, he warns Lil, and a masseur for his back. He worries his wife will not recognise him: 'I think you will see more change in me than all the rest of the war. My hair has come out so and they have taken out so many teeth. The hope of seeing you has cheered me up tremendously and I feel much better. I have felt absolutely done since I had this accident.'[145]

He also hopes to see Vincent Sandilands,[146] his brother-in-law, now commanding the 2nd Scottish Rifles, before he goes. Sandy has his own health issues, which will shortly remove him from the front for three months: 'I did not think it sounded very well when Baby said he was having nightmares about the war . . .'[147]

But most of all Chaplin hopes to get home. Imprisoned by his duty to his men, he counts the days till his precious month-long release commences, he focuses on just keeping going till he can board the ship to Britain, he prays that the army does not change its plans for the Cams.

Friday, 24 November 1916 [from billets in Citerne]

My darling,

We went for a route march today. I walked all the way and my leg was quite good and I did not feel it walking, although I did not dare to ride it.

Major Murphy came over from the 2nd Bn – he says that Sandy has got three weeks' leave home.

Major HS went off today, so if nothing unexpected occurs I should get home on the 5th or 6th and I should be home for Christmas – we will have a great Christmas tree for the kids if I am.

Major Murphy said that Col Vandeleur expected soon to return – I hope the hope will not be fulfilled.

You must have your hands full with Eileen's teeth and Jim seedy. I hope he is alright now – it frightens me when children are seedy.

Saturday, 25 November 1916 [from billets in Citerne]

It has been a miserable day – it has rained the whole day.

This afternoon we spent the whole afternoon at a boxing tournament – our men did quite well. I was very cold and would have liked to have retired.

Two terrible youths arrived from the 2nd Bn to arrange about the football.

I am going to have a later morning in bed tomorrow as it is Sunday and I am not going to church.

I am simply counting the days now till I go home and can think of nothing else.

Sunday, 26 November 1916 [from billets in Citerne]

I went for a good long walk alone this morning for exercise. In the afternoon Stirling and Campbell came over from the 2nd Bn – they said Sandy was in hospital in London.

I feel depressed today. I think it is the continual rain and the anxiety to get away home. I am afraid of something cropping up to stop my leave.

Monday, 27 November 1916 [from billets in Citerne]

I received three letters from you today, the last dated the 23rd. I feel very worried about Jim having a temperature of 103, but the Dr says it is nothing unusual in a child. Also your headaches and neuralgia worry me – what does Dr Wildridge say?

I got the leather jersey – a thousand thanks. It is awfully nice and the very thing I want. It has turned awfully cold again.

I have been inoculated again today for enteric. I did it to give the men a lead as they were rather shying – I shall probably have a temperature tomorrow. I have to be teetotal for six hours.

Yes, the air seems full of sickness. Our Brigadier is in bed. I am afraid I shall have to go there, which I do not want to do at present.

Tuesday, 28 November 1916 [from billets in Citerne]
The General is bad so I had to do the Bde work in addition to my own. I have had a lot of walking. I walked with Col Crawshay all of some ground in connection with a scheme and got back to find it was all useless as the scheme was off.

There is a tremendous lot of influenza so called – there are more officers sick in the Bde than I have ever known.

Wednesday, 29 November 1916 [from billets in Citerne]
I am very anxious about Jim. There has been no mail for two days. I would wire, but I am sure if he was bad you would wire to me – but I wish the mail would come.

My leave for a month has been sanctioned, so unless anything turns up unexpectedly I should be home about the 7th. It depends when Major HS returns.

Thursday, 30 November 1916 [from billets in Citerne]
There is still no mail, so I am very anxious about Jim. If there is no letter tomorrow I shall wire.

The 2nd Bn beat us at football today by 3 to 0.[1] Col Jack came over to

---

1 Battalion War Diary records the results as 0–5.

see the match. He commands an English regiment in the same Brigade[1] as Sandy.

This will just be a short letter as we are leaving to dine with the 2nd Bn very shortly.[2] The Division have provided us with a char-à-banc motor.

The General is still sick. I walk to Bde twice a day to transact business, so I am fairly busy.

Friday, 1 December 1916 [from billets in Citerne]

I cannot tell you how relieved I was to get two letters from you today and to learn that there was nothing serious in Jim's illness. It is awful having a lapse of three days without a post in these times.

We had a great dinner with the 2nd Bn. They had the divisional band – a string band who played very well and one quite forgot the War. Col Jack was there with his hunting horn.

No, dear, I never thought for a moment that it would make any difference if I lost my hair to you.

General P came tonight and was very pleasant – he is a nice man.

Saturday, 2 December 1916 [from billets in Citerne]

I hope to be home on the 7th. There is no way that I can see of arranging for you to meet me as I cannot possibly let you know till I arrive at Folkestone. It depends whether Major HS arrives and if I catch the boat at Boulogne. Of course one can never be certain but it looks a certainty that I shall get my leave.

I have a letter from Ronnie M who said nothing fresh and also from RO, who has not passed his board yet. Col Jack came to tea today – he had no news particularly. I am glad your mother is better.

---

1 23rd brigade, 8th division.

2 One of the first occasions in which officers of the two rivalrous battalions had ever dined together. The two units were rarely in the same country, as they took turns in their postings abroad. The friendship of Chaplin and Sandilands, and their link by marriage, doubtless helped to thaw previously frosty relations.

Sunday, 3 December 1916 [from billets in Citerne]

I am very glad to hear that Jim is getting on so well – it frightened me to hear that he had a temperature.

Did I not say that my leave was for a month?

I had a letter from Sam Darling's brother in answer to mine to his mother. He said that his mother had had a sort of breakdown.

I am just counting the time to go home.

With all my love and thoughts and heaps of kisses to the children. For ever your loving husband, Graham

Extracts from the battalion War Diary,
December 1916,

Kept by Major Herbert Hyde-Smith
[Colonel Graham Chapman on leave]

Billets in Citerne
8 December – Battalion marched to Airaines from Citerne, starting at 6.40am and entrained there for Méricourt, and from there marched to Vaux-sur-Somme, where the battalion billeted for the night.

Billets in Vaux-sur-Somme
9 December – Paraded 1.30pm and marched to Camp 111 near Bray arriving 5.30pm. Draft 53 OR.

Camp 111, Somme
10 December – Day spent cleaning up.

11 December – Paraded 10am, marched across country to Camp 17 near Susanne. Transport by Méricourt Road, draft 120 OR.

Camp 17, Somme

12 December - Improvements made in Camp and also cleaning the surroundings, which had been left in a very insanitary condition. CO and two Company Commanders reconnoitred road to trenches.

13 December - Improvements to Camp continued.

14 December - Battalion paraded 1.30pm to march to trenches near Rancourt. 150 men per company inclusive of Lewis gunners and bombers only were taken. B Echelon at Maurepas. Three officers and 170 OR not for trenches remained in camp. Battalion took over from 16th KRR.

Trenches near Rancourt

15 December - Trenches very wet and muddy. No work was possible by day: by night a certain amount of work was done to improve the line but companies were chiefly involved in carrying.

16 December - During the night the two companies in front line were relieved by the support and reserve companies.

17 December - Day comparatively quiet, except for a little shelling, 4 men wounded.

18 December - During the day there was rather heavy shelling of the front line. There were only a few casualties. The battalion was relieved by the 20th RF at about 9pm and went back into support at Priez Farm. One company sent back to Le Forest.

19 December - Working party of 200 men sent up to front line during the night.

20 December - Working parties again sent up to front line (200 men).

21 December - Working party (150) for front line, for laying floor boards, one man wounded. Lt & Quartermaster G Wood was tried by court martial, charged with drunkenness. He was found guilty of the charge and the court sentenced him to be severely reprimanded.

22 December - Battalion relieved by 1st Middlesex and were brought down in motor lorries to Camp 17 arriving about 10pm.

Camp 17

23 December - Companies cleaning up. CO inspected companies.

24 December - GOC inspected the battalion. Church Parade service 10.30am.

25 December - Christmas Day.

HOWITZER WOOD

'A staff officer said to me the other day that I was probably
the only officer who had served with a regiment continuously
throughout the war . . .'

British commander-in-chief Haig promoted to field marshal — troops suffer
as coldest winter in decades sweeps Europe — British forces push Germans
back on the Ancre — new infantry training manual introduced for British
army — organisation of artillery revised — German army starts to withdraw
to stronger defensive position

A month at home with his wife and two small children for Christmas. What
effect would that have on a man after two full years at war? Four and a
half weeks spent in the knowledge that he must return to the battlefields,
and the continuing likelihood of his own death. Perhaps Graham Chaplin
is inured to it now, he has seen so much and lost so many. And will he
talk about what his battalion has been through? The question is whether
anyone would want to listen. Some in Britain are already fed up with the
war, and the demands it makes of every family. Few would understand
what it was like to be fighting over fields of corpses in bitter cold, standing
waist-deep in mud with shells exploding back, side and front, for days on
end. Most soldiers continue the avoidance instigated by the censorship of
their letters – they leave it all unsaid, a habit that becomes a tradition and,
over decades, a defining characteristic. They rarely speak about the war.

The Britain Chaplin sees on leave is different, too, finally bearing the mark
of events across the Channel. The newspapers are full of casualty lists, dotted
with greying photographs of the fallen. The streets are mournful places,
so many wearing black. Food shortages have taken hold, as the Germans'
ruthless submarine tactics – sinking anything – restrict the nation's imports.
Prices of basic foodstuffs are rising, the poor are being squeezed, social
unrest is palpable. No one talks of outright victory any more.

Some feel it is pointless carrying on. There are rumours of peace talks
offered by the Germans and dismissed out of hand by the British and
French. All this Chaplin must ignore as he spends the month slowly

getting to know his children while Christmas in Sunningdale flies by. But eventually the dreaded day dawns when he must pack his bag and prepare to travel dutifully back to his men, and the coldest European winter anyone can remember.

The British army he returns to is in another bout of recasting itself, evolving as different technologies and tactics take hold. In an attempt to learn from the mistakes of 1916, new methods of attack have to be mastered, the old ways discarded – no more advancing by the line into a hail of fire. Instead, officers and men must practise staggered advances, spaced out in 'artillery formation'; a more thought-out integration of the specialisms of Lewis gunners, bomb throwers and rifle grenadiers is introduced; and more control is given to divisional commanders over artillery, increasingly recognised as the key to any breakthrough.

For the Cams, it means more work. In December, they briefly man the trenches outside Rancourt, then are withdrawn west again to the village of Épagne-Épagnette, two miles south of Abbeville, just twenty miles from the coast, for training in the new methods: physical fitness, night exercises, repeated drills, attacking in formation, classes for bombers, classes for Lewis gunners, bayonet fighting, baths, more bayonet fighting, more classes.

Chaplin has problems to fix, too. In his absence, Tubby Wood, the Cams' longstanding, hard-drinking quartermaster, appears before a general court martial – judged by officers of another regiment – charged with drunkenness. Wood, forty-six, his nerves suffering from the perpetual bombardment of the transport areas in the Somme, is now an alcoholic.[148] But under Chaplin, his weaknesses have been managed while he continues to prove himself an able quartermaster. On 7 November, however, while Chaplin is still in hospital and the battalion is supplying working parties for the front line at Flers, Wood drinks himself to a standstill in the officers' mess, and is drunker still the next morning, when the battalion is on parade for its move back to Méaulte. And that morning he abuses the transport officer in front of other ranks. Hyde-Smith, as stand-in commander, feels he has to act, and formally charges Wood, who must face a court martial when circumstances allow.

By the time the trial takes place, nearly two months have passed, during which time Chaplin and others have organised a compromise.[149] Wood pleads guilty to being drunk in the officers' mess, but not guilty to being drunk the next morning – and has two officers and a sergeant major to back him up as witnesses. So justice is seen to be done. He is 'severely reprimanded' but allowed to continue as quartermaster.

Wood is such a fixture in the battalion – joining the Cameronians in 1889, serving in India with Chaplin, fighting in Africa, rising to sergeant major and drilling many of the young officers who started pre-war – that no one wants to see him jailed, or sent home in ignominy. His booming voice and cockney wit have followed the Cams from Mons to High Wood. Chaplin, who has clearly discussed what happened with Lil at home,[150] will know this is now a situation that must be handled with care, but he is also a man who remains loyal to the old army ties. Later that summer, he will promote Wood from lieutenant to captain, almost as if in recompense for his Christmas reprimand.

Chaplin also has new orders. After training is completed at Épagne-Épagnette, the Cams are heading back to the Somme, to part of the line previously held by the French army. There they will find the frozen river itself and the front around Cléry, due south of Bapaume, with its woods and marshes and islets and an enemy that will shortly surprise them.

Tuesday, 9 January 1917 [from billets in Épagne-Épagnette, south of Abbeville]

My darling,

I had a very dull man sitting opposite me in the train to Folkestone, so there was nothing to divert my thoughts and I felt very sad at leaving you. We had a smooth passage, rather to my surprise. We got to Calais about 5. I went to the RTO and found that my train did not leave until 8.30 this morning. I went to the hotel on the quay – I think it is called the Terminus. I could only get a bed in a passage, which I took in preference to hunting for another hotel as it was raining hard. I went to write to you but there was no writing paper. To my disgust I found a notice to say that all officers had to report to the Base Commandant, so I had to trek off in the rain and found the place after some difficulty in the dark. When I got back it was time for dinner. I had a rotten dinner and afterwards met Col Carr,[1] who used to command No2 district (Hamilton), and also a Col Holling who used to be in the DCLI in Lucknow. You may remember Col Carr's boy in the Seaforths. They were both commanding base depots.

I had a most uncomfortable night – I do not think I slept at all. I kept thinking of you all. I got up at 6am and had a wash and had coffee and a roll and started for the station. The train should have started at 8.30am but did not start till 11, which was pretty annoying. I arrived at the station from which I started[2] on leave at 4.30pm. I went and saw the RTO, who told me that the train to my railhead[3] started at 8pm and it would be an hour's run. I went into the town to get some food and fortunately met a man in our 5th Bn who told me where Bde Hd Qrs were, only six kilometres from the town – so I got an old cab and drove off there at once. After an hour's drive I duly arrived and saw the General and Major Twiss – the latter had been home on 10 days' leave. I then drove on here another two or three miles[4] and found everyone well.

The Quartermaster was severely reprimanded[5] and is back at work, but I have not seen him yet. The doctor, padre, transport officer and Mr Becher are all on leave, so the mess is small.

They got the turkey alright – it was very good but arrived late. Parcels are taking a long time to come. Gunter's cake has not come yet.

Everyone said I was looking much better – no-one noticed my hair.

I feel very homesick and could not think of anything but you all.

---

1 Lieutenant Colonel E. E. Carr.
2 Abbeville.
3 Pont-Remy.
4 The battalion was billeted in two villages, Eaucourt and Épagne-Épagnette.
5 Quartermaster George 'Tubby' Wood had been court-martialled for drunkenness in Chaplin's absence.

I hope you went to the Money[1] wedding today.

I miss you dreadfully.

Thursday, 11 January 1917 [from billets in Épagne-Épagnette]

There has been no mail and no paper today. Tomorrow I hope to get a letter from you.

It has been a very dull day and I feel depressed and bored.

I got up at 7.45 and had breakfast at 8.45 and then went for a route march I enjoyed – we did eight miles. I walked the whole way as it was so cold and snowed hard at the end. I then held the two orderly rooms – it was then time for lunch. After lunch I went for a long walk with Major HS along the main road – not very interesting. Capt Hunter came to tea. I read Blackwood till dinner time as it was raining. Mr Craig,[2] a subaltern – a funny little Scotchman, a mathematical master in private life – dined with us. We played bridge and I lost.

Could you send me the *Daily Mail* map of the war area? It is so long since I have seen a map of the whole of France that I do not know how the line runs.

I am off to bed now.

Friday, 12 January 1917 [from billets in Épagne-Épagnette]

I did not sleep so well as usual last night for some reason. I was up at 7 and had orderly room at 9 and then spent the whole morning walking round the companies at work – especially looking at the new officers. There is one nice fellow amongst them named Walker,[3] a Ceylon tea planter, who took my fancy. After lunch and the usual correspondence I went for a ride with Major HS. We went to see Col Garnett,[4] who is amusing and cheerful.

The padre got the MC. I did not see it in the honours list. I am very glad –

---

1 Lieutenant Robin Money, one of the original Cameronian officers to sail to France in August 1914, was wounded in 1915 and later transferred to the Middle East.

2 Second Lieutenant William Craig, the son of a lighthouse keeper, was a maths teacher at Hutcheson Boys' Grammar, Glasgow, before enlisting. He joined the Cameronians in October 1915 and was killed at Villers Guislain in September 1918.

3 Second Lieutenant S. T. Walker.

4 Commander of the 20th Royal Fusiliers, transferred to the 2nd Royal Welch in February 1917.

he jolly well deserved it. Did I tell you that he is leaving us? I am very sorry.

We had a company commander, Capt Kennedy,[1] to dinner and played bridge. I could not hold a card and lost every rubber.

Saturday, 13 January 1917 [from billets in Épagne-Épagnette]

I got up at the usual time today and we paraded at 9.30 for General P who gave away medal ribbons.[2] He was very kind and said several times how pleased he was that I was back. He made a short speech, saying that one more effort and we should finish the war – I hope that it will come true. He then went off. I had a lazy morning – held the two orderly rooms. After lunch I walked with Major HS into the big town,[3] about three miles. We went to the Officers' Club – quite a nice place – and had tea. We then read the papers and walked back in time for dinner. We met Col Clayton[4] there and also General Mayne, otherwise no-one we knew.

We start packing up tomorrow, getting rid of surplus kit.

Two years and five months since we left Glasgow – it seems much longer.

How I wish I was playing bow-wow and trit-trot with Jim and nursing Eileen. I wonder if they miss me but don't suppose they do.

Sunday, 14 January 1917 [from billets in Épagne-Épagnette]

I got your two letters today dated 8th and 9th, and also your wire. I am very sorry indeed to hear about your mother's relapse and that the new doctor talks of gallstones. It looks as though Dr Wildridge was right. Of course you would have to go up to Scotland and I hope you will find her better. You will have a horrid journey I am afraid with no sleepers.

I went to bed early last night and slept till 8 o'c. I did not breakfast till nearly 10. I went to the orderly room and did a little work and then Major HS

---

1 Killed five months later in trenches at St Leger.

2 Captain Brown and Second Lieutenants Scott and Sussex won Military Crosses, Privates Anderson and Garvey won Military Medals.

3 Abbeville.

4 Commander, 5th Scottish Rifles.

and I walked to Brigade Hd Qrs – two or three miles. I saw Major Twiss[1] and heard General P was leaving tomorrow, so determined to go and see him today about the Brigade. We walked back in and had lunch somewhat late. Almost immediately after lunch I rode off to Divisional Hd Qrs, a six- or seven-mile ride. I found them located in an enormous chateau. I handed my horse to a groom and went into the chateau. I found some difficulty in finding anyone. I went into several rooms which were empty and then found the ADC.[2] I was taken by him to the General, whom I found writing in the bathroom, being the only warm room on account of the heater. He could not have been nicer. He said that the question of my Brigade had been hung up over my health. He said that they only wanted people in the best of health – "bounding good health". I said that it was impossible to expect that I should be that after all I had been through, but pointed out that I had never been a day away except through an accident and that I was in quite good health now. He said that he was going to GHQ tomorrow and that he would represent my case and find out how I stood.

I then went for a walk with him for about half an hour and had tea. He came out and saw me off and said "I cannot promise you anything definite, but I will do what I can."

I feel very unsettled now and fed up about the Brigade business, but hope it will turn out alright.

With all my fondest love and heaps of kisses to Jim and Eileen and you. For ever your loving husband, Graham

*   *   *

Up at 4.15 a.m. to get the bags to transport, marching at 6 a.m. to Pont-Remy station over icy January roads in pitch darkness. Army orders dictate arrival at 7 a.m. for embarkation. The train will leave at 8 a.m. But as usual it fails to appear until 11 a.m. Chaplin watches his officers oversee the boarding, chatting to Twiss, the brigade major, who is a friend of long

---

1 G. K. Twiss, brigade major of 19th brigade.
2 Aide-de-camp, acting as secretary to the General.

standing now. They travel together as the train trundles slowly east, back to the battlegrounds. It takes seven hours to cover the fifty miles to Bray-sur-Somme and then a two-mile march, tramping over newly repaired roads in pitch darkness again, with only the flare and thump of occasional shells in the distance to herald their destination. By 7.30 p.m. they have arrived at Camp 112, a spreading collection of army huts and tents, close to Camp 111, their base before Christmas. The snow lies deep all around. Chaplin is met by the adjutant of 2ⁿᵈ West Yorks, Colonel Jack's new regiment, asking him to dinner: 'So we went and had a very good dinner.'[151]

Chaplin organises a return match two days later. Jack brings port. His gossip will have left his host with conflicted feelings. Jack, thirty-six, has been selected for a 'higher leaders' course at a senior officers' school, evidence that he has been hand-picked for rapid promotion. He is already filling in, commanding the 23ʳᵈ brigade, when his own brigadier goes on leave. Only recently he had attended a brigadiers' conference[152] at 8ᵗʰ division, arranged by its Canadian-born commander, General Heneker, 'for the purpose of sifting every detail of organisation with a view to improvements'. How Chaplin would like to be so consulted.

Increasingly isolated – even Padre McShane has moved on to a new brigade – Chaplin walks to keep warm. In the HQ hut, he sleeps in a curtained-off corner, 'which I said was as it should be as I did not like taking out my teeth *coram populo*.'[153] There are few like him now: those who have survived in the front line from the start. Such survivors quickly build a reputation. For his men, that will be a reassurance. Chaplin is a stickler, a soldier of the old school who will insist on formalities that New Army recruits find irrelevant amid the horror of war, but he is also a lucky leader in a brigade once dubbed lucky itself,[154] initially unattached to a division, and often used to replace shattered forces after the worst fighting is over. But how soon before that luck changes?

By midnight on 21 January, the Cams are back in the front line, tramping eight miles from Curlu to relieve the 2ⁿᵈ battalion, 68ᵗʰ regiment of the French 17ᵗʰ division in trenches overlooking bleak hills and frozen marshes, beside deserted, shattered Cléry-sur-Somme. Once a village that sprawled along the north side of the pond-pocketed river, where the land dips gently down from the plain above, nothing now remains but pounded bricks and a broken tractor with the word 'Cléry' chalked helpfully on its side. Three companies are posted to hold the line north of the river, two platoons to the south. The 98th brigade are posted north of them, the French XV Corps to the south, giving the Cameronians command of the right flank of the entire British army, stretching north of them to Ypres.

It is not a glamorous posting. Despite the deep French dugouts, cold weather takes it toll. Temperatures drop far below freezing, coke is in short supply for braziers; first frostbite, then trench foot and measles are rife. Soldiers start burning the wooden crosses left on graves for warmth, reasoning that their need is greater. In the frozen River Somme, great spouts of water are thrown up by occasional shells as the artillery attempts to break up foot-thick ice, determined to prevent any enemy incursion. After three days in glacial desolation, the Cameronians are relieved by the 20th Royal Fusiliers and go into support in Howitzer Wood, a blasted scrub of forest whose purpose is now to hold the troops ready, a mile behind the front line, in case a German attack pushes through. Here at least the soldiers can keep warm by working tirelessly, carrying to the front line, repairing communication trenches, sorting provisions. Canteens have also been set up, serving tea, replacing the rum tot which General Pinney removed.[155] Four days later the Cameronians return to the front line, relieving the Fusiliers. And so it goes on, cold day after cold day, as the Cams rack up casualties from the continual mortaring and rifle grenading.

Chaplin's letters are brief and clipped. He is exhausted: 'I did not get to bed till 5am this morning and was up at 8am so my head is not very clear.'[156] And he worries that his own endurance may be wearing thin, that the cold will be too much for him, that his wife may be pregnant again . . . He has started sleepwalking again, too.

Thursday, 25 January 1917 [from support trenches in Howitzer Wood]
My darling,

This is the first time for about a week that I have been able to sit down in peace and write to you. This morning I had to go and look at some ground. I had a tremendously long walk, principally through communication trenches – not very exhilarating. I went on my way back to Bde Hd Qrs. Major Twiss is probably going to get a month's leave and Major HS is going to do Bde Major and then go on to the Division to learn staff work there, so I suppose we shall see no more of him. I am sorry. Capt Hunter will be 2nd in command. Our General[1] said that General P spoke to GHQ about me, but they would not tell him anything definite but said that they had my name and all my recommendations.

Your letters of the 19th and 20th came in also. I am very distressed about the cut on your nose – poor Jim, I expect he is too. I have been thinking about the K too. I cannot imagine that anything can be wrong and hope, my darling, that it will be alright the day after tomorrow.

Yes, it is very satisfactory that you have settled with Connie and Lindsay[2] and that is all finished with – but I shall hope to be able to give all back to you. I feel much more hopeful about what you and I both want now.[3] I would rather get it at home, for a short time, at any rate.

I saw today a German aeroplane brought down in flames. I saw the pilot or observer fall out – it fell a few hundred yards from me.

I have got an enormous box of chocolates from the Sisters of Notre-Dame, Glasgow, by post tonight. I wish you were here to eat them.

We are in dugouts here, but very comfortable – we all have beds, including the men. We are not in a bad part, so do not worry about me. I feel extraordinarily fit, better than I have been for a year. Your coat is a tremendous success in this cold weather and has been of the greatest use.

I can think of nothing but you all.

---

1 Brigadier General Mayne.
2 Money owed to Graham's sister and brother has been paid off by Lil.
3 His promotion to brigadier general.

Sunday, 28 January 1917 [from front-line trenches in Cléry]

We were moved suddenly yesterday – hence no letter. We are in dugouts, very comfortable but the cold is intense. I don't even remember such cold before. Two of our men were frostbitten.

Col Crawshay has been wounded. I am sorry that we shall lose him, but he is fortunately not badly hit.

I hope the K has come.

I walked in my sleep the night before last and woke up to find myself in the snow with only socks on. It has given me a bit of a cold. I think it is due to not having had much sleep lately.

Tuesday, 30 January 1917 [from front-line trenches in Cléry]

You cannot imagine what a relief it was for me to hear that your old friend [K] had arrived safely.

It is now early in the morning and I am trying to write on a very shaky table and in very bad candlelight.

The towels and socks arrived safely – also the pencil refills. Alas the pencil holder is lost. I am awfully upset that I have lost your cigarette case. With my new servant I am afraid I shall lose all I have. He is very worthy but extremely stupid.

At present I am so tired and so short of sleep that I cannot think. I have never known such cold – it still continues to freeze hard – and the river close to us is frozen over.

Poor little Eileen! What an event biting her own lip. When will she walk?

I cannot tell you how I long to see you all and wish some good chance would let it come about.

Thursday, 1 February 1917 [from billets in Suzanne]

I meant to have written you a tremendous letter – yesterday – the anniversary of a very happy day for me – and we were to have had an especial dinner, but the fates ordained otherwise. Everything went wrong and we did not get here till 1 or 2am, and I did not get to bed till 4am. These are the worst we have ever struck in the way of rest billets. The mess is a half dugout – cold, dark and the fire smokes. Our sleeping place is a bit better.

I did not get up till 11am and after lunch walked to a place to see another camp with Capt Hunter. On the way we met Wardrop, my old groom, with the transport of the 2nd Bn. He told us the 2nd Bn was only a mile off. On our way back I went into the Bde and found Capt DG Foster[1] who came out with us there – he had come to join again. Major Stirling and the adjutant of the 2nd Bn came to tea. I had a bath this evening, not having had one for over a week – I wanted it badly.

With all my love and thoughts and heaps of kisses to you and with the sincere hope that we shall spend all the 31st of Januarys together in future.

Friday, 2 February 1917 [from billets in Suzanne]

I am writing under adverse conditions – the hut is frightfully cold and full of smoke.

I got up pretty late, had orderly room, walked round the camp, talked to various people, mostly padres with a view to Sunday services. Padre McShane came to see us for a short time and Col Jack came to tea. He had a very bad cold and was not very cheerful.

Our pipers and buglers played retreat tonight and played very well. The buglers I was especially pleased with as they did not get much practice to keep their mouths hard.

I got the *Daily Mail* map alright – it just shows our part. Many thanks.

We have not been so uncomfortable as we are now for a long time. If it was not for your waistcoat and coat I should be perished. I slept well last night, but as a rule we all wake up from the cold.

If I sent my washing home could you get it done? We have been having difficulty in getting our clothes washed.

---

1 Sent home sick from Septmonts on 27 September 1914, later returned, before returning home despite Chaplin's objection. See the War Diary entry for 6 July 1915 and Chaplin's letter of 30 July 1915.

Saturday, 3 February 1917 [from billets in Suzanne]

The bitter cold still continues. We have improved the mess a little. We have had an unexciting day. Major HS and Col Jack came to tea – no news from either.

I dined tonight with the Divisional Staff – very comfortable, but I felt out of place.

Monday, 5 February 1917 [from billets in Suzanne]

Last night I was frozen stiff and could not write – my hands were too cold. Today we are much better off. We have got a stove which works, have closed up the open spaces and had a table and forms made. I got very little sleep on account of the cold, which shows no signs of diminishing.

I have had no letter from you for two days, but I got three together three days ago. It was funny the servants hearing of us on the film[1] – if it was us, we did not know that we were taken.

Yesterday I had tea with Col Jack and heard his drum and fife band – quite good. I should think he has a good battalion.[2] I went for a walk with him.

We are all anxious to hear what America is going to do about Germany's blockade.[3] I hardly think they will declare war.[4]

I am very anxious to get your photograph in your new jersey.

I am glad General C got the WO to reverse their decision.[5]

I do not expect to be able to write very much after a few days.

Wednesday, 7 February 1917 [from billets in Suzanne]

I do not ever remember being so cold as I was today. I got up at 5am and started on horseback to ride four or five miles. There was a high wind and everyone with a moustache had it frozen stiff. Afterwards I had a long walk

---

1 News film that mentions the regiment.

2 2nd West Yorks.

3 From 1 February 1917, Germany adopted a policy of unrestricted submarine warfare in an attempt to blockade Britain.

4 They did, two months later.

5 Possibly refers to General Cavan, commanding XIV, reversing a decision forbidding the men to wear leather jerkins.

and got back to camp about 11am. I was jolly glad to get three letters from you – I was beginning to be nervous.

About the life policies – I cannot remember exactly what they are or whether the premiums are paid yearly or half yearly. It is written on the policies. If you are in doubt, write to Standard Life and the Oriental companies and ask them and then just write to Cox and ask him to pay the premiums. It does not matter whether the policies are re-assigned to you or myself as you have my will, but I presume Lindsay re-assigned them.[1]

Your pie arrived today and was a real godsend. We are badly off for rations, we have had no potatoes for 10 days, the meat was uneatable, so we enjoyed the pie immensely.

It is very hard to write now, dear, not on account of nothing to say so much as the awful cold. The water is frozen in the mess even with a fire. Also both the Quartermaster and the adjutant are away on leave, so I have a lot to do.

Just fancy Eileen talking – when both of them talk there will be a lot of conversation.

No, I cannot throw the show up as long as I can last, but there will be no-one in France who will be more pleased to go home than I shall be – if the time ever comes.

Thursday, 8 February 1917 [from support trenches in Road Wood]
Just a line to say all's well. It is 2am here and I am frozen. I walked the whole way here, starting at 4.30pm and arriving at 8pm, since when I have walked three or four miles as we are very scattered.

Col Jack came to say goodbye. He has a very bad cold – I should not think he would last much longer.[2]

---

1 The life-assurance policies – three with Standard Life and one with Oriental – were taken out by Graham Chaplin a decade earlier, when he was a captain, and appear to have been temporarily assigned to his brother, Lindsay, perhaps as collateral for the £700 loan which Lindsay made. Lil has now paid the loan back and taken on the policies..
2 Jack is forced to retire sick from 27 February to 7 March.

Friday, 9 February 1917 [from front-line trenches in Road Wood]

I was jolly glad to get your letter of the 4th. I am sorry that you have been worrying about me, as I am very well – only suffering from the intense cold. We are much warmer and happier here than our supposed rest. There is simply nothing to write about. I got up very late, not having got to bed till 3am. Major HS came in about 9am whilst I was still in bed. I walked about most of the morning, making myself acquainted with the lie of the land.

We had potatoes today for lunch and dinner – the first time for 10 days.

Saturday, 10 February 1917 [FSPC]

I am quite well.

Sunday, 11 February 1917 [from front-line trenches in Road Wood]

I cannot understand why you should not have received my letters unless for the same reason that I get yours usually in batches of three.

If the regiment was taken on the cinematograph then I was not with them. It was the day I rejoined from hospital.

It has been uncommonly dull here. All the men on working parties. I have had nothing to do. I might have written letters but in these dugouts and with only candles it is trying to the eyes.

It is not so cold today. I hope the thaw does not come till we are out in rest – very selfish, but it will be extremely unpleasant when it does come.

I don't think the French things will be out for a long time.[1] It is no certainty that I shall get one, but I know that they tried hard for me.

I cannot get you out of my thoughts. A staff officer said to me the other day that I was probably the only officer who had served with a regiment continuously throughout the war.[2] I said that I would much rather they gave me a Brigade than that I should establish a record – although I have been lucky enough.

I wish I was in the nursery seeing the kids bathed.

---

1 French awards for gallantry – Chaplin later received the Croix de Guerre and Légion d'Honneur, which were given to British troops fighting alongside the French.

2 Of the 60,000 or so men who were shipped to France in August and September 1914, around 1,500 would have been infantry officers. It is hard to prove that Chaplin was the only officer left who hadn't been removed from the front line by promotion, death or injury, but it is a possibility.

Saturday, 17 February 1917 [from support trenches in Howitzer Wood]

We came out last night. I was absolutely tired – I do not remember ever being so tired. I simply could not write. I got to bed at 1.30am and slept like the dead till 10am, and woke up much refreshed. All day I have written and not had a moment to myself.

We have lived only in dugouts for a month. The artificial light and restricted life becomes very tiresome. For another week I shall not be able to write regularly, if at all – I will send only postcards. After that if all is well I will resume my daily letters.

I cannot understand Willie's manoeuvres or what he is driving at.

I had a tremendous surprise today – Capt McLellan[1] suddenly appeared to rejoin us. I am still keeping Capt Hunter as 2ⁿᵈ in command.

I should not harass myself too much about the food regulations[2] and I cannot bear to think that you are going to save up for me.

I only wish I could be with you.

Sunday, 18 February 1917 [FSPC]

I am quite well.

Monday, 19 February 1917 [from support trenches in Quarry sector, Howitzer Wood]

Yesterday I had a splendid long walk through miles of trenches, all to no purpose as we did not go there. I also had the same pleasant walk today, only more so.

The past month seems to have been one of the longest.

No, dear, I could not ask to be sent home. I must just stick it out and hope for the best. With all my love and thoughts and heaps of kisses to Jim and Eileen and yourself. For ever your loving husband, Graham

---

1 McLellan was tried by court martial in July 1915 on two charges 'for certain inaction' and acquitted on both. He appears to leave the battalion later that year, although no mention occurs of him in the battalion War Diary until June 1917.
2 Reports in British newspapers in early February stated that the government wanted to avoid compulsory rationing, but was keen for civilians to restrict themselves to 3 lb flour, 12 oz sugar and 2 lb, 8 oz of meat a week.

Thursday, 22 February 1917 [FSPC]

I am quite well.

Friday, 23 February 1917 [FSPC]

I am quite well.

ARMY SCHOOL

'Two years and seven months since we left Glasgow – it seems to me that I am 10,000 years older.'

The thaw comes and makes the ground around Cléry impassable. Simultaneously, divisional HQ pushes for a policy of aggressive raiding. General Pinney even agrees to restore the rum ration before assaults, in order to bolster men's morale. On 23 February, the 2nd Worcesters, 100th brigade, capture forty-three Germans in a surprise attack. More prisoners are taken by the Glasgow Highlanders in the same brigade.

The pressure is on Brigadier Mayne in the 19th to match these exploits. He proposes an attack to bite off a salient that protrudes into the line held by the 19th below Cléry. Battalion commanders are summoned to a conference to discuss how the assault should be planned. Chaplin and Captain Robert Graves, temporarily in charge of the 2nd Royal Welch, argue against it, pointing out how long it would take soldiers to advance across thawed open marsh, sinking in with every step, exposed to German machine-gun fire. None would survive. Mayne listens. The assault is cancelled.[157]

Then a call comes for Chaplin to head back to school – the Fourth Army is trying to re-educate senior officers in a war where lessons are slowly being learnt, and has commandeered a large three-storey chateau halfway between Abbeville and Amiens, many miles from the front, to give its men classes. The officers come in batches of twenty-five, and are billeted in the pretty village of Flixecourt, higher up the marshy Somme river, while attending a week of courses, interspersed with educational trips to mock battlefields and army depots. The classes range in subjects from gas and bayonet use to tactical thinking, and an overview of battles past.

It is Chaplin's first experience of a general, formal presentation of where the army stands after two and a half years of war.

It is also, for all front-line officers, a chance to discuss the war's progress, compare thoughts on methods, and sleep. In most cases, they leave behind battalions that have endured one of the worst winters on record, and are now exhausted, depleted and low in morale.

Sunday, 25 February 1917 [from Camp 19, Somme]

My darling,

I came out last night to get a bath before going to a conference down country which lasts a week. I go off tomorrow in a car.

I have never been so done. I don't think we have had such a long spell. I feel quite knocked up – the weather has been awful – but I feel alright tonight.

To my intense surprise I met Sandy – he was in a car – he is going to command his divisional school, very sick at not going back to his battalion, but I expect Baby will be pleased.

I had not heard from you for a week till today when I got six letters. I am very distressed that you are all so seedy and that you are having a bad time with the children. Everything seems to have come at once.

It makes me wish I could come home more than ever. You seem to be worse than anyone and there is nothing I can do to help you.

Tuesday, 27 February 1917 [from Army School in Flixecourt, outside Amiens]

After I wrote to you on the 25th I had no sleep as something went wrong[1] and I was up all night. I felt so seedy in the morning I almost thought that I could not start.

However I did alright. I travelled in a car with Col Scott of the 93rd[2] who is

---

1 Guides leading the Middlesex to relieve the Cameronians in support trenches at Road Wood got lost.
2 2nd Argyll & Sutherland Highlanders.

out again. We came through the place where I was in hospital.[1] We had a very good lunch – the first decent meal I have had in a long time. We arrived here[2] safely and got our billets. I have a nice room in an ironmonger's house. It is a treat to be in a house again after five weeks in dugouts and huts. There are 25 of us – it is nice to meet different people. There is a good mess, everything well done. I went to bed immediately after dinner and slept like the dead till 7am. This morning we went over all the various departments of the school and this evening had a very interesting lecture on the Somme Battle by an Army Staff Officer.

As soon as I had finished dinner I came back to the billet to write this and go to bed as soon as I have finished. I want to sleep as much as I can.

I do pray that you are all better. Unfortunately I shall not get your letters till I return on the 7th, when I hope the regiment will be back in some pleasant spot.

All the talk here is about the Germans withdrawing and how far they are going back.[3]

Wednesday, 28 February 1917 [from Army School in Flixecourt]

I got up at 8 this morning, had breakfast and we all went in a bus some distance and discussed a tactical scheme.

This afternoon we went by bus to the place where I was in hospital to see some things connected with the war. Some remained there to dinner but a few of us came back. I want to get in sleep whilst I have the chance.

The worst of being here is not getting your letters. I did not have them forwarded as I might miss them altogether. I am very anxious about you and simply pray that you are better.

Thursday, 1 March 1917 [from Army School in Flixecourt]

I did not go with the remainder this morning. The long ride in the open bus

---

1 Amiens.

2 Flixecourt.

3 The Germans were withdrawing to better defensive positions at the Hindenberg Line, constructed over the winter months.

yesterday made my eyes bad. We had two lectures, one rotten one and one very interesting one by a gunner.

They forwarded my letters – I got four from you. I am most thankful that you are all so much better.

We had a divisional band to play to us tonight – rather nice, but I wanted to get to bed.

Saturday, 3 March 1917 [from Army School in Flixecourt]

We had two more lectures, both fairly interesting.

I sleep about 10 hours every night, which makes all the difference to one.

Yes, Mabel has had rotten luck. It is extraordinarily inconsiderate of Reggie never to take any sort of interest in her. Give her my love.

No, I don't think I could apply for a job at home, but if they do not soon give me what we want I shall have to do something. Thank heaven the winter is practically over, or will be by the time we have had our rest.

Thursday, 8 March 1917 [from 33rd divisional HQ, Somme]

I have been travelling for several days, hence no letters. I could not write the night I left – my eyes were so inflamed I could not see.

We went by bus and train down to a pleasant place on the sea and then travelled about seeing training depots and bases.

We came back 50 miles in a bus – very cold and miserable. In the morning we left. The Army commander[1] gave an address to us – it was very interesting, a sort of review of the whole war – and then we went back to our regiments. I came back with Col Scott – another 50-mile bus ride. The regiment had not moved as soon as I expected. They march today but I have not seen them. I was put up at Divisional Hd Qrs and made very comfortable – a good dinner and a good night's rest.

---

1 General Sir Henry Rawlinson, responsible for many of the tactics that failed on the Somme.

I am commanding the Brigade[1] until the General[2] comes. They come here today and I move with them tomorrow.

I am awfully pleased to hear that you and the children are alright again but sorry to hear of your mother's relapse. I will write to Edith if I have time.

We have had a lot of snow. I suppose this is the last of the winter – I hope so. I could not write whilst we were on this trip as there was no way of getting the letters censored.

Friday, 9 March 1917 [from Camp 13, Somme]

I took over the Brigade last night. Col Clayton[3] and Major HS[4] came in about 11 o'c – we talked for a bit and then I went to bed. I got up at 8 o'c and was glad to find my eyes much better – not having to ride in an open bus for a day. We breakfasted and rode to this place[5] – we have a pretty good but cold billet. It is still snowing.

Capt Hunter and the Dr came to see me after lunch and I walked up to their camp with them. They are all well and everyone cheery after a very long spell without much rest or comfort.

I feel very much better than I have for a long time – no doubt after another week's sleep I shall be walking on the tips of my toes.

I hope we do not remain here long as the regiment is only in huts, which are none too comfortable in this weather.

Saturday, 10 March 1917 [from Camp 13, Somme]

I have not had a very exciting day. It has started to thaw and the mud is awful.

This afternoon I walked round the camps – it was very heavy going. I saw Capt Wright in our camp and he came back to tea with me. He told me that Capt Minchin is engaged to be married – he did not know the lady's name. Capt Wright is applying to come back to us.

---

1 19th brigade.
2 Brigadier General Mayne.
3 Commanding officer, 5th Scottish Rifles.
4 Major Hyde-Smith is commanding the Cameronians in Chaplin's absence.
5 Camp 13, near Bray-sur-Somme.

Major Twiss also came to tea. He is looking very fit after his month's leave, which he spent mostly in Devonshire.

Major HS is going to the Division and Capt Foster is going to the Army as a learner.

I suppose Eileen will soon begin to talk now as she will be a year old next month.

I go to bed very early these days – I have plenty of sleep to make up.

Sunday, 11 March 1917 [from Camp 13, Somme]

The post came today and I got five letters from you, which pleased me immensely. I am very glad that Jim and Eileen are quite fit again. I am sorry you still have neuralgia – it is funny that the Dr can do nothing for it.

I got a nice pie and cake from Edith.

As it is Sunday I have had a quiet day. I rode round the camps this morning and saw all the regiments and went for a walk with Major HS in the afternoon.

I saw General P for a minute today – he is coming to inspect us tomorrow morning and lunching with us probably.

I am beginning to think also that it is time that I had a rest at home soon or had an easier life. It has defeated everyone why I have not got a brigade – I cannot understand it – but perhaps it will come soon.

Monday, 12 March 1917 [from Camp 13, Somme]

The General came and inspected the regiments today. He cantered all over the place. I was not very pleased as the ground was very muddy and I got splashed from head to foot.

It rained in the afternoon and I have not moved out, so it has been very dull.

Tuesday, 13 March 1917 [from Camp 13, Somme]

There is no mail today. I am back with the regiment. We have a fairly comfortable hut, but the whole place is surrounded with mud.

We are all pleased about Bagdhad[1] falling.

Two years and seven months since we left Glasgow – it seems to me that I am 10,000 years older.

Tomorrow we are going to have a day in the country – lectures in the morning and lectures in the afternoon.

I am glad that the winter is over. I could not stand another tour in the trenches – this last one nearly finished me. Three winters up to my middle has begun to start rheumatism.

Wednesday, 14 March 1917 [from Camp 13, Somme]

This morning all COs went into a town[2] about six miles off by bus. We had a lecture in the morning, had lunch in a café and in the afternoon another lecture. I came back in a car with the General, had tea at Bde Hd Qrs and then rode back to camp and have been busy since – writing etc.

I had three letters from you today – I am very sorry to hear about your mother.

I am glad Jim and Eileen are getting less shy – they do not do themselves justice when they cry.

I am afraid, dear, that there is no chance at all of leave – at least that is the general impression. I would give anything to see you and the children. I have never felt so tired.

Thursday, 15 March 1917 [from Camp 13, Somme]

This morning I had a fairly long ride. I went out to see companies route marching, came back to lunch, had orderly room and then had a fairly long walk, doing a regimental exercise with all officers, and got back for a late tea – then lots of writing and dinner.

Mr Becher came back today, looking more delicate than ever.

It has dried up a bit – the sun has been shining and the camp looks a little

---

1 Baghdad was captured by British forces, led by General Maude, on 11 March 1917, after the occupying Ottoman forces withdrew.
2 Albert.

less dreary – but we shall all be glad to move away but we don't know yet when that will be.

It is an awful nuisance that you cannot get a cook. If they are going to send a lot of women out here I suppose the servant question will become more difficult still.

Friday, 16 March 1917 [from Camp 13, Somme]

No post again today, at least no letters.

This morning I walked most of the morning going round the camp and seeing the companies at work. In the afternoon I rode out to inspect our transport. Capt Wright came to tea – he was looking very well and has put in to rejoin us.

Afterwards I had to go to a Brigade conference. It was very dark and misty coming back. I got absolutely lost riding across country and was jolly glad to find myself back.

I am feeling quite fit again. I began to think I was done the last time I came out of the trenches – I felt awfully ill. We had a severe time of it in the way of weather. I have never seen the men so done, but they are looking much better now.

I wish to goodness I could get leave but I am afraid it will not be possible.

Everyone seems to be very optimistic about the end being near. Kiss Jim and Eileen for me.

Saturday, 17 March 1917 [from Camp 13, Somme]

I got two letters from you today and was very glad to get them. I am very sorry you have had so much trouble with your teeth and glad that they are finished. Yes, I suppose that Jim is getting quite a man.

This seems a bad business in Russia[1] – there have been rumours of trouble for a long time. I hope that it will not affect their taking a part in the war, but it must affect them.

Major HS has come back to the Brigade to do Major Twiss's job – who

---

1 First reports had emerged of the February Revolution in St Petersburg, when mutinous Russian soldiers supported protestors in clashes with police.

has been ordered back to India, much to his disgust. I am like the mill stream which goes on forever – I have seen the Brigade change twice over.

There was a poor fellow in the Flying Corps killed here today. His machine crashed to the ground – the only accident I have known.

My hair is very bad – in spite of the hairwash which I am afraid does no good and is not worth going on with. The doctor has painted my eyes with nitrate of silver[1] – I hope it will have the desired effect.

My temper is getting very short these days – I really get quite angry sometimes.

I wish you could send me a snapshot of Eileen with her new hair.

Sunday, 18 March 1917 [from Camp 13, Somme]

Today being the Sabbath I went to the Presbyterian Service and was very sorry I did. It was in the open and very cold and lasted ¾ of an hour and the parson was very dull and boresome. The General was there.

I did some work after lunch and then went for quite a long walk by myself, which I quite enjoyed. I passed a man working in the road in RS[2] uniform, who said to me "Have you the time on you, Jock?" I said "Don't you know an officer when you see one?" He replied "I have not been in the Army that long." I asked how long he had been and he said six weeks.[3]

I hope this revolution in Russia does make them buck up and get on with the war. The withdrawal of the Germans[4] seems to extend a long way now.

We have got to lighten our kits so I shall probably send some kit home.

Monday, 19 March 1917 [FSPC]

I am quite well.

---

1 Used for removal of small quantities of unwanted tissue, e.g. warts and verrucas – now considered unsuitable to use near tissue areas which do not regenerate, such as eyes.
2 Royal Sussex.
3 Regular soldiers, such as Chaplin, found the easing of old habits, such as automatically saluting an officer, very hard to accept, unless under battlefield conditions – the gulf between the old and New Army recruits was wide.
4 To the more easily defended Hindenburg Line.

Tuesday, 20 March 1917 [from Camp 13, Somme]

Last night I had to retire to bed instead of writing – I got a chill standing on Church Parade on Sunday – but I am alright today. The companies went route-marching but I did not go out in the morning as there was a high wind and I wanted to save my eyes. This afternoon I took all the officers out and did a scheme, which took all the afternoon. It has been a miserable day – cold and windy.

We are all sick that the German retirement did not start whilst we were in the line – it would have been interesting following them up.

General R[1] will be in the same Corps as ourselves. I am going to tell him that I hope he will do what he can – if he can do anything – for me.

Wednesday, 21 March 1917 [from Camp 13, Somme]

I had a very unexciting morning – walking all over the country looking at the companies.

This afternoon we had a Brigade scheme – also very dull.

Tonight I dined with Col Garnett[2] – Major Poore[3] who is now their second in command and who came from the Yeomanry married Marjorie Denistoun, Capt Despard's[4] step-daughter.

You know nowadays sooner than we do what is happening. We get our latest news from the English papers. No-one knows what is going to happen but we expect to be here another week.

I got a cake yesterday and one today from Gunter – they came opportunely as I had no more cigarettes.

Thursday, 22 March 1917 [from Camp 13, Somme]

It has been a miserable day – the whole countryside was covered in snow when we woke and it has snowed in blizzards during the day.

I walked a lot in the morning seeing the companies and in the afternoon did a scheme. Major HS came to tea.

---

1 Robertson, commanding 17th Division.
2 Commanding the 2nd Royal Welch.
3 Major Roger Poore, killed by a shell outside Ypres later that year.
4 Captain H. J. Despard was the chief constable of Lanarkshire.

This evening we played bridge.

I wonder why Lindsay[1] has suddenly been inspired with a desire to come out here – it is a bit late.

The news is interesting now about the German retirement – I wonder what it all means?

Friday, 23 March 1917 [from Camp 13, Somme]

It has been a more Christianlike day today – it was quite warm in the middle of the day.

I rode out this morning and saw the companies route-marching and this afternoon after seeing a company on the range went for a walk with Major HS.

We don't know yet when we move but I don't suppose we shall be here much longer and I shan't be sorry.

I shall be very glad to get the snapshots of Jim and Eileen. Cotton my servant stupidly left my photos behind with the spare kit – not knowing my ways – so I have no photographs of any of you, for the first time in the war.

I have got to get a new string to my identity disc – the old one has become so rotten that I can tie it no longer. I quite dislike parting with it.

With all my love, darling, and many kisses to you and Jim and Eileen.

Saturday, 24 March 1917 [from Camp 13, Somme]

It has been a splendid day today – the only real fine day we have had. In the morning I walked over the country looking at the companies in training and then went to a very dull lecture. I went to tea at Bde with Capt McLellan and afterwards went for a walk with him and Major HS.

When we were out walking I saw two English nurses, the first I have seen in this part of the world.

We advance the time an hour tonight.

I shall be anxious to see the snapshots of Eileen and Jim – I hope they are a success.

---

1 Graham Chaplin's elder brother.

I am going to make a desperate effort to get a belt tomorrow. I shall have to go to Church, much to my annoyance, as General P is coming.

I have not heard from RO again or ever from Harriette and do not know where they are.

Sunday, 25 March 1917 [from Camp 13, Somme]

Today was spoilt for me by having to go to Church owing to General P coming to the service. It was bitterly cold and I was very cross. Afterwards it became fairly warm. I had lunch here and afterwards Major HS came and after tea we went for a long walk.

I wonder how Mrs Harriette will get on going to Paris? It is an awful journey apparently there and back – and you have to go by Havre.

I should think Devonshire would be the place to take the children to – no danger there from shelling and very fine country I believe, although I have never been there.

It will be three months on the 8th since I left home – the most wearisome months I have had in the war.

We had a chicken tonight for a change. The padre bought it in the village. It is a great thing in this country to have an RC padre.

What brutes these Germans have been[1] in their retirement.

Monday, 26 March 1917 [from Camp 13, Somme]

I am very glad to hear that Nancy[2] is stopping – it will save you a lot of worry and the children will be better for it.

It has rained all day. This morning I walked to the Brigade and in the afternoon acted as judge in a horserace.

Major Spens[3] dined here tonight. He is a brother of the one who married Torky's little friend Miss Donaldson.

---

1 The German army destroyed infrastructure and booby-trapped buildings as they retired to delay the advance of the French and British armies.

2 Lil Chaplin's cook.

3 Hugh Baird Spens later became commanding officer of 5th battalion Scottish Rifles. His younger brother, John Ivan Spens, married Gwendoline Donaldson.

We expect to be here some days yet. I shall be jolly glad when we move.

Yes, I think it would be well worth it if you could come to Paris if I cannot get leave home, but it will be difficult to arrange as you would take several days to get there but if I should send you a telegram could you start at once and also we should have to arrange some hotel so that we should be certain to meet. I still have hopes that I shall get leave home as I am due on the 8th and leave has not yet been stopped as far as I know. Anyway I shall apply for it and if I cannot get it I shall try to get leave to Paris and will wire you.

I simply long to see you again. I have never felt as homesick as I do now.

With all my love, darling, and heaps of kisses to Jim and Eileen and to you. For ever your loving husband, Graham

HINDENBURG

'It was curious in the battle, amongst such a scene of carnage, that my orderly picked up a baby's shoe – I suppose some father was carrying it as a memento . . .'

German army destroys roads, villages and orchards in retreat to new Hindenburg Line – British, Canadian, Indian, Australian and New Zealand troops attack around Arras – French offensive opens on front between Reims and Roye – high casualty rate leads to first mutinies among French troops – America declares war on Germany

The war has taken another twist. As winter turns to spring in 1917, British probings reveal that the German army has fallen back to a new, carefully prepared position, shortening the front it must defend. Now the enemy occupies the heavily fortified Hindenburg Line, stretching from outside Arras, south of Béthune, to Laffaux, near Soissons – the medieval town north-east of Paris where Graham Chaplin had ended his retreat from Mons two and a half years previously. The new German line, marked by two deep trenches, 200 yards apart, has been built over the winter months, and runs for ninety miles, incorporating steel-reinforced dugouts, observation posts and machine-gun nests, linked by heavily protected tunnels and telephone cables. Part of it is built using the reverse-slope defensive strategy popularised by Wellington in his battles against the French – lining troops beyond the crest of raised ground. Thus invisible, they can pick off the enemy as they advance over the top. That allows at least part of the Hindenburg Line to remain hidden from ground-based artillery observers. The Germans also adopt a new strategy of elastic defence, planning for the enemy to overrun positions until lines of communication are stretched, then counter-attacking with well-hidden reserves, kept near the front, to regain lost ground.

The German army starts to pull back in March, destroying roads and railways as it retreats, cratering crossroads, poisoning wells, razing villages, felling orchards, driving all inhabitants out, aiming to leave no cover, food or water for the advancing enemy. The British and French press forward

tentatively, hindered by German rearguard actions, always nervously wondering if the retreat is a bluff before a devastating counter-attack elsewhere
– in particular, an assault in the north to seize the Channel ports. If the
British have an opportunity to harass and overtake the withdrawing German
army, they choose not to pursue it.

Instead, they redraw long-laid plans for a major push south of Béthune,
designed to draw German forces away from a proposed French assault
further south on the Aisne. British forces have increased to fill five armies,
three of which – the First, Third and Fifth – congregate their divisions
around Arras, north of the Somme, ready to assault the new German
defensive positions. The First Army sends in the Canadian Corps on 9
April to take Vimy Ridge, a strategically vital escarpment north of Arras.
To the south, British and Australian divisions of the Fifth Army attack the
village of Bullecourt. Both make initial advances. But between the two,
the Third Army comes to a juddering halt against the Hindenburg Line.

This is the war Chaplin rejoins after a precious week at home on leave
in early April. Spring has lifted the gloom of winter; many in Britain are
optimistic that a breakthrough can now be made with the Allied forces
showing overwhelming superiority in numbers and technology – the new
tanks proving a formidable weapon, when used on suitable ground. And
on 6 April, American Congress, angered by the ruthless sinking of ships
by German U-boats, votes to enter the war. Soon its soldiers will arrive in
France to fight side by side with the British. Despite the likely collapse of
Russian forces in the east, allowing the Germans to shift resources west,
the war looks winnable again.

While Chaplin is away, the 33rd division is sent north from the Somme
to bolster the Third Army, and by Easter Sunday, 8 April, it finds itself
heading towards the battlefields of Arras and now part of VII Corps,
commanded by General Sir Thomas Snow – a senior officer Chaplin knows
all too well.[158] But he must swallow his misgivings and, a day after leaving
Lil in London, yet again find his men.

Tuesday, 10 April 1917 [from billets in Bailleulval, south-west of Arras]

My own darling,

My heart felt like lead at leaving you yesterday and I wonder what you did and whether you caught the 11.00 train.

General Hamilton came up and spoke to me on the boat – it was absolutely crowded – I had lunch on board. I did not see anyone else I knew. The sea was rough and the boat rolled badly. As soon as I landed[1] I got a wire to say which station was our railhead. I went to the RTO and found that the train left at 9.05pm so I went to the Folkestone and read Blackwood and had tea. I then went for a long walk alone round the old town. I met the nice ASC fellow I travelled down with – I did not see him on the boat. We dined together and left in good time for the train. Unfortunately we stood at the wrong end of the platform so could only get a 2nd class carriage, with a family in it. The train crawled along and I did not get to the place where I was told by the RTO to go till 1 o'c. You can imagine how pleased I was when I was told that I had been directed to the wrong station and that I should have to go back to very near Boulogne by a train this morning. I made such a fuss that they put me on a supply train, where I had a seat in the guard's van – very uncomfortable but I slept a little. This morning I found out that when I was near my destination I should have a tremendous wait, so I got out and walked, getting a lift part of the way in a lorry. I arrived at our railhead. I could not find anyone who knew where the Division was, so I walked on till I came to the Headquarters of another division. I walked in the first door I saw and the staff officer in there happened to be a man I had known well in India. They put me on to our Division by telephone and I asked them to send a car for me, which they did. I had lunch and the car duly arrived and brought me back. I found everyone and everything well. Before I forget, the sandwiches you made me take were very useful as I had nothing else between dinner last night and lunch today.

We are in a small village and are quite comfortable. It has been snowing hard this afternoon, so we are glad of a house.

When we got to Boulogne we heard rumours of 10,000 prisoners. It was

---

1 In Boulogne.

exaggerated then, but we have over that now – but you will see it all in the papers before you get this – still everything is going well, which is the great thing.

I feel fearfully homesick for you all and would give anything to be back.

I hope and pray that you are well. With all my love and all my thoughts. For ever your loving husband, Graham

Friday, 13 April 1917 [FSPC]
I am quite well.

Extracts from the battalion War Diary, April 1917,

Kept by Colonel Graham Chaplin

Hénin[1]

12 April – CO reconnoitred ground as far as Hénin. Battn marched to Hénin and took up position in sunken roads in front of Hénin. C&D relieving 18th Northumberland Regt (30th Div).

13 April – A&B Coys moved forward to positions in T4, d55 vacated by 21st Div when they moved forward to attack.

Hindenburg Line

14 April – A&B Coys moved forward and took up position for attack. The 19th Bde was placed under orders of the 21st Div.

A Coy attacked down Hindenburg front and support line with two platoons in each, D Coy in support to A. B Coy failed to get

---

1 Hénin-sur-Cojeul, south of Héninel.

in the proper position. C Coy therefore became the attacking
Coy and took up position from Hindenburg support line to a
point 200 yards north of it. At 5.30am both companies went
forward but were held up in both lines by enemy barricades.
Actual ground gained was in front line 150 yards, in support
100 yards. C Coy on left held up by MG fire got forward and
dug in. Positions gained were consolidated. Casualties killed:
Capt D Foster, Lieut McFarlane. Wounded: Capt I Brown, Lieut
Sloan (died of wounds), Lieut McGregor.

15 April – Bombs etc brought up preparatory to a further
attack by two coys.

16 April – At 4.15am two companies renewed attack down
Hindenburg Line. The officers in command in the support line
failed to start at the correct time, this prevented the
success of the operation. The attack down the front line got
forward 500 yards at dawn, but owing to arrival of enemy
reinforcements and bombs running short, we were driven back
to the original position. Fifty bombers of the Royal Welch
Fusiliers were sent up to reinforce H'Burg front line. The
Battn was relieved by the 4th Suffolks.

Hénin
17 April – Battalion in bivouac along Hénin-Neuville-Vitasse
road. Men cleaning up and overhauling Lewis guns etc.

18 April – Ditto.

19 April – Ditto.

The battalion is still in Bailleulval, south-west of Arras, when the Third Army's main assault begins at 5.30 a.m. on Easter Monday. The Cameronians' War Diary notes proudly that 6,100 prisoners are taken by the Third Army on that first day of assault, 11,000 by the Third and First Armies combined on the second day. By Wednesday, 11 April, Chaplin is marching his men in heavy snow to Mercatel, eight miles further east, all keen to take part in likely victory. The next day they march past the remnants of blasted villages to Hénin-sur-Cojeul, just a mile from the front line where the Germans are now counter-attacking vigorously. The 19th brigade is placed under the orders of 21st division, which has already captured a small part of the Hindenburg Line as it breaks across the La Sensée river. British troops, still confident, have blocked trench and tunnel to prevent German attempts at recapturing the position. The same day, General Allenby, commanding the Third Army, publishes an order stating, 'We are in pursuit of a beaten enemy . . .'

To Cameronian eyes, the Hindenburg is a magnificent creation with yards of thick defensive wiring and twin deep trenches, the second followed underground by a large, wide tunnel, forty feet down, with alcoved chambers offering mess rooms and sleeping quarters. The chambers are so deep that they are unaffected by heaving shelling above. Into this, the Cams are sent with orders to attack the Germans and push on to gain more of the Hindenburg.

It is deadly work, parties of bomb throwers trying to blast past resolute defenders dodging down complicated trench and tunnel networks, often resorting to bitter hand-to-hand fighting with cudgels, blackjacks and bayonets, the worst the Cams have experienced so far. The gains are modest at a high cost. The Germans are anything but beaten.

Chaplin establishes an HQ deep in a captured bunker, liaising with brigade and his companies by runner, walking his battalion positions by day, then retreating into the ground before the attacks start again at night, waiting for news of advances above, balancing that against fighting to left and right, coordination impossible in the heat of battle. Overnight on Monday, 16 April, a party of Royal Welch bombers, under Lieutenant

Sassoon, are added to the Cams as reserve, and put under Chaplin's command. Plans laid by brigade HQ to attack in the tunnel, as well as above ground, are shelved[159] as the Cams throw men into raiding-party attacks over the blocked trenches at 4 a.m. on 17 April. The Royal Welch bombers follow them in, gaining new ground,[160] which is lost over the next day when the Germans counter-attack as the exhausted Cameronians are relieved by the 4th Suffolks, part of the 98th brigade, and fall back to a tented camp to recover. Chaplin moves his battalion HQ to another unused German bunker, and starts writing to Lil again.

Tuesday, 17 April 1917 [from a bunker in the Hindenburg Line]
My darling,

I have not been able to write for several days – till today I have only had about six hours' sleep in five days. The men are in the open but we are in a wonderful German dugout – I suppose Brigade Hd Qrs. We are about 40 feet underground, there is a big mess room and several bedrooms. It had been prepared for demolition but I suppose the Germans had been shifted too quickly. The German trenches are wonderful works – the wire appalling and a passage for living in 30 feet below ground running the whole length I have seen.

Captain Foster was killed – he died most gallantly, leading his company in great style. Capt Wright is slightly wounded by a bomb – he did very well.

I am so tired that I cannot write very well, but I am very fit.

I think of you all the time and hope that you are well and the K will be there.

Wednesday, 18 April 1917 [from a bunker in the Hindenburg Line]
I got three letters from you today. I am very distressed to hear that you are so seedy. I hope and believe that you are alright – I cannot believe otherwise.

I slept till 10 this morning. It was 12 o'c by the time I had breakfast – the Brigadier came then. I walked round the companies, who were living in holes dug by the side of the road.[1] I then had breakfast or lunch with the transport and

---

1 In bivouac along the Hénin–Neuville-Vitasse Road, according to the War Diary.

wrote my official correspondence in a shed. I had tea with the Quartermaster in a forge – the only remaining house in a village. I walked afterwards to a Field Ambulance to ask after a wounded officer. When I got back I found Major Riddell-Webster here looking very flourishing, having motored over to see me.

The day we left the line, Ernest Shepard[1] came into our dugout. He was looking very well and, with a moustache, much improved in appearance.

I got a pie and tart from Edith – most welcome as we only had bully beef for dinner, which we have lived on for the last week.

Can you send me a new electric torch? Mine is broken.

Thursday, 19 April 1917 [from a bunker in the Hindenburg Line]

I got up late this morning and was walking down the road when I met General P – he seemed very pleased to see me. Our late show was a rotten one[2] – it is just our luck – but everyone is very pleased with the regiment. Unfortunately we have lost all our best fellows. I lunched with General M[3] and then went on to another Brigade. I was riding back when my horse got tied up in some wire and fell on me. My foot was jammed in the stirrup and I thought I was for it but some men rushed over and released me. I was not hurt at all, but covered in mud. I stopped at the Quartermaster's to wash and had tea there.

We had a great dinner tonight and bread for the first time for a week.

It is still raining and miserable.

With all my love and heaps of kisses. For ever your loving husband Graham

Saturday, 21 April 1917 [FSPC]

I am quite well.

---

1 Ernest Shepard, married to Graham Chaplin's sister, Florence, enrolled in the Royal Garrison Artillery in 1915. By 1917 he was using his drawing skills to create battlefield sketches for Army Intelligence as a forward observation officer. Chaplin's remark about Shepard's moustache is a typical droll aside from an old soldier regarding the appearance of a new one.

2 A failed attack down the Hindenburg Line, 14–16 April.

3 Brigadier-General Mayne.

Extracts from the battalion War Diary,
April 1917,

Kept by Colonel Graham Chaplin

Hénin
20 April – Relieved Middlesex Regt in left sub sector. Digging
of assembly trenches continued.

21 April – Quiet day.

22 April – Relieved by two coys Middlesex and two coys
Argylls.

23 April – Attack by the 98th and 100th Brigades – 700
prisoners taken. Suffolks driven back to original position.
Two coys (Argylls and Middlesex) held out in very advanced
position.
   At 2pm the Bn moved up to sunken road. Two coys carried
bombs up for 98th Bde.
   At 5pm Bn moved up in support of 98th Bde.
   At 11pm one coy sent up Hindenburg front line coming under
orders of OC 4th Suffolks. One coy carrying bombs to H'urg
support. One coy relieved one coy on left of H'burg support.

24 April – Coy on right of Hindenburg line brought back and
kept in the tunnel. Relief of 4th Suffolks in front position
finished by 8pm. Enemy reported to be retiring on left of
Hindenburg support line. Patrols pushed forward down both
front and support lines. Reported enemy has retired down
these lines also. Final position taken up on sunken road in
support line T6 and 9.6 and 150 yards in front of sunken road
T6 and 4.4 in front line. Blocks made at these two points.

20th Royal Fusiliers relieve A Coy on left. A coy brought
back into reserve. 20 prisoners, three machine guns, seven
trench mortars, three *minenwerfer* taken. Two coys 18th Middx
Pioneers dug trenches to protect left flank just north of the
Hindenburg support front T5.6.9.8 to T6.6.3.0. Four trenches
dug to be held by A Coy. Blocks in both lines strengthened,
also in second block in rear of front block made, and a block
in tunnel in support line.

25 April - At dawn A Coy occupied the trenches dug by the
pioneers north of H'burg Line, keeping sentries in each by
day, remainder of men in the tunnel. The Battn relieved by the
9th KOYLI (27th Div) and go in bivouacs at Boiry-Becquerelle.

26 April - March to tents at Ficheux, five miles.

27 April - March to Bailleulval, six miles.

Thursday, 26 April 1917 [from tents in Ficheux, near Bailleulval]
My darling,

We have crowded so much into the last few days and had so little sleep
that I can hardly remember dates.

We came out of the battle on the 21st – I think I wrote last on that day. We
were ordered back on that day – we were relieved at 1am on the 23rd, and at
3pm on the same date went back once more. We were all up that night, took
over in the front line on the morning of the 24th. At 8am we advanced, took
prisoners, machine guns, and had the most interesting day we have had in
the war. We came out of the battle last night. I had only had about 10 hours
sleep since the 21st so I slept like the dead. We are now going back to where
I rejoined the regiment when I came out from leave.

General M congratulated me today on how the regiment had done and General

P came this afternoon and shook hands with me most warmly and congratulated me. We had the hardest time of any regiment and they did splendidly.

I am afraid I forgot poor little Eileen's birthday[1] owing to the battle.

You must not worry, dear, about the letters – naturally things don't run smoothly in these shows and you would hear soon enough if I was hit.

I am afraid I shall have to get a new coat as I look rather shabby now.

Major HS[2] has come back to us, I am glad to say, but no orders have come to us as to whether he is to stay.

In the fighting we retook some of our own men who have been wounded and taken by the Germans. They said the Germans were very kind to them.

I want some toilet paper badly.

Well, my darling, I must close and go to sleep. I think of you and Jim and Eileen the whole time.

Friday, 27 April [telegram]
All well Graham Chaplin

Saturday, 28 April 1917 [from billets in Bailleulval]
I am ashamed to say that I did not write last night. I waited till everyone had gone and then could not find any paper, the servants having packed away my block. I thought I would be awake early enough to catch the post but of course I never woke till it had gone.

Yesterday we marched from our camp at 9.30 in the morning – a short and pleasant march. General P watched the regiment go by and was very pleased with their marching and turnout after the hard time they had been through.

We are in a different farm to what we had before, but it is quite nice and I have a room to myself, which I like.

We did not get lunch till late – after which I rode with Major HS about seven miles to see a famous part of the old German front line, where we had

---

1 Eileen was one year old on 18 April.

2 Hyde-Smith, who had worked as brigade major at 19th brigade headquarters since January. See Chaplin's letter of 25 January 1917.

held the trenches opposite to it[1] – it was very interesting of course to us. It was a pleasant day and we saw primroses and daffodils coming up amongst the appalling scene of desolation. We got back too late for tea.

We played bridge – Capt McL, Mr McFie, HS and myself – and I lost both rubbers.

I slept like the dead till after eight and then took a long time getting up and having a bath – I was appallingly dirty. With new underclothes I felt a new man. I walked over and held orderly room and then breakfasted. One of the staff came to see me and stayed a long time and then General M came. He told me that he was writing a special report on how well the regiment had done in the late operations. He came into my room and was very interested in the portraits of Jim and Eileen.

It was curious in the battle, amongst such a scene of carnage, that my orderly picked up a baby's shoe – I suppose some father was carrying it as a memento.

Capt McL picked up a letter from a French girl to a German officer enclosing her photograph. The letter was full of devotion and love – it strikes me as peculiarly horrible when one sees what the Germans have done to her country.

Now I have to go off to inspect a draft which has arrived.

Sunday, 29 April 1917 [from billets in Bailleulval]

I cannot understand why you are not getting my letters and postcards. I have never missed more than two or three days. I am sending this by an officer going on leave.

I enclose a copy of a letter sent by General M to the Division about me – it is very flattering but I thought you would like to have it, but don't show it to anyone.

It is a most lovely day, just like summer. I walked over with Major HS to the Bde, where we saw General P. We rode back and had a good lunch and afterwards General M inspected the draft.

I am glad you ordered a navy-blue dress as I like you in them so much.

I am sorry about Mrs Harriette being so seedy.

---

1 Beyond Foncquevillers on the Somme.

No, I should not take six guineas a week for the house.

With all my fondest love and heaps of kisses to Jim and Eileen. For ever your loving husband, Graham

BRIGADIER GENERAL MAYNE'S REPORT, dated 28 April 1917
Headquarters, 33rd Division

I wish to bring to the notice of the GOC 33rd Division the excellent work of Lieut Colonel J G Chaplin DSO, 1st Battalion the Scottish Rifles (Cameronians) during the fighting between April 12th and 25th.

The Battalion took over the Hindenburg Front and Support Line from the 62nd Brigade on the night of 13th/14th April and made a bombing attack on the early morning of 14th April. It again went into the Hindenburg Line on night of 20th April till night of 22nd/23rd April when it was relieved, the relief being complete at 1am 23rd.

At 12.40pm it was moved up to close support and at 5pm went back to the Hindenburg Line where it remained until relieved on night of 25th April.

Throughout the period Lieut Colonel Chaplin displayed great determination. His dispositions were in my opinion sound, and he was always cheerful. During the last 48 hours he had to hold a nasty bit of the line with very tired troops to whom he set a fine example. I understand that Lieut Colonel Chaplin has been recommended for the command of an Infantry Brigade and so I submit this report in case the GOC may think fit to forward it to higher authority.

C Mayne Brigadier General
Commanding 19th Infantry Brigade
28th April 1917

*   *   *

Withdrawn to rest and refit, the Cameronians march west to Bailleulval, south of Arras, then further south to the ruined village of Monchy-au-Bois, part of the old German front line in the pre-Hindenburg days. They have seen the fiercest fighting and, despite the army's willingness to learn new lessons, have witnessed little change in tactics. Battalion after battalion has been thrown at strongly held points, in plans laid by staff officers unfamiliar with the territory. Changes suggested by commanders on the ground are frequently treated as challenges to authority.[161] Divisional accounts written after the fighting often seem laughable to those who were there. There is scant progress.

By 24 April, the Germans have at least pulled back from the line being attacked by the 33rd division, partially conceding ground after persistent assault. The corps and the division claim a great victory, and plaudits are shared among the brigades. Just a few note that the German withdrawal was not on account of any strategic masterstroke on the British part, but likely to be because of exhaustion.

If praise is to be handed out, however, every survivor of the fighting above and below ground feels he deserves it. Brigadier General Mayne, in charge of the 19th brigade, will have noted the accolades received by those commanding the 98th and 100th brigades fighting alongside him, and how his battalions are now on occasion being lent to other brigadiers – he needs some gains of his own. His generous, written praise of his most senior colonel is a noble gesture, well deserved by its recipient, but it also has its political uses. Perhaps, too, it eases the pressure being put on him by an officer who is desperate to leave.

The increased likelihood of promotion lifts Graham Chaplin's mood. From 1 May his letters to Lil are more jovial, more hopeful in tone. He comments on the gossip Lil relays: 'Yes, it must be awkward for the lady who has married again to find her husband is alive – I expect he will be quite cross.'[162]

And he notes that, in ground the Cams have moved across, the Germans have given dead British soldiers proper graves: 'It makes one have a better opinion of them.'[163]

Sam Darling's mother sends him apples. Meanwhile, the battalion trains for the next planned attack. General Snow now worries that rifle skills have been lost in the obsession with the bomb. He demands that the Cams relearn their once-renowned technique of rapid fire. New soldiers, old methods, a different mix – everything is tried except, perhaps, canvassing officer opinion. The assaults on the German line remain relentless.

Chaplin is again told he will be held back from the next assault – a regular policy now to preserve some experienced officers. 'This will please you but I hate it,' he writes to Lil. 'It is a thousand times more anxious work sitting behind.'[164]

He also comments about the lack of German graves – 'perhaps they have all gone to the Corpse Factory'[165] – and gossips about families they know, the Draffens and Aitchisons, and the horse races organised as entertainment by divisional HQ. In one race, Chaplin's mare, ridden by a Cameronian subaltern, Thomas Oppe, comes third in a field of thirty-five. At times it seems as if General Pinney organises his race meetings rather better than his wars: 'The division provided drinks and tea. Nothing was wanting but some female society . . . Altogether we enjoyed it and rode back.'[166]

Lil sends pie and biscuits from Fortnum's, and reports that her mother's health is worsening. Her brother, Willie, now overseeing production of explosives for the War Office, is garlanded with new promotion and decorations. Chaplin is not generous with fraternal regard for his brother-in-law: 'Yes, it is pretty hard luck that Willie should get all these things when you think of all the poor devils who do all the fighting, but it is the same the whole way through – not that these things matter really. It is the opinion of those who serve with you that matters. No ribbons can give you their respect if you do not earn it.'[167]

By 11 May the battalion is preparing to move again. Chaplin remarks on the graves of British officers outside the house he must leave: 'The mother of one received a photograph of her boy's grave through the Queen of Spain while the Germans were here. John Champneys was his name – his father was a well-known ladies' doctor[168] – not that I ever heard of him.'

The Cams are up at 4 a.m. on Saturday, 12 May, and marching out two hours later – the early start a boon on a sweltering day. By 10 a.m. they are installed at a tented camp at Boisleux-Saint-Marc, and Chaplin, like a life prisoner, is counting the days of his service again: 'Two years and nine months since we left Glasgow. I think that it is time that I had a rest. I don't suppose there is anyone else who has served that time continuously with a regiment.'[169]

Then rain, then back to the trenches – this time at Croisilles, eight miles south-east of Arras – but with Chaplin held back in reserve at divisional HQ with Pinney: 'I have got a tent to myself and am comfortable. The padre and Capt McLellan are here – we are in a pleasant spot – green fields and everything nice to look upon, except that the villages are destroyed.'

Here, like all officers held in reserve, he must wait to see how the fighting proceeds, and how he might be needed. As ever, he is in equal parts bored and anxious. He spends the following days reading a book lent by the padre – *Pincher Martin, OD: A Story of the Inner Life of the Royal Navy* by 'Taffrail' – and frets about getting home, where Lil is helping to care for her mother: 'You have had nothing but worries lately.'[170] He plays bridge with Pinney, and complains at the endless paperwork he is sent regarding the insurance policies signed over to his brother, Lindsay. And as intermittent reports come in from the fighting, first of a suicidal sortie ordered by division to test the manning of a German trench, then a full battalion attack on the Hindenburg in thick mist, he wishes he was with his men: 'I am terribly anxious about the regiment. I know that Mr Scott the adjutant is wounded, but that is all I know. The last few days have all been the same – one sits behind here with nothing to do but to think about them – I hate it.'[171]

Extracts from the battalion War Diary,
May 1917,

Kept by Major R. D. Hunter

Trenches, Croisilles
16 May – Patrols sent up to enemy wire, all fired on by sentries. In spite of this the division were troubled with a belief that the line was only held by a few men. Orders received for a company to be sent over to make a reconnaissance in force and draw enemy fire.

At 3pm B Coy under Lt Sussex advanced in two lines widely
extended from behind Nos1 and 2 posts, on left of Croisilles-
Hendicourt Road. They advanced to within 200 yards of Germans'
wire without being fired on. At about 150 yards strong fire
was opened on them by rifles and six machine guns.

The Coy took cover in shell holes and remained out till
dark when they withdrew.

Information gained - trench strongly held, wire badly
smashed.

Casualties: five killed, 15 wounded, six missing - total 26
OR.

The following wire was received from 33rd Div dated 17-5-17

"The information gained by reconnaissance patrol of the
Cameronians yesterday is of greatest use to the Army. The GOC
33rd Divn wishes this made known to all officers and men of
19th Inf Bde. He thanks the Cameronians for their sound work."

17 May - A quiet day. A&D coy each sent out in fighting
patrol after dark with a view to getting a prisoner but no
enemy encountered.

18 May - Relieved by 2nd RWF and moved back into shelters in a
sunken road.

19 May - Quiet day.

20 May - 100th Bde attacked H'burg Line at 5.15am, got front
line but failed to get Support.

At about 3pm received orders to move into position of
assembly in Sq. v13a. Moved up Sensée Valley by Coys in
Artillery formation, came under heavy fire. 2Lt Scott severely
wounded, about eight other casualties.

At 5.20pm received orders to attack H'burg Support Line in

conjunction with 20th RF. Our objective Nelly Lane to Oldenberg
Lane. Zero hour 7.30pm.

At 7.25pm Battn advanced in four lines, A&D front lines, B&C
rear lines. The 9th HLI had promised to give guides but these
did not materialise.

From the start the Battn lost direction and went too much
to their left crossing the line of the 20th RF who had not
come up. They crossed the H'burg front line which was not
recognisable and found the barrage still on a line about 60
yards ahead. When it lifted they went on and about 40 or 50
Germans rushed to them with their hands up.

The Coys concluded this was the H'burg Support and reported
accordingly. They dug in about 30 yards in front of it.
Their position was so hard to locate that no water, food or
ammunition could be sent up.

21 May - Reports received in morning showed that parts of all
4 Coys were on a line between Sensée River and Fontaine Road
about 50 yards from H'burg support. The day was fairly quiet
except for persistent sniping and some machine gunning from
the H'burg support. At 11.30pm the Battn withdrew according to
orders.

54 prisoners were taken by the Battn including two officers,
all of the 225th Regiment (Prussians).

Casualties: killed officers 2Lt T A Oppe, OR 14. Died of
wounds 2Lt T Scott, 2Lt A Phillips. Wounded 2Lt Muirie, OR
100. Missing 16.

Total four officers, 130 other ranks.

22 May - Battn got into bivouac at St Léger between 1 and
3am. Lt Col J G Chaplin DSO resumed control.

Tuesday, 22 May 1917 [from bivouac in St Léger, near Croisilles]
My darling,

I was very glad to get your letter and to hear that you had arrived safely at Brentham and that you had found your mother so much better.

I am sorry to say that Mr Scott died from his wounds and now Mr Becher will be adjutant. Mr Oppe, a dear old gentleman, was also killed. Also Mr Phillips, a friend of the Girdwoods, was mortally wounded – otherwise we were lucky. Capt Wright, who is the hero of the battalion, and Capt Hunter are alright, also Major HS. The regiment did jolly well and their advance is the talk of everyone who saw it.

I am thankful to say that I am back with them, but we do not know what is going to happen to us.

Wednesday, 23 May 1917 [from bivouac in St Léger]
You have all my thoughts – it must be terrible your mother being so ill and just waiting and not knowing what is going to happen.

We have had a very quiet day. I walked to the Brigade in the morning and have sat about most of the day. General P came this afternoon and was very complimentary about the regiment – but there is no sign of any rest, which we had hoped for.

Poor Mr Phillips died from his wound.

If I come through this next show alright – if you agree – I am going to ask that my case about what we want should be referred to the C-in-C and if they will not give it me that I may be sent home. I feel so much the injustice of it. I have been strongly recommended by every General Officer under whom I have served since September 1915. Everyone says that I must have an enemy. I hate the idea of not seeing the show through to the end but I am prepared to go home if someone will not see justice done to me. Of course one is extraordinarily lucky to be still alive. One of the Brigadiers of this Division said that I was a human phenomenon – that he knew of no-one who could stand what I had lived through, the physical hardships and mental strain.

I feel so indignant about the whole thing that I cannot think of anything to write.

Thursday, 24 May 1917 [from bivouac in St Léger]

I know that you must be having a most miserable time, which worries me immensely – I can imagine nothing worse. I am glad your mother has rallied and that you think that she has a chance. Poor soul! What an awful time she has had.

I see that I am mentioned in despatches again. It has not done me much good, but I am glad for the regiment's sake as it means that they have done well and God knows that they deserve it.

I have to get up at 3am so I will go to bed. With all my love, darling. For ever your loving husband, Graham

PS: Please tell Edith that I am going to write her a letter of thanks covering about 14 pages for all her pies etc – if they will ever give me a rest for a day or two.

Saturday, 26 May 1917 [FSPC]

I am quite well.

Sunday, 27 May 1917 [FSPC]

I am quite well.

ABSOLUTELY DISHED

'I had a very nice letter from Padre McShane about our losses. He . . . was told by someone who ought to know that the reason that I was not given a Bde was for being so outspoken at Loos. He . . . said if that was so, I wear the invisible cross of military glory.'

Battle of Arras finishes with assault on Bullecourt – Allies hold sections of Hindenburg but are unable to make breakthrough – all sides take significant casualties – French suppress mutinies with over 3,400 court martials and change commander-in-chief again – British attack and capture Messines in Flanders to divert German forces north

The Cams are not out of it yet. Pinney wants more from his division, pushed on by Snow in corps command. Even General Allenby, commanding the Third Army, has made a rare visit closer to the front line – at St Léger, outside Croisilles, where the Cameronians are resting in bivouac. It is not close enough for some in the 19th brigade who have grown cynical about senior staff's remoteness from reality.[172]

On Whitsun Sunday, 27 May, the brigade is ordered to attack the Hindenburg again, the Cameronians side by side with the 2nd Royal Welch and other battalions, targeting 800 yards of tunnel and trench that stretch south from the Sensée river to the Fontaine-les-Croisilles road. They have orders to capture the trench, then block and defend it. That section of the Hindenburg has, of course, been captured and lost already, and lies on the reverse slope of a crest, making observation from ground level impossible. The plan is for a mass attack in the early afternoon, catching the Germans off guard after lunch, following a brief but heavy bombardment. Chaplin sets up his battalion HQ next to others in an old quarry north-east of Croisilles; Brigadier Mayne briefly visits to wish them luck and remind them to send back reports of their progress regularly. Two miles in the rear, the divisional staff stand on a raised spur to watch 'the show'.

The attack is another costly disaster. The Germans beat back the assault, hiding in deep bunkers during the initial bombardment then re-emerging into their trenches with enough time to mow down attacking battalions with machine guns, or fight fiercely hand-to-hand, rebuffing any attempts to push them out of the trench and shell holes they have wired up in front. The enemy also returns artillery fire with a ferocious bombardment on the British line, destroying all telephone communication between battalion and brigade HQs, leaving signallers desperately trying to send coded messages by electric Lucas lamp, and HQs eventually resorting to pairs of runners, hoping one will get through.[173] In the confusion of the mass attack, two companies of Cameronians advance too far too fast, into their own supporting bombardment. Does Graham Chaplin pull them back or is the order given by an accompanying officer? It is never clear, but in the rush to retire and realign, other advancing troops, seeing them fall back, think a total retreat has been ordered. A panic wave briefly spreads from the Cams to the Royal Welch, and some flee back to their original positions. Others are left surrounded by German defenders.

Later, when Snow asks Pinney to account for the attack's failure, and Pinney asks Mayne, and Mayne asks his colonels, Chaplin steps forward to acknowledge that his battalion was at fault – an act that wins him the respect of the 2nd Royal Welch,[174] also implicated in the panicky retreat. At battalion level, all privately acknowledge that, after three attacks on the Hindenburg in six weeks, the soldiers of the 19th brigade are exhausted and demoralised, all too happy now to turn back to the safety of their own trenches in the confusion of such poorly conceived assaults. For Chaplin, it is another setback in his quest to gain promotion, and to have more control over his fragmented, anxious life.

A day later, the men of the 33rd division are told that the attack was only a holding operation anyway, designed to distract the enemy from a weightier assault at Messines.

Extracts from the battalion War Diary,
May 1917,

Kept by Colonel Graham Chaplin

In bivouac, St Léger
26 May - The Battn ordered to take part in another attack on
H'burg second line on the morrow. Moved up to the H'burg front
line after dark. HQ in the quarry as before. Strength of Battn
going up - 13 officers, 350 OR.

Hindenburg front line
27 May - the Battn got out into shell holes in front of the
H'burg line before daylight and lay there until 1.55pm when
the attack commenced.

The Battn attacked on the left with the 2nd RWF on its
right. Objective H'burg support line from Fontaine Road to
about 500 yards south.

The barrage which lasted nine minutes was weak and ragged.
The coys followed it up closely and got into the trench. B
Coy went too far, got into the barrage and had to come back.
The Germans massed and opened heavy machine gun and rifle fire
which compelled B Coy to retire.

On this C&D Coys also retired. The RWF were hung up by
patches of wire but got into the trench. They retired when our
men retired.

By 8am all were back in the H'burg front line. This was the
third time B Coy had attacked in 10 days and although the men
went well, there is no doubt they were apathetic.

28 May - The Battn were relieved by the 1st Queen's Regt after
dark. They came back to bivouacs at Moyenneville.

Casualties: killed officers Capt Kennedy, 2Lt Forbes, 2Lt
Clark, OR two. Wounded Lieut Craig, 2Lt Taylor, OR 46. Missing
2Lt Newlands, OR 24. Total: six officers, 72 other ranks.

In bivouac, Moyenville
29 May - Rests in bivouac.

30 May - Marched at 5pm to Bailleulval - eight miles.

In camp, Bailleulval
31 May - Rest and clean up. Total casualties during the month:
10 officers, 202 OR.

Thursday, 31 May 1917 [from billets in Bailleulval]
My darling,

I sent you a telegram the day before yesterday as soon as we were out
of the show to say that all was well. I could not write – I was too busy and
worried – and yesterday we marched back here to the same place that we have
been in twice before – very comfortable headquarters and now that all the trees
are out very pretty and not much sign of war.

We attacked, I regret, unsuccessfully. Everyone who was looking on said
that the advance was magnificent, when one of those extraordinary things that
happen in war occurred. The left company got into our own barrage and tried
to draw back out of it – this spread and the regiment thought that it was an
order to come back and they came sullenly back. As the onlookers said, the
withdrawal was as good as the advance. I am afraid that it has absolutely dished
me, although no blame can be attached to anyone – the men were worn out with
all they have been through and it was just a piece of extraordinary bad luck.

I saw General P as I said I would, but he advised me not to make any fuss
about what we want under the circumstances. I saw both the Divisional and
Corps Commanders and both admitted that the men had done all they could,

and we have not been in any way officially blamed, but it has worried me tremendously as it is the only time in the war that anything could be said against our soldiering. There were some extraordinarily gallant things done – as good as any in the war.

A lot of the "habitants" have returned. One lady showed me with great pride a baby which she said was a "souvenir de permission". I did not tell her that Eileen was one too.

I told General P that I considered that I had been most unjustly treated and also that it was quite impossible that I could go on much longer. This has been a most unfortunate show for me as I meant to have written to the C-in-C and one cannot very well do it now.

With all my fondest love to you and Jim and Eileen and heaps of kisses.

Friday, 1 June 1917 [from billets in Bailleulval]

My darling,

I had no letter from you today which was a great disappointment. We were not very vigorous today. I had a ceremonial parade, just marching past, and was quite in good form and felt like I was when adjutant nearly 20 years ago. This afternoon I slept or rather tried to after walking round the billets. We had a concert in the evening and had all the company commanders to dinner and the pipers played. Somehow it was not a great success – we are all rather depressed after this failure in the attack.

I had a very nice letter from Padre McShane about our losses. He says – but I can hardly believe it – that he was told by someone who ought to know that the reason that I was not given a Bde was for being so outspoken at Loos. He was quite poetical and said if that was so, I wear the invisible cross of military glory.

I should love to see your new dress and hope I shall soon. It is only another month before I shall be due leave.

I have to write to the relatives of all the officers we have lost, which rather worries me.

Sunday, 3 June 1917 [from billets in Bailleulval]

I did not write last night. I wrote eight letters to relatives of dead officers. By that time I was so depressed and my handwriting so bad that I had not the heart to write.

Tomorrow we start training hard again.

Today being Sunday I did not get up too early and did not go to church. I went for a ride in the morning with Major HS – the country looks lovely now – all the trees being out and the crops up has obliterated to a great extent the scars of war. The inhabitants have come back – the cattle, sheep and women and children make a much more pleasant picture than when we were last here.

We have no idea what we are going to do.

The Corps Commander[1] inspected us yesterday – he was very pleased – no-one so far has said a word of blame for our attack failing. I feel much better now. I was beginning to feel pretty down with all the worry.

I am going to the place where I was in hospital on the 6th and remain there till the 9th. I hope they will get the inflammation in my eyes reduced. When I am there I am going to try and see people who can help me.

I should love to see Jim and Eileen sunburnt. With my love to them and to you and heaps of kisses.

Monday, 4 June 1917 [from billets in Bailleulval]

I got your letter enclosing Mrs Harriette's. I think Harriette[2] was quite right to ask to go home. Last time I saw him he was certainly not fit to be commanding a regiment – we all think he did jolly well to stick it as long as he did.

It has been a lovely day but too hot. We have been doing the usual training. In the evening we had a band from another Division[3] to discourse sweet music. Major RW[4] came in the evening but would not stay to dinner.

---

1 Lieutenant General Snow.
2 His old friend, Harry Lee.
3 Band of the 1st battalion Royal Welch Fusiliers, 22nd brigade, 7th division.
4 Tom Riddell-Webster had left the Cameronians in 1915 to work on staff as deputy assistant adjutant general.

Wednesday, 6 June 1917 [from a hotel in Amiens]

Yesterday I was on a Court Martial – the first time for two years – that took up the whole morning. In the afternoon I slept and inspected our transport at 5pm.

Major HS got the DSO. I am very glad – he ought to have had it before.

In the evening Major HS, Capt McLellan and myself went to dine with Major RW. He sent a car for us, but the man lost his way so he turned up very late. However we got there alright and had a very cheery dinner. Major O'Connor[1] in the regiment was there. The chauffeur lost his way going home and we did not get back till 2am – too late to write my letter.

This morning I started with Capt Wright, who is going home on leave, in a car for this place where I was in hospital. We arrived safely and I booked a room in the hotel. We then went to the station to find out about his train, which left at 7.30pm. We then went to the hospital to see the doctor about my eyes, but he was out. We walked to Cox's, who have a branch here, and got some money. We then went to a restaurant and had lunch and afterwards I saw Capt Wright off. I returned to the hotel and slept all the afternoon. I then went to the Dr about my eyes – he was very nice and gave me a lotion to bathe them with three times a day.

I dined alone at a restaurant and then went for a walk. It is very nice to be in a civilised part again and to have nothing to do for a few days.

I simply long for you and have hardly the patience to wait another month.

Mr Becher is probably going home on leave. If he does, I have asked him to write to you and meet you and tell you all that he can – he is a very nice boy.

Thursday, 7 June 1917 [from a hotel in Amiens]

I cannot discover any way of getting my letters censored, so I am afraid that they will have to wait until I return to the regiment but I will write each day just the same. Last night I wrote almost in the dark as one is not allowed to have a light and the window open. I then bathed my eyes and went to bed

---

1 Major Richard O'Connor had been commissioned into the 2nd battalion Scottish Rifles in 1909, but served initially in World War One as a signals officer. In June 1917 he was appointed brevet lieutenant colonel of 2nd infantry battalion, Honourable Artillery Company. In World War Two, as a general, he commanded the Western Desert Force in 1941.

and slept till eight. I had a fine hot bath and breakfast late. At breakfast I recognised a Col Turner in the Indian Cavalry whom I had not seen for 20 years. He was very surprised at my recognising him. He is a brother-in-law of that Capt Ross who was in the Kensington Palace Hotel. I went for a walk and met Col Rochford-Boyd,[1] who asked me to lunch. We had a very good lunch and a great talk about soldiering. I came back and bathed my eyes and then slept the whole afternoon. I went for a walk when the rain stopped – it rained the whole afternoon, which has cooled the atmosphere. Even my grey hairs do not protect me from the young women. I never go out without getting accosted, but I look straight to my front.

It amuses me just to walk about and see the people after the sort of desert we have lived in. I feel and look much better for my rest and nothing to worry one. If you could only be here I should be quite happy.

Sunday, 10 June 1917 [from billets in Bailleulval]

As I could not get my letters posted I did not write after Mr Becher left. I was quite glad to come back yesterday as I am not very good at doing nothing, although I am much better for the rest and having slept a lot. I wired to the Division to send me a car but it did not arrive, so I started at 6pm by train with Griffiths. I went about halfway by train and then got a lift in a motor lorry which brought us very nearly here, but the three miles or so I had to walk. We got here about 12.30 this morning. I got three letters from you and the snapshots. I thought Eileen was very good but not Jim – I don't think it flattered him. He looks much fatter than when I last saw him.

No, dear, I have not changed my mind about writing to the C-in-C, but perhaps General P is right and I had better wait, especially as the Army Commander is going to be changed.[2] As you very rightly say, you get no credit for all the good work but if anything goes wrong one gets lots of blame.

---

1 Colonel Henry Rochford-Boyd, Royal Horse Artillery. See Chaplin's letter of 1 May 1916. He is killed later in 1917.

2 After the Third Army fails to break through in the Battle of Arras, Allenby is replaced as commander by General Sir Julian Byng on 9 June. Allenby was later put in command of the Egyptian Expeditionary Force which captured Jerusalem on 9 December 1917.

General M[1] is going on leave, probably tomorrow, so I shall go to the Brigade for 10 days.

On the 13th it will be two years that I have commanded the regiment and two years and 10 months since we left Glasgow. It is too long.

I don't know why but I am feeling depressed tonight for no reason whatsoever. With all my love and thoughts, darling, and heaps of kisses to Jim and Eileen. For ever your loving husband, Graham

*   *   *

The air is hot, the weather torpid. The Cams are exhausted, waiting to see how they will be used next. The 33rd division remains close to the front, with the threat of return imminent, as the Battle of Arras, on which so many hopes were pinned, fizzles out into yet more attritional trench warfare. The Germans are proving the most obdurate of foes.

Graham Chaplin is plagued by ailments. He has a cyst cut out of his eye. He yearns to see his children. He must make do with the welcome return of Padre McShane, dining with the battalion on 13 June, and any army gossip he can prise from Lil, principally of those who have got away, home safe: 'What is wrong with Sandy? Why has he applied for a Bn at home?' 'Is Major Draffen home for good?'[175]

There is little to write about, he moans, 'the same old training every day'.[176] Brigadier General Williams, previously commanding the 2nd Royal Welch, drops in to tea with more gossip. Otherwise the days are filled with 'a perfect orgy of sports',[177] as the army struggles to keep the men busy. Chaplin again argues his case for promotion with Pinney: 'He had apparently been to GHQ and reminded them about me. He said my name was much nearer the top and so perhaps we shall soon get what we want . . .'[178]

Will the Cams' performance in the last battle dent his chances? He hopes not, batting back Lil's queries: 'No, there was no question about the failure of the last attack being in any way my fault personally, nor have we in any

---

1 Brigadier General Mayne.

way been blamed for it officially, only as one gets credit for a success so one has to take the blame for a failure.'[179]

And he pleads with her not to go to London, after a long-range bomber attack by twenty German Gotha aeroplanes kills 162 civilians in the capital on 13 June: 'We shall have to blow their towns down – what brutes they are.'[180]

General Snow presents medal ribbons to the brigade on 17 June. And then the Cameronians are sent back to the line, back beyond Croisilles, beyond the camps where swallows, deprived of their usual barns, blasted into ruin, are now nesting in the army's tin huts. The soldiers must prepare for yet another attack on the Hindenburg.

Extracts from the battalion War Diary, June 1917,

Kept by Colonel Graham Chaplin

```
Camp at Bailleulval
18 June - The Battn marched at 6.30am to camp at Moyenneville.
Weather extremely hot.


19 June - Moved up in the evening to trenches and sunken road
behind Croisilles. Relieved 6th Leicesters, 21st Div, in support
to front line.


20 June - Officers visited front line with view to attack to
be made at end of week.


21 June - Remained in support. No shelling. Fifty men working
in communication trenches each night.


22 June - Ditto.
```

23 June – HQ moved up into tunnel in the Quarry at 6pm.
A&B Coys under Capt Wright moved up into Lump Lane before
midnight. One Coy 18th Middlesex Pioneers also assembled in
Lump Lane. Half C Coy moved up into the Quarry in support.
The objective was to capture and consolidate Tunnel trench
establishing a block in it 160 yards from Lump Lane. Zero hour
was fixed at 12 midnight.

24 June – At zero hour a barrage was put on Tunnel trench.
At zero plus one it commenced to creep at 25 yards a minute
back to Oldenburg Lane where it remained for one and a half
hours. At zero plus one the Coys began to advance. They were
fired on almost at once by one or two machine guns and the
centre platoon was soon held up by some wire from behind
which they were bombed by Germans in shell holes. The flank
platoons continued to advance but finding the centre platoons
had stopped and both officers being wounded they fell back
again. The centre platoon dug in where they were and the
Pioneers joined up their trench with Lump Lane. The Germans
fired a lot of trench mortar bombs and rifle grenades from
the exposed flank. At dawn there was no possibility of further
advance and the Coys were withdrawn to Croisilles. The 20th RF
again taking over Lump Lane. Between 6 and 7pm the Battn was
relieved by the 9th HLI (100th Brigade) and marched back to camp
at Moyenneville.

Casualties: killed officers 2Lt Murray, wounded Capt Wright,
2Lt Hourston. Other ranks killed six, wounded 32.

25 June – Rested and cleaned up.

Chaplin makes his HQ in the same old quarry as before, but this time in deeply tunnelled dugouts, much improved even in the three weeks since he last moved in. He puts two companies in the forward line under Captain Wright – the same Wright who sailed with him to France as a young lieutenant back in August 1914, and later, through parental connections, gained a promotion to a staff job before asking to return to his regiment.

The section of Hindenburg they must attack is the same as before, too, still being held by resolute German defenders. Again the Cams rise to fight their way across, following a rolling barrage, and again they are mauled by machine-gun fire and bombs thrown by Germans manning shell holes in front of the main trench. Part of Wright's two companies make progress, part are held, meaning those in front have to dig in and wait, before being bombed out of their positions and retreating again. The cost is seven killed and thirty-two wounded, and they end back where they started.

For Chaplin, sitting with his adjutant in the deep dugout, waiting for runners to bring messages, it must have seemed desperate and demoralising, like banging your head against a wall, repeatedly, getting nowhere. He is losing men, the replacements are low quality; he has few officers he can trust, none who has been at the front as long as he has. But then such men do not exist elsewhere. He is probably now the longest-serving front-line infantry officer in the war, never wounded home, never promoted out of the trenches. He not only wears the invisible cross that McShane has awarded him, he carries it.

By 24 June, the Cams are relieved in the Croisilles trenches by the 9th Highland Light Infantry. By 29 June, they have returned to trenches yet again, this time in Monchy-au-Bois. At the beginning of August, they are pulled back to rest and refit in Condé-Folie, a small rural village beside the River Somme, fifteen miles north-west of Amiens. By then, Chaplin is in England again, on two weeks' leave.

CONDÉ-FOLIE

'I hope with all my heart that we shall somehow soon be together again. You must, I know, be having a wretched time. I am very sorry that you feel nervous alone.'

British commander-in-chief Haig plans new campaign in Flanders despite misgivings of politicians – French fight off German attacks at Verdun – Russia launches Kerensky Offensive in east to divert German forces – British aim to secure Belgian coast and close U-boat ports – French argue for delay until arrival of American forces in 1918

A soldier on leave faces choices. Those at home are interested in good news from the front, and the newspapers daily supply it. And even an officer as weary of the fight as Graham Chaplin would hope that, overall, the gloom of winter has been cast aside and progress is finally being made. But back in Britain that early July of 1917, what would he make of the newspaper reports from the Arras front, so blustering in their bravado, summing up the 'Year of British Triumph'?[181] Pleased to be part of a good story, perhaps, but fully cognizant that the reality is always different. British journalists are almost too keen to allay doubts about the volunteer soldiers that have filled the New Armies raised since 1914.

> In the course of the year these New Armies of ours have taken over 70,000 prisoners, including 800 officers. They have captured 450 German guns, with more than 2,000 minor pieces like machine-guns and trench mortars. This is the capture of a mighty army, an army of 10 whole German divisions as now constituted, with all its equipment. These New Armies have had against them the whole military strength of the German Empire – that is to say, of every division in the German armies. It is these New Armies which in the course of the year have taken all three ridges – namely, the Albert Ridge, the Vimy Ridge, and the Messines Ridge – on which, from Ypres to the Somme, the Germans had drawn their lines as being the strongest positions to hold on this front, and enthroned on which they overlooked all our preparations for attack. No fortress in history possessed one tithe of

the defensive strength of any one of these ridges fortified as the Germans had fortified them, and held by the flower of the German Army under the strictest orders to fight to the death and not yield an inch of ground. Each ridge was not a single fortress, but a mass of clustered forts, and 50 single places from Beaumont Hamel to Messines, from Pozières to La Coulotte, were each much more than any Kronstadt or Sebastopol. This is what our New Armies have done in the course of the year.[182]

There is little discussion of the stalemate away from the three great ridges, but much talk of the 'firm resolution of Sir Douglas Haig', of the great strategic guile of the British commanders, and the immense losses suffered by the Germans around Arras as they fight desperately to cling on to positions, sacrificing their best men and guns, covering the ground with corpses. Just occasionally the lack of any real progress is mentioned, but the erosion of German reserves and morale is key, and even some of the horror of this attritional war is now being detailed. Each blunted British attack brings the fighting closer to the end, wearing down the enemy. For a commander on the ground, such as Chaplin, who has witnessed the worst suffering, it can be the only consolation.

Lil Chaplin's attentions are focused north, where her mother is now seriously ill at the family home in Stirling. Lil's stance on the war is simple: she already knows many widows and she wants Graham away from the front – running a training camp in Britain, or promoted out of danger. To her, it will seem incongruous and terrible that her husband is one of the very few original officers from the British Expeditionary Force of August 1914 still leading his men from the trenches. But it seems he simply doesn't possess the social connections or the political guile to gain that promotion to brigadier general. Day by day the likelihood grows that he will be killed or maimed, shot by the ever-present snipers, or blown to smithereens in the bombardments recounted so proudly by the journalists.

Does Chaplin, in those all-too-brief periods of leave, tell his wife what it has really been like to wage his war from Bois-Grenier to Cuinchy, and the Somme to Arras? The waste of life, the smell of putrefaction, the barricades of the dead, the screams of the injured, the terrors of mutilation and pain and sacrifice which he has witnessed? Everything he has left undetailed in his letters – how can he not try to tell her? The newspapers are already using many of the same terms. But he will also have downplayed it, he will have recounted it with phlegm, because that is what a British officer of the old army does. No advantage is gained in being 'poetic' about it. So much of that would only come later, much later, when the war had finished and tallies were counted, emotions assessed.

His letters now make plain only that he is desperate for promotion, or failing that, a job at home where he can be with his wife and children. Would he be any safer as a brigadier? Not much, as enemy bombardments regularly target brigade HQs, but at least he could assert more control over tactics in a war where he already mistrusts the strategy. He is the colonel who has regularly thwarted his own generals' misconceived notions of when to send the men over the top. As a brigadier, he could better argue against even more stupid plans.

For now, he must return to his battalion, already at rest in Condé-Folie. There, he presents the façade that his men have come to know and expect.[183] They must, of necessity, have few clues as to his true feelings. What they see is the stocky, spiky Bull Chaplin, impatient with incompetence, distant from young officers, often angry with what he sees around him – a commander who rarely attends the Sunday service parade once so central to Cameronian identity. He fights the war his own way. But his men look to him to pull them through. He can be studied as only a commander is studied, a thousand men fixated on his moods and utterances, unpicking the meaning of his words, gossiping on his likes and dislikes, discussing and agreeing on his character, assessing his strengths and weaknesses, building over time an assessment of just what he is made of, because it affects them all. That is how a battalion, focused on the chain of command, works. First and foremost, Chaplin's men know he is a survivor, and in a war where battalion commanders can change month by month, he is a constant. That can be appreciated.

**Saturday, 14 July 1917 [from billets in Condé-Folie, on the River
Somme, midway between Abbeville and Amiens]**

My own darling,

I felt quite stunned when I left you yesterday – I hate these partings more
and more. I wondered all day how you were getting on – I am afraid you had a
miserable journey. I got into the taxi and drove straight back to the club. I had
lunch and left in plenty of time for the train, you may be sure. I got a seat in
the Pullman and then walked up and down to see if there was anyone I knew.
I met a gunner I had not seen for a year and then met a Major Humphreys,[1]
a good fellow who commands a tunnelling company. I was surprised to meet
him as I was told just before I went home that he had been killed. There were
a large number of nurses crossing.

On board I met Captain Cuthbert whom we saw in Princes. The little boy
with him lost his arm on his way to the trenches for the first time. We had a
very smooth crossing – close to Boulogne there were shells dropping into the
sea – whether practice or at a submarine I could not make out.

We arrived at Boulogne at 7pm. To my disgust there was no car for me,
so I went with Cuthbert to the RTO and found that our train went at 9.57
so we walked back to the Folkestone and had dinner. Again we were at
the station in plenty of time for the train. On the way the carriage door of
the next compartment came open and was caught by a passing train and
smashed, injuring one of the occupants rather badly. I could not sleep at
all and was glad when we arrived at our destination.[2] We walked to the
village – it was now 2am – woke up the people at an inn and got a fairly
good room and were soon in bed and asleep. We were called at 8am and
had breakfast and went to the station to catch a train at 9.30am to a place
seven miles away. On the platform I met our Padre, who told me that the
regiment was only 500 yards from the station where we were, so I walked
off at once to headquarters.

We are in the proprietor's house of a big factory. We are more comfortable

1 Major H. J. Humphreys, Royal Engineers, CO 251st Tunnelling Company.
2 Condé-Folie, south of Abbeville.

than we have ever been before. We have a flat with kitchen, dining room and sitting room and each of us has a bedroom.

It was raining but I rode round to see the companies – they are very scattered through the village. After lunch I went to sleep and then went on the range to see a shoot.

I wonder if Jim misses me. I don't suppose that he does. I miss you all dreadfully.

We expect to be here for 10 days or a fortnight yet. I could stand a lot of this sort of war.

Sunday, 15 July 1917 [from billets in Condé-Folie]

I got up quite early – about 6 o'c – and went for a walk by myself. It was nice and fresh and everything very peaceful. After breakfast I read the papers and did not go to church. I had lunch and then walked with the doctor to the Brigade about five or six miles. As we arrived at Bde, General P also arrived. He had no news and only talked about fishing – he looked very ill. We had tea with the Brigade. There were some boys outside who fired off crackers every few minutes, which annoyed us. We went on and saw Col Clayton and Major Spens.[1] We then walked back in time for dinner.

We have got a Staff ride[2] coming off which annoys me intensely. After nearly three years of war one does not want to play at it much.

I miss you all more than I can tell.

Monday, 16 July 1917 [from billets in Condé-Folie]

I should think that this will surpass all my previous efforts in dullness, for this has been an extraordinarily uneventful day. I got up early, went for a walk, had breakfast and then walked round the companies, had lunch and went for a ride with Major HS. We played bridge and went to bed early.

---

1 Both of the 5th Scottish Rifles.

2 A study of former battlefields designed to develop tactics and leadership among senior officers.

I miss you more than I have ever done before and hate everything and have come to the end of my patience.

With all my love and heaps of kisses to Jim and Eileen and YOU.

Tuesday, 17 July 1917 [from billets in Condé-Folie]

This morning I did the usual round of the companies. The training ground and the range are so scattered that it is a good long walk and takes most of the morning. In the afternoon I rode over to the Horse Show about seven miles alone. It was a lovely afternoon, but I was pretty bored when I got there. It was mostly limbers, cookers etc – they were wonderfully turned out, but it is very dull watching the judging. I got back in time for dinner and then played bridge.

I believe we are to be here until the end of the month – it will be the best and longest rest we have had in the war. I feel very slack here. I suppose it is being on the river[1] and that it is relaxing.

We have got a Staff ride lasting 24 hours. After three years of war these paper wars are loathsome. I am very weary and off to bed.

Thursday, 19 July 1917 [from billets in Condé-Folie]

Yesterday we marched about seven miles to the Horse Show – the whole battalion. I got up at 6 and we marched off at 7.15. It was quite nice marching – I walked the whole way both going and coming – it was cool and inclined to rain.

It was a splendid show. My mare, ridden by Capt Hunter, was second. He tied for first place the first round, but lost points in the run off. I enclose the rosette for second place. The official photographer was there – I am afraid I was snapped by him.

There were a good many ladies present. French and nurses – a very pretty French girl gave away the prizes. We marched back at 7pm and got here at 9pm or later. Now we have this beastly Staff ride which will last 24 hours.

I wish they would give me a job at home so that I could be with you. I miss you all horribly and feel very homesick, I suppose more so because one has time to think.

---

1 Condé-Folie lies among fens created by the River Somme.

With all my fondest love and heaps of kisses. Forever your loving husband Graham.

*   *   *

Desperate for rest, Chaplin now finds the days dragging, as if anticipation of its ending makes enjoyment impossible. After nearly three years of war, his battalion is given four weeks at ease, billeted in a small hamlet straddling the bucolic wetlands of the Somme river, forty miles from the front. Condé-Folie is a sprawling village of red-brick homes and barns, barely any over one storey, less than ten miles from the Cams' winter home in Citerne. The village clusters round the rail line running towards Abbeville, just where the flat plain west of Amiens begins to undulate into low hills and dells.

The 33rd division has spread its brigades all around, in villages and towns, black spires poking up through the sycamore woods, amid fields of white sheep and pale brown cows. Here, close to the Baie de Somme, where the river heads towards the sea, the men are kept busy mounting guard, repairing equipment, completing chores, but really just relaxing in the oppressive July heat that drives everyone to shade or river or both. These are the marching grounds of English armies of old, of Edward III and Henry V, tracing the banks of the Somme river, desperately looking for crossings, harried by the French, heading for Crécy and Agincourt.

Now the British soldiers are welcomed, providing honour guards for Bastille Day, sleeping in beds, playing cards, buying wine, often luxuriating in the unaccustomed peace of rural summer life. Beyond the nominal training – bombing, bayonet fighting, rapid firing, formation practice, route marches, physical drill – there are drafts of new men to induct: 245, including six officers, for the Cameronians, many of them veterans who have fought in France or Salonika before.

So what else to do in this drowsy heat, away from the attractions of Abbeville and Amiens? Concerts and sports are organised, boxing tournaments draw big crowds, 'bathing parades' become swimming galas in the broad fishing ponds that pool out from the river. There is also a Pinney favourite, the horse show for officers and men, planned with his usual precision in matters equine. Flat races, jumps, races for officers, races for NCOs and men, turnout prizes, single-horse turnout, pack-animals turnout, pairs horses, pairs mules, teams of six mules, complete-cooker turnout . . . Pinney, an obsessive horseman, judges them all, a leg injury forcing him to limp round his elaborately constructed showground and enclosures, aided by his staff officers.

Even the planned 'staff ride' – a mobile course in tactics detested by veterans like Chaplin, because it implies that staff officers know better – cannot dent the mood of dissipation, underscored with anxiety. Trips to Amiens, even to the seaside, are organised. For many of the men, it must have seemed surreal, as if the war had forgotten them. But it was waiting. And for Chaplin, in the middle of this idyll, there is bad news from home, too.

Saturday, 21 July 1917 [from billets in Condé-Folie]
While I was on this staff ride I received the wire announcing your mother's death. Of course we knew it was inevitable, but all the same I know what a shock it will be to you. You have all my sympathy and love, darling. I wish I could have been with you to comfort you. I should certainly go to Sunningdale as soon as possible and take Edith too. I am afraid that she will be worn out.

The staff ride was awful rot and a waste of time. We left here at 7.45am and went on all day, halting for hours in some places. We got dinner at 9.20pm. We were told we should probably be called up in the night. I slept on top of a bed and did not undress. After all we did not move till 6.30am, went a few miles on and the whole show was over – having combined the maximum amount of discomfort with the minimum amount of instruction.

I hope with all my heart that we shall somehow soon be together again. You must, I know, be having a wretched time. I am very sorry that you feel nervous alone.

With all my fondest love and heaps of kisses to Jim and Eileen and yourself.

Sunday, 22 July 1917 [from billets in Condé-Folie]
I am very tired, so expect a duller letter than usual. I got up early and went for

a walk before breakfast. I did a bit of business – writing etc – and then went for a walk with Capt Wright. After lunch I got your letter and the spectacles which are very good. The drops have not come but I will use them when they do.

I rode over to the RWF sports with Mr McFie. We had tea with Colonel Clayton. Capt Scott who used to be with us has joined them.[1] He had been wounded with the 10th Bn. I also met a RWF who came home from India with me in 1907. He was wounded at Loos as a Lt Col and is now a captain again – such is the fortune of war!

There is some awful form of ophthalmia amongst the horses from which they go blind. My mare shows signs of it – I hope she has not got it. I shall be awfully sorry to lose her after all these years.

The mosquitoes are very bad here and are raising lumps all over me.

Tuesday, 24 July 1917 [from billets in Condé-Folie]

I am ashamed to say that I did not write yesterday. I walked about all the morning seeing the companies and in the afternoon we had aquatic sports – I was judge. We have a very good pond in the marshes, very deep and 110 yards long. The REs[2] made a high dive 17 feet high and a springboard. The high diving was particularly good and all the races were good. We had a greasy pole competition – no-one got to the end. We also had an inter-company punt race – as no-one had been in a punt before it was very amusing. It was a splendid day for it and very warm.

The vegetables and fruit arrived safely and were splendid – many thanks, dear.

I just long to go home to you, dear. I feel awfully homesick and miss the children so. You must be having a wretched time. I shall be glad to hear that you are back in Sunningdale.

I am trying to get Major HS a month's leave or I don't think he will last.

Thursday, 26 July 1917 [from billets in Condé-Folie]

I was very pleased to get a letter from you – I was getting nervous having had

---

1 5th battalion Scottish Rifles.
2 Royal Engineers.

none for two days. You must have – I know – had a very sad time. I am glad that the funeral is over – you will feel more rested now. I am afraid that you will have a bad time with Nanny away but I am sure you will manage alright. I wish I could be there to help.

It has been unbearably hot. I am going to the seaside tomorrow for the weekend. I think it might buck me up, besides being a good thing to take the last chance to get away from the soldiering for a bit.

Monday, 30 July 1917 [from billets in Condé-Folie]

Owing to my trip to the seaside I am afraid that you will have two blank days as there was no means of getting the letters censored.

I left here at 12 noon and arrived about 3pm. Our late doctor, O'Grady, was on the same train but I did not see him until we arrived.[1] I walked with him up to the camp to enquire for Col Mason[2] but found that he was on leave. I then got into a fiacre[3] and drove four miles to the place where I stayed last year. I was lucky to get a room in the hotel as the place was crowded for the weekend. It was a lovely day and I went for a walk to see the place and the people. The crowd mostly consisted of subalterns from the adjacent base camps and lots of English women of all classes and apparently doing all sorts of work, regular nurses, VADs, women's auxiliary corps, YWCA – the last are all ladies, I think. Their main object seemed to be the same, namely man hunting. I had tea in a tea shop and then walked down to the bathing place to have a bathe in the sea. I felt rather shy in such a crowd largely consisting of women as one had to walk about ¼ mile to the sea. However, clothed in a magnificent bathing suit – two francs for the cabin, suit and towel – I went off. I enjoyed it immensely and had a good long swim and felt like a giant afterwards. I walked till dinner time and went to bed almost immediately afterwards. There were lots of the ladies dining with the officers and it amused me to watch them.

---

1 It is unclear where the trip is to – the reference to staying there in 1916 suggests it may be a resort close to a port such as Boulogne.

2 Formerly in the Cameronians, now running a base on the French coast.

3 Hansom cab.

I was called at 6.30am and meant to have a bathe, but there was a tremendous storm on and so I went to sleep again and slept till 11 o'c. It rained the whole morning, so I read the paper and then had lunch. I met a lot of people I knew, but no-one interesting – the most interesting another CO with whom I discussed the training of recruits.

I went for a walk after lunch with a fellow who used to be in the 19th Bde and meant to have had a bathe but it again rained hard. I had dinner alone but much amused with the efforts of the fair sex to captivate young men.

I drove to the station after dinner. They would not allow me to travel without a movement order so I had to walk to the Commandant's office and get one. I then learnt that Col Mason had just come back, so I went to his house. I found him at dinner and very fit. I had a glass of port but could only remain half an hour. He is very anxious to go into action with the regiment to see what a modern battle is like.

My train went punctually at 10.20.

I was afraid of passing my station – very easy to do as they don't call out the names – however I arrived home safely at 1am feeling much better for my trip.

I got up at 5am and we did a seven-mile route march starting at 6.30am. I walked the whole way and when I got back found General M[1] here – he did not however have anything interesting to say, except that they will not allow Major HS a month's leave.

We shall be in the train tomorrow so I am afraid that I shall not be able to write regularly after this but will send a postcard when I cannot write.

I was very pleased to hear that Eileen could walk alone. Seeing the French kids playing on the sands made me very homesick. I wished Jim and Eileen could have been there and most of all you.

With all my thoughts and fondest love and heaps of kisses to you all. For ever your loving husband, Graham

---

1 Mayne.

THEY MINDED
MORE THAN I

'I feel that going home without a Brigade I have been a failure, but if I go on any longer I run the risk of breaking down altogether.'

Germans attack at Nieuwpoort to pre-empt British plans to land troops on Belgian coast – Allied forces launch large-scale offensive at Passchendaele in third Battle of Ypres – Prime Minister Lloyd George warns Haig that the nation will not tolerate another drawn-out offensive with high casualties – Allies fail to reach objectives after first month of fighting

The idyll cannot last. Three weeks after arriving in bucolic Condé-Folie, the Cameronians receive orders to prepare for a return to the front. But it is not to where the men expect. The 33rd division is returning to the XV Corps, and is being hurried to the coast where the Germans are attacking around Nieuwpoort, where the River Yser flows into the North Sea – end point for the vast trench line that stretches down to Switzerland. The 33rd had long heard rumours of a shift to the north as the British prepared yet again to break out of the Ypres salient – as a division, it was now used to being sent in to bolster attacks by less experienced battalions. But Nieuwpoort is twenty-five miles north of Ypres, and overlooks a very different terrain.

It was here, nearly three years previously, that the Belgian army opened the river sluices and flooded the low-lying land to halt the German advance through Belgium. And it is here that the attention of all sides has turned as the war grinds towards stalemate further south. For British commanders, breaching the line, supplementing any attack with ship-borne troops and sealing the U-boat harbours of Ostend and Zeebrugge looks an attractive option during the summer of 1917. The stalling point is whether it should be in combination with a renewed push at Ypres, or as an independent action.

The argument becomes unnecessary, as the Germans, guessing British intentions, launch a pre-emptory attack around Nieuwpoort on 10 July, capturing and holding defences east of the Yser, and unveiling a new weapon: mustard gas. The British delay plans to counter-attack, in order to build up artillery and men. And so Lieutenant General Du Cane, who had replaced Horne as commander of XV Corps in September 1916, is given Pinney's battle-hardened 33rd division to hold the line. Du Cane, an artilleryman by background, had previously worked at the Ministry of Munitions in Whitehall. He would very likely know Willie Alexander, Graham Chaplin's brother-in-law.

That would be scant consolation for the Cameronian colonel as his men enter yet another arena of war. On 31 July, his battalion packs its bags and parades after lunch, before marching to the rail station at nearby Pont Remy – Chaplin, as ever, riding at the front. The trains to the north are quicker now, staffed by British railwaymen, and once the battalion has been decanted in Dunkirk, it is loaded onto barges and pulled through small canals to the main army camp in Bray-Dunes, part of the slow flow of the 33rd division closer to the Nieuwpoort battle zone. Over 18,000 men – twelve infantry battalions, three field ambulances, divisional headquarters, divisional artillery, divisional engineers, divisional pioneers and assorted administrative staff – are now all beside the sea at the start of August, less than fifty miles from the tip of the Kent coast, as if about to start a very British holiday. For three days, it rains consistently. Then the sun comes out and the soldiers swim, by company, by battalion, by brigade – at times by the thousand – playing in the waves like children. And at night, while they wait for final orders, they watch German planes make bombing runs at the border towns around them.

By now, the full text of Lieutenant Sassoon's 'Soldier's Declaration', sent in July to his commanding officer in the Royal Welch, has been read out in the House of Commons[184] and printed in newspapers. Sassoon, who fought through the Battle of Arras with the 2nd Royal Welch alongside the Cameronians, has refused to return to the front after a period of convalescent leave. He believes the war is being 'deliberately prolonged by those who have the power to end it'. Sassoon's impassioned outburst will have reached the 19th brigade, where many remember his bravery, and some will share his views – there is widespread unease at the profits being made by those with a vested interest in keeping the war going. All will also have heard the government's response, voiced in the House of Commons, that Sassoon is suffering from a nervous breakdown on account of his experiences in battle, and has been committed for treatment to Craiglockhart War Hospital in Edinburgh.

For old soldiers like Chaplin, who stood in admiration of Sassoon's abilities as a soldier, the idea that his declaration is being used to lobby against conscription would be detestable. Chaplin has his own doubts as to the way the war is being conducted, and has made plain to Darling and others what he thinks of some of the generals in charge, but he believes that everyone should be involved in this fight, with no exceptions. In what other way can Germany be stopped?

Wednesday, 1 August 1917 [from billets in Bray-Dunes, outside Dunkirk]

My own darling,

I did not write yesterday as owing to our being on the move there was no mail in or out.

We marched at 3.30pm – it was very hot and I went very slowly and had lots of long halts. We had to march about seven miles to the station where we entrained. One has to be at the station 1½ hours before the train starts so there is no chance of missing it. The men took off their equipment in the trucks and then had their teas and we had a mixture of tea and dinner. One company, Capt Wright's, was left behind and follows tomorrow. We started about 8.50pm. We lighted candles and played bridge till about 2am. I did not expect to sleep but slept fairly well for two or three hours. We arrived at our destination[1] about 6am. We all fell in as quickly as possible and marched about a mile through the town to barges. There was a barge for each company and all the officers got on the tug. The transport followed by road. We were about two hours on the barges. I talked to the man in charge who was quite interesting and had been a sailor. We disembarked very quickly and had a short march to the camp. It

---

1 Dunkirk.

was one of the worst days I have known for rain – it came down in buckets. Burberrys were no good and everyone was soaked to the skin.

This is quite a nice camp on the seashore.[1] The men have good huts with concrete floors and the officers all live in one hut, with a separate compartment for each officer to sleep in. Major HS and I have rooms in a seaside bungalow which is also the mess.

We had breakfast at 12 and then I went to bed and slept till late in the afternoon and then put on dry clothes.

I was delighted to get three letters from you tonight and also your mother's will, as I had not heard from you for three days.

The will could not be fairer. I should like you to have the diamond ring if you have the choice.

Yes, we could have been very happy at Nigg.[2] On the 13th it will be three years since we have been separated, so I hope that it will not last much longer.

I have read today a book called 'Letters from a General to his son on receiving his commission'.[3] I liked it very much – it puts down on paper what we all believe.

Friday, 3 August 1917 [from billets in Bray-Dunes]

I am getting very bad at missing the mail – but yesterday I got up early and went to the Brigade and a large party of us went off to visit the Divisional front. I went in a car with the General. It was a long drive – we got to the furthest point we could go in the car about 11am and we walked till 4pm, at

1 Camp B in Bray-Dunes, on the French–Belgian border.
2 Army base in Scotland.
3 Published by Cassell and anonymously written by Major-General T. D. Pilcher, former GOC 17th division, *A General's Letters to his Son on Obtaining His Commission* is a heartfelt if sentimental account of what the values of a soldier should be. Pilcher, an experienced senior officer, was removed from command after attempting to dissuade his superiors in XV corps from the policy of frontal, daylight attacks near Mametz Wood at the Somme in 1916. The book, published in 1917, makes no mention of the Somme and carries a forward by General Horace Smith-Dorrien. The fact that it was circulating in XV corps, where Pilcher had irritated corps command under Lieutenant General Sir Henry Horne, is pertinent, to say the least.

which time we got back to the car. After not having heard a shell for nearly five weeks it was not particularly pleasing to hear them again. We had quite an interesting tour but had no food and a lot of walking was through heavy sand. I got back here at 5 or 6 and had tea. I meant to write after dinner but was so sleepy that I thought I would write in the morning, but of course did not wake in time to catch the mail. It rained pretty well all yesterday and has rained hard all today.

I got two letters from you last night. I am so sorry, dear, that you are so nervous at being alone. I wonder if Nanny has gone off and if Jim and Eileen are good. I am glad that Mabel is alright. I will write to Edith.

Saturday, 4 August 1917 [from billets in Bray-Dunes]

I have absolutely nothing to write about. I got up fairly early, had breakfast and went to the range[1] and then walked to see two companies doing an attack.

After lunch I read the papers and went for a walk with Major Scott.

Padre Stewart who used to be with the 93rd came to tea.

Today is the third anniversary of the war – it seems like the third century to me.

Sunday, 5 August 1917 [from billets in Bray-Dunes]

You must be having a terrific time with the children. I hope that Jim has settled down or both you and he will be worn out.

Major HS has gone off today on 10 days' leave, which greatly improved his spirits.

It has been fine today for the first time and has been very hot. Nearly everyone bathed but I did not – I had no costume and felt very slack.

I had intended to go to the Church of Scotland service but the padre started off too soon so I did not go.

I should certainly invest the money you get from your mother's estate. I should not have too much in any one stock. I am a great believer in having your money well spread out.

---

1 Firing range.

Thursday, 9 August 1917 [from billets in Bray-Dunes]

I started to write to you last night but the lamp struck work and all the servants being in bed, I could get no light.

Fortunately I had both your letters together saying that Eileen was sick and that she was better and you thought alright. I have no letter today but they never come regularly now. No, dear, I would much rather know if anything is wrong – I hope that all is well now. I am very distressed that you should have hurt your hand to add to your troubles and hope that it is not going to be troublesome.

I spent the usual day going round the companies yesterday – very dull. In the afternoon I had an interview with the Corps Commander.[1] He said that the last time I was in the Corps he had sent a special letter about me getting what we want – he could not understand it and that he would do all he could for me again. He was very nice. I have never seen him before.

Isn't it an extraordinary thing? Griffiths has gone away with the same disease as Manser.[2] It makes me feel rather nervous but the doctor says there is practically no danger of infection.

I have had exactly the same day today, round the companies all day. It is a monotonous life enough, but it is quite a change to be so long out of danger. We expect to have another week here.

I hope that there is nothing seriously wrong with Edith.

Mr Pirie[3] was tried today – I hope we have seen the last of him.

I have bought a bathing costume and if the weather is propitious mean to bathe tomorrow. There are a lot of jellyfish here, which rather puts me off.

---

1 The 33rd division has joined the XV corps, commanded by General John du Cane.
2 Blood poisoning.
3 Brechin-born Alexander Pirie joined the Cameronians as a private from the Canadian Divisional Mounted Troops in August 1915. He was later promoted to 2nd lieutenant. The London *Gazette* of 2 November 1917 records his dismissal from the regiment following a general court martial. The battalion's War Diary carries no mention of his court martial, but if Lil already knows of it, then it is likely to be linked to an incident occuring during the assaults on the Hindenburg Line, before Graham Chaplin's last leave.

Friday, 10 August 1917 [from billets in Bray-Dunes]

I have had no letter again today. I feel very anxious about Eileen and pray that she is alight.

We went for a route march this morning. I walked most of the way. After lunch I slept and after tea went for a walk. We had dinner early and had an open air concert which was really very good.

My new servant's name is Brown, a young soldier. I hope he will be more fortunate than his predecessors.

Sunday, 12 August 1917 [from billets in Bray-Dunes]

I was awfully pleased with the photographs of the children and also with the cases they were in – many thanks for them.

I was delighted to get your letter dated the 6th as I had had none for three days and was anxious about Eileen as I was not sure from your previous letter if it was certain she was alright again.

Col Jack was wounded[1] but I do not know how badly.

I think it is possible that Major HS will go to the 2nd Bn.

I want over to see General P. He is in bed – he has something wrong with his leg – some burst blood vessel, serious I should think at his age.[2]

Today being the Sabbath I have been at a Bde conference and ridden all over the place looking at defence works.

Many happy returns of the 15th, dear. I hope that we shall spend them in future together.

Tuesday, 14 August 1917 [from billets in Bray-Dunes]

I was delighted to get two letters today. I said in one of my letters that I had the cigars and clothes so it must have gone astray.

I should certainly take on Brabazon[3] again but should not renew the agreement until the last possible date.

---

1 Jack was wounded by a shell on 31 July, near Ypres, while commanding the 2nd West Yorkshire.

2 Pinney had just celebrated his 54th birthday.

3 The house Lil was renting in Sunningdale.

No, dear, I do not want any new clothes or new waterproof yet a while.

Our delightful rest has come to an end – we shall be on the move soon, so I am afraid the postcard may have to be resorted to again. In a way I am not sorry. I am tired of training.

I wish I could be with you for your birthday!

Thursday, 16 August 1917 [from Australia Camp, Koksijde, thirteen miles east of Dunkirk]

I was too tired to write yesterday. I got up at 3.30am and we had a fairly long march. I walked all the way for exercise. After we had settled down we had lunch and then I got an order which necessitated riding and walking till dinner. I then turned in.

It was unfortunate that I was away as the Army Commander[1] came and asked to see me.

Today we are on the move again. I shall not be able to write much for some time but there is no necessity for you to worry.

I am sorry that I gave you the impression that I should be out another year if all was well. I sincerely hope that I shall not – I think I should be quite dotty by that time.

Harriette's job[2] does not seem to be much of a catch. I should certainly hate those hours. I can't imagine who could have told Mrs Lee that I was not well – I have never been better.

There seems to be a lot of peace talk. I hope there won't be except on our terms. It makes me mad to think of all the misery the Germans have inflicted on the world if they are to get off scot free – although no-one will be more pleased than I shall to see the end.

With all my love and heaps of kisses for Jim and Eileen and yourself. For ever your loving husband, Graham

---

1 General Sir Henry Rawlinson commanded the Fourth Army and, for a period in 1917–18, the Second Army around Ypres.
2 Lee has taken an administrative role in Aldershot.

Friday, 17 August 1917 [FSPC]
I am quite well.

*   *   *

Eight more field-service postcards follow.

Extracts from the battalion War Diary,
August 1917,

Kept by Colonel Graham Chaplin

Australia Camp, Koksijde
16 August - Battalion relieved 7th West Ridings in reserve sector
Lombartsyde B Ech. Casualties: one OR killed, three wounded.

17 August - In reserve Sector Cas.

19 August - Ditto.

20 August - Ditto.

21 August - Ditto. Casualties: three OR killed, five wounded
(gas).

22 August - Relieved RWF in the line, B & C Coys in advance
posts. Casualties: six OR killed, 23 OR wounded.

23/4 August - B Coy raided and post captured. Casualties: five
OR killed, two OR missing, 17 OR wounded.

25/6 August - B recaptured post. Capt E W Sussex killed in
action. Casualties: seven OR killed, 14 OR wounded.

26/7 August - Battalion relieved and moved back to Koksijde.
Total casualties for this tour: 23 OR killed, two OR missing,
62 OR wounded.

28/9 August - Battalion marched to De Panne and stayed there
for night. Battalion moved by buses to Capelle in Synthe area
arriving 2pm. Remainder of day cleaning up.

Billets in Synthe[1]
30 August - Cleaning up, checking deficiencies and inspecting
anti gas appliances.

31 August - Bn moved by buses from Petit Synthe to Moulle,
seven kilometres from St Omer, arriving 3pm.

This is war again. Reveille at 2.15 a.m., march at 4.15, ever closer to the
guns and the danger. Streams of ambulances pass the marching men as
they move nearer the front, bodies on stretchers, horses in gas masks, fresh
cemeteries right and left. The new German weapon of mustard gas enforces
a change for the 33rd division's kilted battalions – 2nd Argylls, 9th Highland
Light Infantry – as the gas not only chokes the lungs but scorches skin
on contact, and lingers in shell holes and puddles. Much to the delight of
their fellow soldiers, the 'kilties' are given long cotton drawers that must
be worn at all times.

Nieuwpoort is ghostly, battered by bombing, the last town in Europe's
long line of trenches. Chaplin leads his men past the broken buildings and
north, back towards the beach, crossing the swirling Yser on undulating
pontoon bridges and then moving up to the reserve trenches, where they
must wait for their turn in the line. Up ahead, HQ is a small brick fort, part

---

1 Outside Dunkirk.

of seventeenth-century fortifications that once denoted the French border, now under constant bombardment. Beyond that, a mix of concrete outposts and breastworks – necessitated by the floodplain – form the front, with few connecting trenches, all too easy for an attacking force to penetrate. Behind here, the Cameronians assemble, running working parties back to Nieuwpoort for provisions and ammunition, supplying the Royal Welch, who hold the line for the first six days.

Then, on 22 August, it is the Scots' turn. Just as the Cams' B and C Companies set off to relieve the Royal Welch, a German raiding party is spotted and artillery fire called in. In the ensuing chaos, the shelling hits the British outposts, killing six and wounding twenty-three Cameronians. Fighting continues for two long nights, the Cams losing and then winning back one outpost. In retaliation, German shells also bombard Nieuwpoort, scoring a direct hit on the fortified house where the 19th brigade has based its HQ. The targeting is so accurate that it soon becomes clear they have a map of British positions, taken from a captured officer. The Germans are also mixing their shells – high explosive, tear gas, pepper gas, mustard gas. It adds a new level of anxiety to the battle, every soldier unsure what each shell will bring.

Brigadier Mayne escapes the collapse of his HQ unscathed – even being a mile back from the front is no protection in an artillery blitz. For Chaplin, such fighting is another pitch into the sleepless maw, where night attacks and constant alertness make recuperation impossible, and exhaustion quickly sets in, pushing him closer to resignation. One month on from his forty-fourth birthday, he can see the age of the commanders around him dropping with each appointment, as the army looks for younger men, better able to take the strain. Nearly every lieutenant colonel in the original British Expeditionary Force had been over fifty. Now most are under forty. At forty-four, he feels an old man set apart.

For some of Chaplin's men, the stress of such fighting has other consequences. One private, Ernest Mackness, a regular soldier from Leicester, already under suspended sentence of death for desertion, is arrested

again after running away from the fighting on 22 August.[185] He is shot
for desertion six weeks later, in the village of Blaringhem, outside St
Omer. He is the only Cameronian under Chaplin to receive the ultimate
penalty.

Thursday, 30 August 1917 [from billets in Synthe, outside Dunkirk]
My own darling,

You must be beginning to think I had given up writing to you, but we have
been in the line since I last wrote and have had a very trying time. The Germans
are using a lot of gas shells. We were in the front line six days, out of which I
only had about 11 hours' sleep. We carried out a successful raid on a German
post, took prisoners and a machine gun, and received the congratulations of
the Corps Commander.

RO wrote and asked if I would like to go to Farnborough. I had no time to
write but have sent a wire to say yes.

We came out of the line and marched a good many miles to quite a nice
place. We all slept till dinner time. I took a room in the hotel and stood a
farewell dinner to Major HS who has gone off today to take over the 2nd Bn.
I got up at 5.30 yesterday and we came here in lorries. Again I slept most of
the day. I sent you a wire to say all well.

This morning I walked over to see General Mayne. He showed me the draft
of a letter he had written saying that I was probably the only regimental officer
who has served continuously from the beginning of the war and recommending
that I should not be employed as a regimental officer any longer and especially
recommending me as an instructor for the CO's school at home if I was not
given a Brigade. I agreed to it as I can no longer stand these prolonged periods
without sleep. I feel that going home without a Brigade I have been a failure
but if I go on any longer I run the risk of breaking down altogether. My nerve
has not gone in the slightest but I feel I must have a rest.

We move again by bus tomorrow and will probably have 10 days' rest. The
probability is that I shall not go into action again, so that you need not have
any more anxiety about me.

I wonder if you will see Mrs RW. If you do, give her my love. I should like to see Ronnie M[1] again.

Friday, 31 August 1917 [telegram]
All well Col Chaplin

Sunday, 2 September 1917 [from billets in Moulle, five miles north-west of St Omer]
We came by buses the day before yesterday to this place. We all went to bed early – the first proper night's sleep for a long time. I did not write yesterday as the padre goes home today and will take this.

It is almost certain that I shall come home at once, either to go to Farnboro' or if my telegram to RO was too late then to command a regiment at home for six months, as they are sending regimental officers who have been out a long time home for that time.

I feel quite fit again now I have had a good sleep, but I have had enough for the present.

Wednesday, 5 September 1917 [from billets in Moulle]
The General[2] has gone on leave and I am commanding the Brigade – very comfortable quarters. I have just arrived here and am told that the post goes at once so this will be a hurried note.

Yesterday I spent all the afternoon in a car going over to see General G[3] to see if he could get me a brigade. As bad luck would have it, he was away for the day, so my journey was in vain – so that I shall just have to leave it to Fate what happens to me. I hate the idea of being scrapped, but I know that it would be foolish to go on any longer with a battalion. I have gone to my

---

1 Ronnie MacAllan, taken prisoner in 1914, released in an exchange of prisoners two years later.
2 Brigadier General Mayne.
3 Major-General Hon Frederick Gordon, formerly in charge of 19th brigade, GOC 22nd division from June 1917.

limit. I cannot any longer stand the long periods without sleep which one has to do as a Bn commander.

It is almost certain that I shall go home. I love to think that we shall be together again and to be with the children. I shall love to see your new coat and skirt.

The padre said he was going to see you. If wonder if he has been – you will be amused. He is a great comic but a good little fellow. Very scotch and likes whisky.

Have you seen Mrs RW?

Sandy seems to be always on leave. I hope that Baby is getting on alright. Give my love to Edith.

With fondest love and heaps of kisses to Jim and Eileen and yourself.

Thursday, 6 September 1917 [from billets in Moulle]

I had a jolly good sleep last night in a very comfortable bed. This morning I rode out with the Staff Captain to see two battalions at training and got back in time for lunch.

This afternoon I walked round to the regiment to see if there was any letter from you – alas there was none.

Our GSO1[1] was wounded yesterday and the new GSO1 is Maxwell-Scott.[2] He is expected to arrive today. I shall be glad to see him again. It is nearly three years since I saw him last.

I wish definite orders would come through about me. It is rather unsettling not knowing when I shall get home or what I am going to do.

This Russian business[3] is awful and will buck the Germans up. There is not much hope of ending the war now till the Americans are ready.[4]

I still feel very tired. I think it must have been the dose of gas I got.

---

1 General Staff Officer, grade 1.

2 Major Walter Maxwell-Scott, Cameronian officer.

3 Following civil unrest and the abdication of the Tsar, Russia was descending into chaos, out of which would emerge the Bolshevik Revolution in October.

4 Despite declaring war on Germany in April 1917, America would not send troops to France until 1918. It only maintained a small army, and needed first to enlist and train a large body of men – a fact known to all sides fighting in France.

Friday, 7 September 1917 [from billets in Moulle]

This morning I rode out to the training ground and saw the battalions at work. I got back just in time for lunch. After lunch I went in a car to Divisional Hd Qrs for a sort of conference and then walked back for exercise.

I am glad you are having good weather. I should love to see the children paddling.

I wish I could hear what is going to be my fate – I hope the Farnborough business. I would of course still prefer a brigade out here but I am afraid it is too late now, besides I want some rest.

If I come home I shall have to get new uniform and also field boots, which will be expensive.

I am very sorry about Pratt[1] being killed.

With all my fondest love, dear, and heaps of kisses to you all. For ever your loving husband, Graham

Graham Chaplin, billeted in the quiet hamlet of Moulle, just a few miles north of St Omer, waits to discover his fate. The battalion has been bussed down from the coast and spends the following fortnight training. The War Diary lists the routine: inspection of tailors, shoemakers and armourer sergeants; training by company; brigade route march; practising artillery formation and trench-to-trench attacks; general musketry course; more route marching; more practice on the firing range. Chaplin has overseen it time and time again since he took command back in 1915. This time, however, the training is more intense, more focused, as the army acknowledges the value of proper preparation.

In such training weeks, a commanding officer can be superfluous. He inspects, he oversees, he eyes his men on parade one last time, taking the salutes. He barks a greeting – his thoughts or his gratitude – but rarely instructs. That is left to other officers.

---

1 Major Audley Pratt, 9th Royal Irish Fusiliers, a family friend (see letter from Pratt to Lil, 1 November 1915), was killed by a shell in August 1917.

Chaplin knows where this current bout of training is heading – east towards the Menin Road where the Third Battle of Ypres is raging. As ever, the 33rd will be used to plug the gaps, to push the army on where others have stalled. And so Chaplin watches, while everything around him changes again. Pinney, suffering from the gammy leg which has pained him all summer, is finally withdrawn as commander of the 33rd for hospital treatment, and temporarily replaced with an 'acting GOC', Brigadier General Wood, formerly in charge of 43rd brigade. Pinney's most senior staff officer, Colonel Forster, is wounded while inspecting the front line at Ypres, and also withdrawn, replaced with Major Maxwell-Scott, a fellow Cameronian.

As a longstanding soldier of the Great War, Chaplin is accustomed to this now. So much has been learnt so rapidly. So much is new – tanks, poison gas, intensive artillery barrages. It is a very different army from the one he joined in 1894, out in India, suppressing Pashtun uprisings, imposing order and protecting commerce, in between tiffin and polo.

He has, as one of the longest-serving regimental officers in this war's front line, experienced a complete tactical revolution in how his army fights, and a social revolution in who it inducts and how it promotes. But here, with the plains of the Pas-de-Calais stretched around him, Chaplin is close enough to where he started to have come full circle. Close enough to Mons, to Armentières, to Loos, to remember this war's earliest days, with its hopes and friendships, and to know that he is close to no one now.

Enough is enough. He has decided to take a desk job at home, bartered by his old friend, Harry Lee, if that is the best he can get, in order to leave the front. He knows it is a young man's war now, and he knows his superiors have doubts about his fitness. As ever, he worries about the cost of going home – though his wife's inheritance from her own rich parents, recently deceased, would presumably cover the new boots needed. Perhaps the worries are just a nervous tic, covering his real anxiety about the cost to his ambition. In a war of rapid promotion, a desk job at home will see him fall far, far behind.

Then, on Sunday, 9 September 1917, he is summoned by Brigadier

Wood, the acting commander of 33rd division, who has news. The next day Graham writes Lil a long letter.

Monday, 10 September 1917 [from billets in Moulle]
My own darling,

Col Maxwell-Scott and General Stockwell came in yesterday and prevented me writing for the mail. Col M-S is just the same – I forget if you met him, I think you did, he is very nice.

I do not know whether you will be pleased or not. The Divisional General sent for me yesterday and said that the Army Commander said if I would withdraw my application to go home they would give me a month's leave and the first brigade that went at the end of it. Of course I accepted. So I expect to be home in about a week. I am very pleased as I should have felt that I had been a failure if I had not got a brigade, but at the same time I hate this continued separation from you, dear, and the children. However you will not have so much to worry about as there is not much danger – it will be nothing compared to what one has been through.

The regiment – in fact the whole brigade – are very pleased that I am to be promoted. I think they minded more than I did.

General P is expected back soon – his leg turned out not to be so bad as they thought.

I am glad you are going to see Mrs RW. I hope she sees the children – I am sure she will love them. She was always most kind to me.

I am going to dine with Col RW – he is sending a car for me.

What are we going to do with a month's leave?

I am writing to RO that it is off my going to Farnborough.

It is most lovely weather now.

I am not sure what date you return to Brabazon.

With all my love and thoughts, darling, and heaps of kisses to the kids and yourself. For ever your loving husband, Graham

Graham Chaplin returns home the following week. By 25 September, the Cameronians, without their colonel, have moved to the Ypres sector. Part of the battalion joins the 100th brigade in an attack on the Menin Road on 26 September. The Cams lose seventeen men killed, ninety-two wounded and fourteen missing.

On 3 October, at Racquinghem, south-west of St Omer, the 19th brigade is inspected by Field Marshal Sir Douglas Haig, commander-in-chief of the British army, for the first time. He does not address the men.

Extracts from the battalion War Diary,
November 1917,

Kept by Major Clifford Scott

18 November – Lt Col J G Chaplin, who had been in France with the battalion since August 1914 and in command since May 1915, ordered to take command of 103rd Brigade, 34th Division. Major C C Scott took over command of the battalion.

TO THE END

'But he that shall endure to the end, the same shall be saved.'[186]

Allied forces attack at Cambrai using tanks — initial gains halted by lack of support — German forces launch large-scale offensive in March 1918 and break through at the Somme — Germans launch second front in Flanders — American forces fight first major battle at Cantigny — German army attacks on Marne — Allied forces counter-attack and drive east — German navy mutinies — Germany surrenders in November 1918

If Graham Chaplin sends more letters as a brigadier general, Lil does not keep them. The family's collection of letters ends in September 1917.[187] But Chaplin's war continues. After two months at home, in late November he is given command of the 103rd brigade in France. The brigade features four 'pals' battalions of Northumberland Fusiliers, originally raised from Kitchener volunteers and known as the Tyneside Irish. The 103rd, along with the 102nd (Tyneside Scottish) and 101st brigades, form the 34th division, which joined the war in early 1916 and went on to take the heaviest casualties of any division on the opening day of the Somme offensive. The 103rd brigade, in particular, had suffered terribly in a frontal attack on La Boisselle.

By November 1917, the 34th division, led by Major-General Sir Cameron Nicholson – one of the army's ablest divisional commanders – is recovering from another bloody encounter, the third Battle of Ypres (Passchendaele), where it had again suffered heavy casualties, fighting along the Broenbeek river. The 34th-division history, written by Lieutenant Colonel J. Shakespear, notes that Brigadier General Chaplin replaces Brigadier General Trevor 'whose health had succumbed to the rigours of the [Ypres] salient'. It is a division under constant stress and in constant flux. By the end of 1917, the 34th has replaced its numbers twice over. If many soldiers felt they were simply feeding the machine, joining the brigades of the 34th would not have dissuaded them.

In early 1918, shortly after Chaplin joins and perhaps at his instigation, the 103rd is reorganised while it is in training near Gommecourt. The brigade's recruitment area around Newcastle no longer has enough men of fighting age to fill its infantry units. So the Northumberland battalions are shrunk, and the 103rd takes in the 10th Lincolns and the 1st East Lancashires, the first regular unit to join the division. By February, the new-look 103rd is with the 34th division in general headquarters reserve, north of Amiens.

At the beginning of March, the 34th goes back into the line south of Arras, in the centre sector of the VI Corps front. Chaplin's 103rd is held in reserve at Hamelincourt, just four miles from Croisilles, where the Cams manned the trenches in May 1917. On the morning of Thursday, 21 March, at 5.30 a.m., the Germans – bolstered by divisions brought in from the Eastern Front after the Russian surrender – start a prolonged offensive, using new tactics, sending in elite storm-trooper units to bypass the front line and attack HQs and artillery positions. The initial assault threatens to sweep through the 34th division, many of whose battalions find themselves rapidly outnumbered, encircled and confused. By the morning of 22 March, Chaplin's 103rd has been swiftly put into a new front line, pulled back after German advances. By 23 March, after forty-eight hours of continual, desperate fighting, the 34th is relieved by the 31st division, having lost over 3,000 men killed, wounded or missing, and pulled its line back nearly three miles, without breaking.

After a brief period behind the fighting, the 34th division is sent north, back into the front line at Erquinghem, where it had spent the spring of 1916. They must man a quieter stretch of trenches previously used to train new troops or allow battle-fatigued battalions to recover. Lying just outside Armentières, it is also a terrain familiar to Chaplin, who won his promotion to colonel there. Much, however, has changed. Armentières had been regularly shelled during 1917, and many of its inhabitants have left. The division must hold a stretch of line running from the River Lys to the Rue du Bois, where the Cameronians so often patrolled in early 1915.

Unluckily for the 34th, it is also the sector where the German army intends to start its second major offensive of spring 1918. Having drawn British forces south to reinforce positions against its first push, it will now attempt to drive through defences in the north and seize the Channel ports.

All is quiet for a week around Armentières, then a bombardment of gas shells starts just south of the 34th's position, then to the north, and finally the Germans attack, threatening again to encircle Chaplin's division. The 34th makes a fighting retirement, slipping across the River Lys on temporary footbridges. There begins a week of courageous rearguard action and retreat, as the German offensive gains ground. Nicholson is continually lent reserve battalions and brigades to delay enemy progress, as his own resources are whittled down.

After taking heavy losses and following the death of its brigadier, the 101st brigade is combined with the 103rd under Chaplin. By mid-April, the 34th is fighting desperately to hold a line around Bailleul, close to where the 33rd division, including the Cameronians, has been brought in to reinforce the position. On 19 April, the Cameronians' War Diary notes simply, 'General Chaplin DSO GOC 103rd Bde visited the Bn', before the unit moves rapidly to relieve the 147th brigade in hastily dug trenches along the road between Bailleul and Saint-Jans-Cappel.

The 34th division is eventually relieved by the 133rd French division on 21 April, after being in action continually for twelve days, attacked in front and on both flanks, yet again remaining unbroken, for which it was commended by commander-in-chief Haig. In the course of the action, it lost nearly 5,000 men, killed, wounded or missing.

This time there are simply not enough new recruits to replenish the division. So its battalions are reduced to cadres of ten officers and forty-five ranks, and for two months it is assigned to the training of American forces, newly arrived on the battlefield.

Then, in June, Nicholson rebuilds the 34th with experienced infantry brought in from service in Egypt, Turkey, Palestine and India. For the 103rd brigade, Chaplin is given the 5th King's Own Scots Borderers, the 5th Argyll & Sutherland Highlanders, the 2/4th Somerset Light Infantry and, no doubt with a nod to his old regiment, the 8th Scottish Rifles. After a brief period of training, the 34th division returns to general headquarters reserve in early July, awaiting orders.

On 16 July, the division is suddenly told to entrain for Senlis, north of Paris, from where it marches towards Soissons, close to where Chaplin ended his retreat from Mons back in September 1914. Here, the French army has attacked the Germans and driven the enemy back five miles, and urgently needs fresh troops to exploit the victory. The 34th is put under the command of General Penet, of the 30th Corps, 10th French Army, and thrown into the fray.

Despite being untested in battle and with little knowledge of the terrain, the brigades of the 34th start ten days of continual fighting, side by side with the French, pushing the Germans back from Villers-Hélon towards Beugneux, taking heavy losses, but contributing to the victory known as the Second Battle of the Marne. By the time they are relieved at the end of July, 153 officers and 3,617 ranks have been killed, wounded or declared missing.

The 34th returns north to Bergues, south of Dunkirk, to rest and refit. A grateful French army then shows its appreciation by decorating the division's senior officers[188] with the Légion d'Honneur, which Chaplin can add to his Croix de Guerre. To the south, the British army initiates a major offensive west of Amiens, driving the Germans back from gains made in their spring offensive towards the Hindenburg Line. The British, French and American forces then prepare for a series of attacks along the whole front line to rout a demoralised enemy. By 23 August, the 103rd is in trenches again, this time around Ypres, where a major assault will start in September that will lead, eventually, to the war's end. But, before then, Chaplin has gone. A note in the 34th division's history says simply that on Friday, 30 August, the brigadier is 'sent home for six months' rest'.

It is four years and fifteen days since Chaplin set foot on the quay in Le Havre, at the start of his war. He has fought through Mons, Marne, Armentières, Loos, Cuinchy, Somme, Hindenburg, Arras, Nieuwpoort, Arras again, Armentières again, Soissons, Ypres. Perhaps he had had enough – perhaps he was, in a term already prevalent, 'cooked', made incapable of command through nervous exhaustion and sleeplessness. Or perhaps he just needed time with his family. No reason is given. But it seems he is determined to see out the campaign away from Flanders, having earned his peace. By the war's end, he has been mentioned six times in despatches – confirmations of which have been assiduously collected by Lil. He has nothing left to prove.

But Graham Chaplin does not leave the army. Midway through October 1918, he is given a new post, commanding the 2nd Cyclist Brigade – a renaming of the old mounted yeomanry battalions, which had remained in Britain as home-defence troops. He is immediately posted to Ireland, where the Cyclist Brigade forms part of the security force overseeing an increasingly turbulent country. And by the time Germany surrenders to the Allies in November 1918, he is back in the thick of it again, but in a very different war, keeping the peace as Ireland revolts.

This time, it seems, Lil is determined that the family will go with him – her police papers for Ireland show she certainly intended to travel. And the Chaplin family grows. In 1919, Lil gives birth to a second son, Ivor. In 1921, she gives birth to a second daughter, Brenda. By then, her husband has been promoted to colonel commandant of the army's Galway Brigade in the west of Ireland. Here he spends two difficult years, as British security forces first try to suppress Irish republican agitation and then later briefly administer martial law over much of Ireland during the elections that precede independence.

After a stint in Britain, Chaplin is posted to Iraq, where he serves for two years, initially as commander of an infantry brigade and latterly as a staff officer at military headquarters, Baghdad.

He eventually leaves the army in July 1927. His official record states that he retires 'on account of ill health' – no detailed reason is given. He is granted 'the honorary rank of Brigadier General'. Chaplin is fifty-four. Lil is one month short of forty-one.

They return to Berkshire, where they live happily in retirement for another three decades. Relations with the rest of the Chaplin and Alexander families are good. Graham is reconciled with Willie, who, having been knighted in 1920, becomes Conservative MP for Glasgow Central[189] from 1923–1945. Willie proceeds frequently to ignore the party political whips as he pursues his own interests, principally a burgeoning business career, two wives – one the sister of the other – and a home in Jersey, where the Chaplins visit him often.

Meanwhile, Graham, in retirement, now has time to hunt, shoot and ride to his heart's content. According to the memories of his grandchildren, he also devotes himself to a new hobby: keeping chickens. He rarely talks about the war. Lil is very much in charge. His children, and later his grandchildren, know him only as 'Da', a kind, quiet man who loves the outdoors.

Graham Chaplin dies on Sunday, 15 January 1956, at New Farm House in the village of Chieveley, near Newbury, aged eighty-two, and is survived by Lil and three of his children. Writing his obituary that year in the *Covenanter,* the magazine circulated among veterans of the Scottish Rifles, his old war friend, Brigadier General James Jack, describes Chaplin's stubborn courage in France, and recites the examples of his willingness to challenge orders when he thought them nonsensical. He sums his comrade up simply: 'The soul of integrity, of courage, the nigh perfect example of an officer.'

A newspaper clipping kept by Lil records that Graham's memorial service, held at St Mary's, Chieveley, was attended not just by family but by his brother-in-law, Colonel Vincent Sandilands, his friend, Major-General Robert Money, and Major-General Sir Eric Girdwood, representing the Cameronians. Forty-two years after his fellow officers assembled their archway of swords at the wedding of Graham and Lil in Stirling, they are there to see him off.

He had outlived many with whom he fought. Philip Robertson died in 1936, Tom McLellan in 1942, Harry Lee in 1946 and Richard Oakley in 1948. But James Jack, Francis Hamilton, Robert Money, Tom Riddell-Webster, James Cotton Minchin, Douglas Moncrieff Wright and Jacobus Hill all survive him.

On 26 November 1956, ten months on from Graham's funeral, and shortly after moving to a smaller house in Chieveley, Lil Chaplin also dies, aged seventy. Among the possessions she leaves is a large tin box, found by Eileen, her eldest daughter. Stuffed inside are three years' worth of pencil-written letters and field-service postcards, assorted press cuttings, photographs and more. Eileen takes the box and stores it carefully away. But she never reads the letters, and eventually passes them on to her own children.

Perhaps Lil knew, as memories are lost and characters blur with time, that the letters will become all that remains – a memorial to early love, one half of a long conversation stretched over terrible times. So she left it for others to piece together their story.

'The unchanging Man of history is wonderfully adaptable both
by his power of endurance and in his capacity for detachment'

Joseph Conrad, from the 1921 'Author's Note'

added to *Victory*, first published in 1915

AFTERWORD

Drive to High Wood today through the Somme's wide, summer wheat fields and you will see the same countryside, replanted and resculpted, that Graham Chaplin and his men fought through – the open plain, the villages nestling in dells, those strange isolated copses standing on ridges. At High Wood itself, regrown, wired off and plastered with shabby signs saying *Propriété Privée*, you can peer over steel farm gates at the gloomy woodland rides disappearing off into the scrubby undergrowth, malevolent with mysterious shadows. Access is forbidden, ostensibly on account of the undefused ordnance that still remains inside its seventy-five acres almost a century after its defining battle. So the wood sits defiant, lowering ominously over the yellow fields that encircle it.

The London Cemetery on its western side is, in contrast, immaculate, its yew arches mirroring the robust design of its red-brick loggia, its book of remembrance now filled with messages left to so many uncles, its belts of tombstones poignantly marking so many unknown soldiers – so many uncles because few of the dead were old enough to have started families; so many unknown because perpetual bombardment had shredded their bodies. One grave near the main entrance even says, *An Unknown Cameronian Officer* – an indication that not even the regimental pips were enough to provide a name.

For an old sweat, a professional soldier like Graham Chaplin, High Wood would have been a place not just of terror, but of frustration and anger: that the strategy was ill thought out, the tactics wasteful of men, an overview of the general position impossible to process. His commanders were struggling with the problem of penetrating formidable German defences, just as the men he commanded struggled to follow through their orders effectively.

Chaplin's unease is palpable in his letters, though he rarely makes overt reference – that would go against his training, and perhaps be unwise in front of a censor. But it is clear from the very telling reference in John Stormonth-Darling's letter to Lil, in September 1916 – 'If he would not tell Generals what he thinks of them it would be better really for himself' – that he made his views known. It is also evident in the accumulation of references to his tiredness. It appears to be an exhaustion entwined with depression, as the scenes he witnessed took their toll.

What is remarkable is how calm and upbeat so many of his letters are. His is a voice that became submerged in the welter of memoirs and excitable accounts that surfaced a decade after the war, written by all ranks, but mostly by the volunteers – junior officers and privates – who came to the war after 1914 and were rightly shocked by what they found, and what was done to them. Read a collection of first-hand accounts in books such as Lyn Macdonald's remarkable *Somme* and you will note how few of the witnesses are battalion commanders. Senior regimental officers are bound by duty to avoid controversy, and are uncomfortable giving opinions – it is what makes the spiky diaries of Chaplin's friend, Brigadier General James Jack, published in 1964, all the more interesting.

Chaplin's letters are equally valuable because here we have the authentic voice of the veteran soldier, the experienced commander of men, engaged in the moment. He is detached in his professionalism, yet rapidly feels powerless to affect anything, and becomes victim to the kind of internal politics found in all large organisations put under stress. He is also a man very much in love. The tropes of most war letters – 'It's raining and the food's terrible, but our boys' spirits are tiptop' – are there, but so too is the intimate chat he continues with his wife, as if determined to maintain this 2 a.m. conversation. Somewhere in his head each day, as he tours trenches, attends burials, organises raids, plans defences and signs off his paperwork, he keeps a space free to continue their talk, almost as if holding her hand throughout the carnage. After he sets off for France, she worries when she doesn't hear from him. She frets that he is dead. So he writes to reassure her. By 1916, as the war progresses and his family grows, she is writing to reassure him. He is nervously anxious when her letters don't arrive. He is dependent on her voice. That is how a marriage can work.

The fragmented form of many of the letters – individual sentences answering earlier questions, piled up in a stack of seeming non sequiturs, Lil's letters burnt – are part of that intimacy; no need for formal structure. It reflects the broken, desperate world he fights in, where every second alive is precious yet boredom predominates, and change makes so much unfamiliar. Questions are put. Answers must be given. Sense can be lost. In a curious way, it echoes the bitty writing of Modernist poets (an allusion that would doubtless make the very unliterary Chaplin scratch his balding head and scoff – but it's there). Cut up and disjointed, parts missing as understood, coded and alluded, they reflect the rhythm of broken, intimate dialogue.

And Chaplin's tone of detachment? It is hard to see how he could have written about the war he was fighting in any other way, given his desire to alleviate Lil's worries, and his position as a battalion commander, overseeing 1,000 men. Perhaps that detachment is a very twentieth-century capacity – to be witnessed again and again as the period's atrocities accumulated – but, in truth, it has long been a human characteristic: to switch off in order to survive, to drain oneself of empathy. Prolonged exposure to horror inevitably hardens the participant. It does not mean that Chaplin feels little. He is disturbed when a local newspaper, writing up the death of one of his men, makes a ready presumption by describing him as a commanding officer 'inured to the horrors of war'.[190] Yet he must protect himself. If the writer of these letters is feeling horror or compassion, he usually hides it as he hides his fear, because an examination of his own feelings might render him useless.

What hangs over any discussion of Chaplin, of course, is exactly what happened on the battlefield at Loos during that fateful September of 1915 – six months, incidentally, after my own grandfather, the battalion medical officer, had left the Cameronians. It is not hard for us now to believe that Chaplin, having witnessed a particularly cack-handed British attempt at releasing poison gas, might baulk at his orders to send his men over the top to face certain death. But his decision to tell his brigadier general that further attack was senseless is certainly brave, especially for a leader in the earliest days of his command. It is clear both he and his brigadier refused to carry out the written order unless a staff officer came to the front line to observe the battle. It was a refusal they repeated again before their part in the battle ended.

Now, his brigadier was his old commanding officer, Philip Robertson, former colonel of the Cameronians, so no surprise, perhaps, that he had the confidence to query orders from on high. It is likely, too, that he put up a detailed defence of his actions when questioned by staff officers. Perhaps it is no coincidence that, later in the war, Chaplin should have been so taken with the anonymously authored book, On the Art of Command,[191] which was quietly circulating among officers. He may even have underlined the following lines from chapter six: 'If you are ever in doubt as to whether an order still holds good, ask yourself: was the officer responsible for the order in possession of the main facts as I now know them to be when he issued it?'[192]

At Loos, the officers in corps command, who had drawn up the orders weeks before the battle, were plainly not in possession of the main facts as he now knew them. But what if every battalion commander raised the same query? It was unthinkable. So someone, somewhere, appears to have marked Chaplin's card. From then on, at a time when experienced officers could expect rapid promotion as the fighting destroyed so many lives, his career stood still. He was left forever wondering if he had done wrong, talking sense in an insane world – an officer other soldiers seemed to admire and senior commanders seemed to mistrust, simultaneously. In the process, denied promotion and stalled at colonel, he became probably the longest-serving front-line officer on the Western Front.

What is not debatable is that Graham Chaplin was a lucky man, fighting in a lucky battalion, assigned to a lucky brigade. The 19th brigade, unallocated to a division initially, dodged serious fighting at Mons, Le Cateau and the Battle of the Marne. They were attacked repeatedly at La Boutillerie, but held their own before moving to the quieter front around

Armentières. Until Loos, in September 1915, the Cams never had to make a serious frontal attack, such as that which devastated their sister battalion, the 2nd Scottish Rifles, at Neuve Chapelle and Aubers Ridge. And at Loos, the Cams were spared the casualties of other battalions in the 19th brigade simply because Chaplin quite rightly queried his orders. Or did Brigadier Robertson query them for him? And then at the Somme, at the moment the battalion is to be tested against High Wood, a site of terrible slaughter, Chaplin is pulled back to be held as a reserve brigadier. Later, he is sent into High Wood, but to hold the line, not to attack. And then, before the battalion is thrown against German trenches at Lesbœufs, losing one hundred men, he is laid flat in hospital, crushed by his horse. Those are the cards Fate deals.

And so it goes on, until he leaves the Cams just as the battalion is trudging wearily into Passchendaele. No shell hits him; no sniper drills his forehead. Every night he keeps writing. Gruff and determined, he appears to go through the whole war almost unscathed – only for nervous exhaustion to pull him apart in other ways: his hair gone, his teeth extracted, his eyes inflamed and infected. Yet on he forges, worrying about his family and his men, but also about money and pay, loans and insurance premiums, promotion and contacts. His world, extraordinarily, is not that dissimilar to that of the executive in a modern-day multinational, posted overseas and spotting opportunity, moaning about head office, worrying about being left behind. That is what these letters reveal. For professional soldiers, this war was their chance for rapid advancement, a fact that is sometimes forgotten in the sentiment that clouds World War One.

For veterans like Chaplin, it was also an opportunity to catch up with friends they had made in a necessarily peripatetic career. Suddenly, the vast majority of the British army was squeezed along a line less than ninety miles long in northern France, not spread across the Empire. Little wonder the letters seem to carry endless lists of old faces recognised, memories jogged. Little wonder, too, the letters reflect the unease felt when their tight little army swells to over one million strong, with first volunteers then unwilling conscripts filling the ranks – what price their professionalism now?

It wasn't a view that garnered much sympathy at the time. Hence the stereotype of Colonel Blimp, the popular 1930s cartoon which became a byword for ignorant pomposity, and drew on the blustering conservatism of the old sweats. Such officers were well remembered by those who signed up in World War One, regaled with how it was always better before. And they were depicted as a danger to progress long before the next war began.

Yet Chaplin is hardly a Blimp, so in love with his wife, plainly delighted by his children and tortured by the thought of being forgotten – torn between home and duty. But he is a man of his time, intolerant and unforgiving, snobbish and sentimental to our contemporary perceptions. Even during the war, informed observers such as Lord Crawford,[193] who worked as a medical orderly in a clearing station in northern France, noted how odd were the obsessions of army officers, divorced from the normal world: they talk 'chiefly of billets and personal grievances', and lack any strategic understanding of the war.[194] Crawford thought the new volunteer intake were the worst – 'swankers' – and the old sweats more likeable, but still difficult. 'The officer of old standing is much more modest in his manner, though more touchy about trifles'.

Those trifles are what we today might see as the lifestyle expectations built up by a pre-war career in the army: free servants, good food, subsidised leisure and obsequious respect from the lower ranks. But there is another side to it: a sense of order, of respect and community, in which all ranks of a regiment look after each other, to the end. Read the letters held in the National Archive appealing for the reinstatement of Tubby Woods' pension. A regiment does not walk away. And many of the values are not so very different from those still seen by some as worthwhile: don't complain, get on with it, look after those around you and love your family. Following Chaplin's progress across three vital years through these letters, you can sense his very human struggle. His is a depiction of war that a survivor creates to ensure his own sanity, all the more revealing for what it leaves out.

ACKNOWLEDGEMENTS

This book pieces together an untold story from the fragments of an one-sided, epistolary conversation, and as such has been akin to assembling a jigsaw puzzle – albeit one with a number of missing parts. The process of finding those parts, putting faces to names and plotting a narrative's progress, has been daunting yet fascinating. I would like to thank all of those who have supported me along the way.

Firstly, it would not have been possible without the encouragement of the surviving grandchildren of Graham and Lil Chaplin – Peter Roberts, Jeremy Roberts, Edward Chaplin and Catherine Chaplin. Their assistance has been invaluable. I am also grateful to Pat Barr (granddaughter of Graham Chaplin's brother Robert), Peter Slater (grandson of Graham's sister Alice) and Honora Smith (granddaughter of Graham's brother Lindsay) for additional information provided.

Outside the family, I owe a debt to Barrie Duncan, overseer of the Cameronian archive at South Lanarkshire Council in Hamilton, for diligently answering my queries on the Cams; to Paul Alexander of Tennants Consolidated Ltd for discussing with me the history of Charles Tennant & Co; to staff at Stirling Library for sourcing press coverage of the Alexander family; to librarians at Surrey University's E.H. Shepard archive, for allowing me to read the letters of Florence Chaplin; and to staff at the Imperial War Museum, whose reading room provided an indispensible resource for finding the memoirs and histories relevant to the Cams' progress in France.

I would like to thank Antony Topping at literary agency Greene & Heaton and Susan Watt at publisher Heron Books for believing in the vision, and ably bringing the book to publication. I am also grateful to

Penelope Price for her detailed copy editing, and David Eldridge at Two Associates for his striking cover design. Finally, I must thank Vanessa Nicolson for her advice on the manuscript and for her constant love and support – *grazie mille di nuovo* – and our daughter Elena Davidson for always keeping an eye on us. It's appreciated.

I would like to dedicate this book to Richard Roberts, Eileen Chaplin's youngest son, whom I never met. He spent the last years of his life sorting, filing and typing out on foolscap all his grandfather's pencil-written letters, yet he never lived to see them appear in print. Without his input, this book would have been much harder to complete.

APPENDIX 1

British army terms, chains of command and fighting strengths, 1914.

Section (part of a Platoon) – twelve men – commanded by an NCO.

Platoon (part of a Company) – fifty men – commanded by a lieutenant.

Company (part of a Battalion, lettered A–D) – 200–230 men – commanded by a captain or major.

Battalion – 1,000 men – commanded by a lieutenant colonel, assisted by a major as second in command and a captain as adjutant in charge of administration.

Brigade (comprising four or five infantry battalions plus engineers, pioneers, field ambulance, veterinary and sanitary sections) – upwards of 5,000 men – commanded by a brigadier general plus staff.

Division (comprising three brigades plus artillery and divisional transport) – upwards of 18,000 men – commanded by a major-general plus staff.

Corps (comprising two or three divisions) – upwards of 36,000 men – commanded by a lieutenant general plus staff.

Battalion HQ – including lieutenant colonel as commander, major as second in command, captain as adjutant, lieutenant as quartermaster and an officer from Royal Army Medical Corps as battalion doctor. Supporting the officers in the HQ company were the regimental sergeant major and specialist sergeants, typically armourer, cook, drummer, pioneer, shoemaker, signaller and orderly room clerk. Up to sixty-five privates were also attached in a variety of roles, including medical orderlies, signallers, transport drivers, stretcher bearers (usually pipe-band members), officers' servants and pioneers.

APPENDIX 2

J. G. Chaplin obituary, *Covenanter* magazine, January 1956:

It is with the deepest regret that we announce that Brigadier General J G Chaplin died on Sunday the 15th January, at the age of 82.

James Graham Chaplin, or 'Bull' as he was always affectionately known to his contemporaries in the Regiment, was born on the 1st July 1873, and was gazetted to the 1st Cameronians in India in 1894, where he saw his first active service during the North-West Frontier Expedition of 1897–98. From 1898 to 1902 he was adjutant of that battalion, becoming a captain in 1900. He continued to serve with the 1st Battalion in India as a company commander from 1902–1909, during which time he was a regular member of the battalion polo team, which was then meeting with fair success. From 1909 to 1912 he was an adjutant in the Special Reserve, thereafter returning to the 1st Battalion as a company commander and becoming a major in October 1913. On the outbreak of the First World War he went to France with the 1st Battalion and commanded his company throughout the five main battles of 1914. In the spring of 1915 he took over the command of the battalion and was awarded the DSO that summer. He was given the brevet of Lieut. Colonel in June 1916, and late in 1917 he was given command of a brigade on the Western Front, with which he served without any respite from sickness or wounds throughout the remaining battles of the Great War. In October 1918 he was transferred to Home Forces as Commander of the 2nd Cyclist Brigade and was given the brevet of Colonel in 1919. His last appointment was as a brigade commander in Iraq, which he held for two years.

Brigadier General Jack quotes two instances of 'Bull' Chaplin's remarkable strength of character:

Firstly – 'At the battle of Loos in September 1915, Chaplin's Battalion was to have made an attack, *provided that* the units alongside his were successful in their advance. As these units had failed in their objectives, Chaplin stood fast. To staff officers who complained about his not going forward, he calmly replied that he was carrying out orders, and that if it was now intended that his battalion should attack, he must have the order to do so *in writing*. No such order came, so, thanks to his judgement and firmness, 'Bull's' men escaped a costly and useless adventure.'

Secondly – 'After two years on the Western Front as a regimental officer, Chaplin's horse fell and crushed him just before his battalion was due to go into the line. Being unable to walk, he arranged for the mess cart to take him as near the front as possible and for a stretcher party to carry him into the trenches. This plan was only frustrated through Higher Command discovering it and placing 'Bull' in the care of the medical officer until he was sound again.'

He (Brigadier General Jack) sums up 'Bull' Chaplin in the words: 'The soul of integrity, of courage, the nigh perfect example of an officer.'

ENDNOTES

Foreword

1   See chapter one, *The Cameronians, A Concise History* [Mainstream] by Trevor Royle. The regiment provided two generals, two lieutenant generals, five major-generals, and nineteen brigadiers in World War Two, many of whom gained their experience in World War One.

2   Section five, part eight, *Memories of an Infantry Officer* [Penguin] by Siegfried Sassoon.

3   *The War the Infantry Knew* [Abacus] by Captain J. C. Dunn.

4   *Recollections of an Infantry Subaltern* by Jacobus (John) Hill, in the Cameronian archive.

5   Letter, 23 November 1914.

6   Letter, 15 December 1915.

7   Letter, 2 July 1915.

8   Letter, 14 August 1914.

The Want of Sleep

9   Letter, 2 October 1914.

10   Letter, 5 October 1914.

11   Major Vincent Sandilands is engaged to Lil's sister, Bee.

12   Irish-born Lieutenant Lauriston John Arnott resigned his commission in early 1914, only to re-enlist on the outbreak of war, when he was posted to the Royal Irish Rifles. He later followed his father as proprietor of *The Irish Times*.

Armentières

13   Ernest Shepard's autobiography, *Drawn From Life* [Methuen], paints a brief portrait of the Chaplin family in Earl's Court. He married Graham's sister, Florence, and recounts that her mother insisted he take out life insurance

before the marriage – a result, perhaps, of the straightened circumstances in which she was left by her husband, Jimmy Chaplin.

14   First in Longridge Road, then from 1889 in Barkston Gardens.

15   As the war settled, long-serving officers were allowed home on leave for eight days every three months, the ranks for far less. It does seem to have varied between divisions, and good relations with certain senior officers organising the rotation may have been key.

Here We Are, Here We Are, Here We Are Again

16   See *The Campaign in Tirah* [Macmillan, 1898] by Colonel H. D. Hutchinson.

17   Letter, 13 January 1915.

18   Ibid.

19   Letter, 25 January 1915.

20   Letter, 26 February 1915.

21   Letter, 22 April 1915.

22   Letter, 4 April 1915.

23   Letter, 19 January 1915.

24   Letter, 19 March 1915.

25   The 1st battalion was drawn from the 26th Cameronians, and the 2nd battalion from the 90th Perthshire Light, amalgamated into the Cameronians (Scottish Rifles) in 1881, the only regiment of rifles among Scottish infantry units. The 1st battalion preferred to use the title 'Cameronians', the 2nd battalion the title 'Scottish Rifles'.

26   Money later became well known for the photographs he took during the Cameronians' first nine months in France.

27   One of the ways army officers showed their dislike of change was to refer to battalions in amalgamated regiments by their pre-amalgamation names – hence the 2nd battalion was often called 'the 90th' as it was drawn from the 90th Perthshire Light Infantry in 1881.

28   Letter, 9 May 1915.

29   Letter, 11 May 1915. The deputation included the moderator of the Church of Scotland.

30   2nd Lieutenant J. L. Loder-Symonds and 2nd Lieutenant H. A. C. Sim.

31   Letter, 12 May 1915.

32   Letter, 4 May 1915.

33   Letter, 12 May 1915.

34   Letter, 16 May 1915.

35   Letter, 20 May 1915.

A Certain Inaction

36 Incidences of court martial tended to increase after a battalion had suffered a period of heavy pressure and casualties. That in turn forced the army to look at how it administered justice. Chaplin writes in the battalion War Diary at the end of June that 'several men have rejoined from prisons under the Suspension of Sentences Act' – legislation passed to prevent men using casual theft as a means of avoiding front-line service.

37 See 14 June 1915 entry in memoir of medical officer Travis Hampson MC, serving with 19th Field Ambulance in Armentières – available online.

38 See Chaplin's letter of 7 November 1914 and remarks on Lieutenant Newman. There is evidence that officers received far more sympathetic treatment than ranks with regard to nervous exhaustion and suspected incidences of cowardice.

39 Letter, 17 February 1917.

40 McLellan is posted home to a role at a UK base in early 1918 and leaves the army in 1919 as a major, aged thirty-five. When he dies in 1942, aged fifty-eight, the *Covenanter*, the Cameronians' regimental magazine, publishes a short obituary, citing his roles as scout commissioner for Kirkcudbright and member of Kirkcudbright district council, and barely mentions his war service.

Loos

41 Letter, 11 August 1915.

42 Letter, 15 August 1915.

43 Letter, 28 July 1915.

44 Letter, 15 August 1915.

45 Sandbags.

46 The question of Robertson's bias towards the 1st (Cameronian) and 5th Scottish Rifles in the 19th brigade is raised by Robert Graves. See chapter fifteen, *Goodbye to All That* [Penguin]. Though, as ever with Graves, it is unclear how much of his fiction is based on fact, or vice versa.

47 John Baynes, in *Morale: A Study of Men and Courage* [Pen & Sword], describes the pre-war relationship between the battalions as one of occasional 'animosity', which wearied the more sensible members of the regiment.

48 See note 25 on the 1881 amalgamation.

49 See the privately published memoir by Patrick Hardinge in the Cameronian archive, Low Parks Museum, in Hamilton.

50   See obituary of Graham Chaplin, written by James Jack for the *Covenanter*, January 1956.

51   Graves asserts in *Goodbye to All That* [Penguin] that the adjutant of the 2nd Royal Welch, left in command after senior officers are killed or wounded, raised a similar query with brigade HQ about continuing the attack.

52   Owen was standing in for Colonel Williams, CO of the 2nd Royal Welch, injured in the first attack.

Such Is Our Life

53   *The Times*, 6 October 1915.

54   *The Times*, 6 October 1915.

55   Letter, 12 October 1915.

56   Letter, 16 October 1915.

57   Letter, 10 October 1915.

58   Letter, 19 October 1915.

59   Letter, 18 October 1915.

60   One of the mines blown before the battle.

61   See chapter twenty-seven of *Undertones of War* [Penguin Classic] by Edmund Blunden: 'Mutual molestation, at first unnoticed, gradually increased, until the ground was liberally shelled in routine.'

62   Letter, 22 October 1915.

63   Near Albert, north of the River Ancre.

64   Irish-born Major Audley Pratt, aged forty-one, served with 1st Royal Scots in the Boer War and was second in command of 9th Royal Irish Fusiliers in 1915. He was killed by a shell in August 1917.

65   Letter, 5 November 1915.

66   Regimental Quartermaster Sergeant F. Powell, quoted in *The War the Infantry Knew* by J. C. Dunn.

67   First mentioned – in response to her suggestion – in Chaplin's letter of 7 December 1915.

Rain and Shells

68   Frederick III of Germany, father of Kaiser Wilhelm, married Princess Victoria, the eldest daughter of Queen Victoria. He died of cancer in 1888, only ninety-nine days after becoming emperor.

69   Letter, 12 December 1915.

70 Letter, 6 December 1915.

71 Letter, 8 December 1915.

72 See Robert Graves' summation in *Goodbye to All That* [Penguin Classic] of the 'top-notch divisions' pre-1916: the 2nd, the 7th, the 29th, the Guards and the 1st Canadian.

73 Letter, 19 December 1915.

74 Letter, 12 December 1915.

75 Letter, 13 December 1915.

76 Letter, 15 December 1915.

77 Letter, 13 December 1915.

78 Letter, 14 December 1915.

79 Letter, 17 December 1917.

80 Letter, 18 December 1915.

Cambrin, Cuinchy, Auchy

81 The same trenches are described by Edward Blunden in *Undertones of War* as 'a slaughter-yard' [chapter four]. Robert Graves, in *Goodbye to All That*, describes the same spot as 'not my idea of trenches' [chapter thirteen] because the lines run in and out of the brickstacks, rather than in a logical, defendable progression.

82 See entry for 7 February 1916, battalion War Diary.

83 Letter, 25 February 1916.

84 Letter, 27 February 1916.

85 Letter, 23 February 1916.

86 Letter, 22 February 1916.

87 Adjacent parish to Sunningdale, Surrey.

88 Letter, 26 February 1916.

89 See entry for 22 February 1916, battalion War Diary.

90 Letter, 24 February 1916.

91 Letter, 28 February 1916.

92 See the private papers of Major G. K. Twiss, staff captain, 19th brigade, Imperial War Museum, on the cancellation of a planned attack: 'I should hope so too. I hate these Cavalry people commanding infantry corps.'

93 Shallower trenches dug at right angles to the main trench.

94 Letter, 16 March 1916.

95 Ibid.

96 Letter, 27 March 1916.

97   Letter, 24 March 1916.

98   Letter, 30 March 1916.

Never Better

99   See Twiss papers, IWM, regarding corps and divisional staff requests: 'The
      way these people talk about "raiding" the German trenches is really puerile
      – I wish they had been as much as some officers have in the trenches.'

100   Letter, 16 April 1916.

101   Letter, 4 September 1915.

102   Letter, 18 May 1916.

103   Letter, 18 May 1916.

104   'K' is a likely abbreviation for 'Kurse' – substituting *K*s for *C*s was a common
      battalion affectation. The New Year's Menu drawn up for Chaplin's A-Com-
      pany dinner in Armentières on 31 January 1914 carried the exhortation; 'A
      Happy New Year To You All is the sincere wish of all the Knuts Konnected
      with the company'.

105   Letter, 18 May 1916.

106   Letter, 19 May 1916.

107   Letter, 28 May 1916.

108   Letter, 29 May 1916.

109   For more on Monro's role in the disastrous Battle of Fromelles, in which
      the 51st Australian Division suffered 5,533 casualties between 19 and 20
      July 1916, see chapter fourteen of *Somme* [Penguin] by Lyn Macdonald.

110   Letter, 3 June 1916.

111   As a temporary colonel, he would have reverted to major if injured or
      retired.

112   See entry for 3 June 1916, battalion War Diary.

113   Letter, 5 June 1916.

114   Kitchener was lost at sea on 5 June when the ship carrying him to Russia
      on a diplomatic mission struck a mine off the Orkneys.

115   Letter, 7 June 1916.

116   Letter, 3 June 1916.

The Somme

117   See G. S. Hutchinson in *The 33rd Division in France and Flanders 1915–1919*
      [Naval & Military Press] who provides an uncritical portrait of Mayne,
      noting his 'great height and rugged strength' and his 'unwearying patience

and good cheer'. For all that, his battalions were often lent to other brigades, suggesting his divisional commanders were unconvinced of his
abilities.

118 See chapter twenty of *Goodbye To All That* by Robert Graves for one
contested account. The author had to revise his version after protests from
surviving soldiers, and his assertion that Scottish troops fled is disputed.
Graves, an officer in the 2nd Royal Welch at the time, had been injured by
shelling and missed the battle, and based his version on an account he
heard in hospital. It is widely acknowledged, however, that Padre McShane
helped to gather together retreating men. *The Cross On The Sword: Catholic
Chaplains in the Forces* [Chapman] by Tom Johnstone and James Hagerty
refers to an account by a medical officer of McShane assuming 'virtual
command of the Royal Fusiliers' at High Wood.

119 G. I. Gordon had rejoined 1st Cameronians as lieutenant in June 1915.

120 Letter, 18 July 1916.

121 See chapter six of *The Hell They Called High Wood* [Leo Cooper] by Terry
Norman.

122 Montgomery rose to Field Marshal in World War Two, but was criticized
late in the war for being unwilling to countenance heavy losses – partly
because of what he felt was a waste of life on the Somme.

123 Letter, 19 July 1916.

124 See chapter three of *Her Privates We* [Serpent's Tail] by Frederic Manning
for an eloquent account of post-battle parade.

125 Letter, 3 August 1916.

126 Letter, 1 August 1916.

127 See chapter nine of *The War The Infantry Knew* by J. C. Dunn on High
Wood: 'No-one from the Staff came to examine the position in our time.
Once the Brigadier did come – and go after a hasty look at it.'

128 See chapter two, *The 33rd Division In France And Flanders 1915-1919*
[Naval&Military Press] by G. S. Hutchinson.

129 Letter, 29 August 1916.

130 Letter, 30 August 1916.

131 Erich von Falkenhayn is replaced by Paul von Hindenburg.

132 Letter, 1 September 1916.

133 Letter, 4 September 1916.

134 Letter from Colonel Sam Darling, 5 September 1916.

135 Chaplin's acquaintance with Geddes adds credence to the stories heard by

his grandchildren that he 'moonlighted' in the police force, protecting the Indian railways, to supplement his pre-war army income.

136 Letter, 6 October 1916.

Before You Go

137 By which time Tennant has left government, following Asquith's replacement as Prime Minister by David Lloyd George.

138 Letter, 6 November 1916.

139 Married to his sister, Florence Chaplin.

140 Letter, 10 November 1916.

141 Letter, 12 November 1916.

142 Letter, 15 November 1916.

143 Letter, 17 November 1916.

144 Letter, 20 November 1916.

145 Letter, 20 November 1916.

146 Colonel Vincent Sandilands, married to Lil's sister, Beatrice (Baby).

147 Letter, 22 November 1916.

Howitzer Wood

148 Robert Graves, in chapter sixteen of *Goodbye to All That*, posits that most officers over forty who survived two years of front-line service became dependant on alcohol.

149 See papers filed in the National Archive: Wood was finally dismissed from the army for drunkenness in 1919 – and stripped of his pension – after he was found unconscious on Calais beach. Despite testimonials written to the War Office by Robertson, Vandeleur and Hamilton, Wood dies penniless in a Glasgow mental asylum in 1931.

150 See mention of the reprimand in Chaplin's letter of 9 January 1917.

151 Letter, 17 January 1917.

152 See entries for 12 January and 18 January 1917 in *General Jack's Diary* [Cassell].

153 Letter, 19 January 1917.

154 See chapter fourteen of Robert Graves' *Goodbye to All That*, in which he quotes a 2nd Royal Welch officer, pre-Battle of Loos, as stating, 'This is the 19th Brigade, the luckiest in France.'

155 In Graves' *Goodbye to All That*, he states that Pinney's removal of the rum ration led to 'the heaviest sick-list the battalion had known'.

156 Letter, 22 January 1917.

Army School

157 See chapter twenty-two of Robert Graves' *Goodbye to All That*.

Hindenburg

158 See Chaplin's letter of 1 June 1915.

159 See Sassoon's account in chapter twelve of *The War the Infantry Knew 1914–1919*. Although it is not stated that Chaplin dissuaded brigade HQ from its initial plan to attack below ground, it would be characteristic of his command to argue against something which seemed foolishly wasteful.

160 According to Sassoon's account, *ibid*, the Royal Welch bombing party could have pushed further. 'My activity was only quelled by a written order from the Cameronian Colonel, who told me that we must not advance owing to the attack having failed elsewhere'. Sassoon was already badly wounded, shot through the shoulder – the injury that was to take him back to Britain, where he would start his celebrated campaign against the war. Chaplin's order to cease fighting probably saved his life.

161 See chapter thirteen of *The War the Infantry Knew 1914–1919*, which contains a scathing account of the 'bull-at-a-gate attacks' on the Hindenburg, officers at brigade HQ being 'remote in action and ineffectual', and the competitive distrust between brigadiers in the 33rd division – 'not a band of brothers'.

162 Letter, 1 May 1917.

163 Letter, 2 May 1917.

164 Letter, 3 May 1917.

165 The Germans were rumoured – falsely – to boil down human corpses for tallow. In fact, they only collected animal corpses for the purpose.

166 Letter, 8 May 1917.

167 Letter, 8 May 1917.

168 Sir Francis Champneys, baronet, eminent obstetrician and chairman of the Central Midwives Board.

169 Letter, 13 May 1917.

170 Letter, 16 May 1917.

171 Letter, 20 May 1917.

Absolutely Dished

172 See chapter thirteen of *The War the Infantry Knew 1914–1919*: 'The Army Commander came up to a vantage point near St Léger to look on. What

did he learn of realities from back there? Only in the midst of reality can opportunity be seized, and it is rare for anyone who combines authority and nous to be on the spot.'

173 See chapter nineteen of *Old Soldiers Never Die* by Frank Richards for a vivid description of signalling during the assault.

174 See chapter thirteen of *The War the Infantry Knew 1914–1919*: 'Colonel Chaplin, with the generosity which distinguished his relations with us, took the blame for his battalion.'

175 Letter, 12 June 1917.

176 Ibid.

177 Letter, 14 June 1917.

178 Letter, 13 June 1917.

179 Ibid.

180 Letter, 15 June 1917.

Condé-Folie

181 *The Times*, 6 July 1917.

182 Ibid.

183 See the description of Chaplin on parade, written in a letter by a newly-joined Scots-American officer, Lieutenant Joseph Maclean, on 21 July 1917, published in *A Tale of Two Captains* [Pentland Press] by Rory Baynes and Hugh Maclean: 'The Colonel is back from leave and we know he's here, as he is *très moutarde*. When he barks out "Cameronians!" at the head of the battalion the earth trembles and is silent – and we are too, you bet. He is a good man, a DSO, and that's the right sort.'

They Minded More Than I

184 Sassoon's letter was read out by Hastings Lees-Smith MP in a House of Commons debate on 30 July 1917.

185 See chapter seven of *Shot at Dawn* [Pen & Sword] by Julian Putkowski and Julian Sykes. Five soldiers from various battalions of the Scottish Rifles were shot for desertion during World War One. Mackness was the only soldier from the 1st battalion.

To the End

186 Matthew 24:13 [King James Bible] – a line abridged for the libretto of Mendelssohn's oratorio, *Ejiah*, and occasionally sung in jest by officers on the Western Front, according to Robert Graves.

187 It is difficult to think of a reason why Graham Chaplin would have stopped writing after his promotion to brigadier. Given Lil's efficiency in collecting his letters, it seems more likely that the batch covering October 1917–November 1918 has at some stage in the last one hundred years been separated from the main collection and lost to the family.

188 As Shakespear puts it in his history of the 34th division: 'With promptitude which fairly astonished the recipients, a shower of French decorations descended upon us.'

189 In one of life's ironies, Willie Alexander contested the Glasgow Central seat against fellow Tennant's director and former friend, Harold Tennant, standing for the Liberals.

Afterword

190 See Chaplin's letter of 3 April 1916.

191 Letter, 1 August 1917.

192 Chapter six, 'On the Art of Command', from *A General's Letters to His Son* by T. D. Pilcher.

193 *Private Lord Crawford's War Diaries* [Pen & Sword], edited by Christopher Arnander – Crawford inherited his title in 1913, but went to volunteer for service in France, refusing to take rank. He later sat as a government minister.

194 Ibid. See entry for 30 August 1915.

Da James Graham Chaplin
a.k.a. "Da" 1873 - 1956